课堂互动视角

中丹高中文学课堂教学实证对比研究

Dialogic Perspective on Classroom Interaction:
A Comparative Study in Danish and Chinese Literature Classes

刘婷婷 ◎ 著

上海大学出版社
·上 海·

图书在版编目(CIP)数据

课堂互动视角：中丹高中文学课堂教学实证对比研究/刘婷婷著.—上海：上海大学出版社，2021.12
ISBN 978-7-5671-4387-6

Ⅰ.①课… Ⅱ.①刘… Ⅲ.①中学教育—课堂教学—对比研究—中国、丹麦 Ⅳ.①G632.0

中国版本图书馆 CIP 数据核字（2021）第 237850 号

责任编辑　柯国富
助理编辑　祝艺菲　邹亚楠
封面设计　谷　夫
技术编辑　金　鑫　钱宇坤

KETANG HUDONG SHIJIAO: ZHONGDAN GAOZHONG WENXUE
KETANG JIAOXUE SHIZHENG DUIBI YANJIU
课堂互动视角：中丹高中文学课堂教学实证对比研究
刘婷婷　著
上海大学出版社出版发行
（上海市上大路99号　邮政编码200444）
（http://www.shupress.cn　发行热线 021-66135112）
出版人　戴骏豪

*

南京展望文化发展有限公司排版
江苏凤凰数码印务有限公司印刷　各地新华书店经销
开本 890mm×1240mm　32　印张 10.25　字数 305 千
2021年12月第1版　2021年12月第1次印刷
ISBN 978-7-5671-4387-6/G·3410　定价　56.00元

版权所有　侵权必究
如发现本书有印装质量问题请与印刷厂质量科联系
联系电话：025-57718474

序

在人类文明的发展进程中，教育始终起着举足轻重的作用。可以说，教育不但决定着一个国家的文明程度，而且在很大程度上，还决定着一个国家的社会发展走向。作为一种有目的、有组织、有计划的社会活动，教育系统地传授知识，在我国历史中始终置于核心的地位。而课堂教学则是教育的典型代表形式，课堂中教师和学生的角色地位、互动方式等与课堂教学效果有着密切的联系。在中西方的课堂上，由于传统思想的影响，教师的角色地位、教学思路、课堂组织形式、师生互动等都存在着一定程度的差别。

在传统的中国课堂上，教师常常被定义为主动的、具有很高权威性的角色，在数千年来敬畏知识、崇尚知识甚至"敬惜字纸"的课堂语境中，这是再自然不过的事情了。虽然西方教育家都把他们数百年的大学历史当作雄厚知识积累的资本，中国许多学人也对西方动辄具有几百年历史的大学顶礼膜拜，为自己国家多数几十年、至多一百多年的大学历史自惭形秽，但西方的教育历史远远无法与中国延续数千年的教育历史相提并论。绵延了数千年的中国传统教学方式对于促进中华文明的发展和延续起到了至关重要的作用。

在现代教育体系中，发源于西方的教育理论和教学方式自有其优越之处，主要诞生于西方国家的科学知识体系像马力充沛的发动机带动着人类社会快速发展，自然而然地，西方的教育理论和教学方法也逐渐成为各国教育体系的重要范本。它山之石，可以攻玉。通过中外教育对比交流，取长补短，无论是孔子的"三人行，必有我师""见贤思齐"，还是魏源的"师夷长技以制夷",都反映了我国向他人学习、吸取他人优点的传统。因此,对比中西课堂教学模式,研究课堂各要素的比例,社会参与关系等,对于促进我国的教育研究和教学改革无疑具有重要的作用。但是在对比的过程中,如何不盲从,不先入为主,不预设立场,这是每一个严肃的科研工作者都要认真思考的问题,只有这样,得出的结论才是令人信服的。作者通过课堂观察、访谈、调查问卷等多种方式采集数据,认真整理分析,其结论无疑是令人信服的。

无论哪一种方式,没有绝对的优和劣。教学方式都会随着时代的发展而发展,随着社会的人才需要而不断更新。本书的研究课题让我回想起我第一次走出国门,到美国去访学的情景。

2008年,我受邀到匹兹堡大学访学。初到美国,一切都那么新奇。我的办公室所在的教学楼——学术圣殿(Cathedral of Learning)高达42层,是当时全美最高、世界第二高的教学楼。每天在这座教学楼里漫游一番,就会让人产生深深的敬佩并为之折服。其包罗各国文化特色的国际教室,代表了美国知识界的开放和包容。匹兹堡大学开放的课程体系,灵活的选课机制,看似随意、没有督导检查的课堂,让人耳目一新。时至今日,国外许多的概念被借用了过来,但是非常遗憾,一些优秀的教育理念仍没有能够为我所用。

2008年5月初,我还趁着看望老师的机会拜访了一所美国小学。我的老师,当时已经80岁高龄的格莱蒂斯·凡切尔(Gladys Fancher)太太仍然担任着一所小学的校外辅导员工作。这所小学位于阿拉斯加首府安克雷奇附近。学校的建筑风格是典型的乡村学校的风格,但是教室的设施和陈设则与我熟知的小学课堂截然不同,没有固定的桌椅,中间是可以席地而坐的地毯,教室前方的一角是电脑台,另一侧是一架钢琴。我向这群不到10岁的孩子介绍了中国。孩子们好奇地问:中国在哪里?中国人吃什么,住什么样的房子?是不是有很多熊猫?长城到底有多长?从孩子们的问题中,我能感到凡切尔太太经常给孩子们讲起她在中国生活的故事。孩子们好奇的神态,天真的问题,稚嫩的声音至今仍历历在目。

但是，在这短短的几个月里，我也感觉到，部分教师对中国抱有偏见且一无所知，无论是在大学还是在小学。可悲的是，10多年过去，这些偏见和无知没有消失，而是日益强烈。凡切尔太太，这位把中国当作第二故乡的老人、不断向美国学生宣传中国的友好使者，也在2014年4月故去。在此，我特意提到这段插曲，也是想借一角纸页，向她表达心底的敬重和哀思。

让我没有想到的是，在亲眼观察了美国对外交流的课堂后，我的职业生涯就与对外交流深深地交织在一起。

愚以为，无论是专注于教学的教育者，还是从事对外交流的教育者，都应该平等地看待教育对象，不存偏见地对待各种文化，求同存异，和而不同，遇到跨文化冲突时能够恰当处理，有不同意见时能够得体地表达出来。同时，教育者要怀有一颗包容之心，待人谦和、提携后学，创造和维护充满正气的文化环境。

自2011年进入上海大学国际教育学院（当时叫上海大学国际交流学院），已10年过去。非常欣慰地看到，学院的学术氛围日渐浓厚，学术成果正不断涌现，一批年轻的教师正在成长起来。刘婷婷老师就是其中一位佼佼者。工作上任劳任怨，不推脱，不滞后，精益求精。自进入学院以来，从事了繁重的行政工作，还要兼顾家庭和孩子，在这样的情况下，仍孜孜不倦，笔耕不辍，成功获批了上海市哲学社会科学规划青年课题。本书是刘婷婷老师以博士论文为基础修改而成的，从中可以看出她扎实的科研功底和严谨的科研态度。

长江后浪推前浪。希望刘婷婷老师百尺竿头更进一步，也祝愿学院的老师们在人才培养和科学研究两方面都成果丰硕，再创佳绩。

姚喜明

2021年5月12日

Foreword

Situated in the fields of dialogic pedagogy and literature education, the study of this book explores the patterns of framing classroom interactions and the applications of the patterns in the literature teaching in different upper secondary schools in two countries. The study uses a comparative view to develop new understandings of dialogic teaching in the literature classroom theoretically and empirically based on the explorations.

The study is designed with two considerations. The first is the consideration of the gap between the ideal theory of classroom discourse and the reality of teaching practice. The second consideration leading to this comparative-study is the heated discussion between Danish and Chinese secondary schools raised by a Danish TV program *9.Z mod Kina*[①]. These two considerations set up the general context of the study, indicating the importance and necessity of the comparative study on the classroom discourse in distinct contexts.

The study comprises both theoretical research and empirical research. The theoretical foundation is grounded in a combination of positioning theory, envisioning theory, and the Cross-model of teaching method. The empirical research employs a qualitative case-study method combined with descriptive, interpretive, and comparative approaches. The empirical data are collected from the classrooms of two Danish teachers and two Chinese teachers.

---

① *9.Z mod Kina* (Danish) means Ninth-Grade Danish Students Compared with Chinese Students.

By comparison, this study identifies the differences in the Social Participation Structure (SPS) in the classes, which indicates the divergent roles and relationships of participants in the different classes. The study reveals two common phenomena that are notable in both Danish and Chinese classes. One is termed *Dancing with Shackles*, and the other is the *Double-Bind Problem* of literary teachers. The findings of the case studies support revision and supplementation of the Cross-model of teaching. Built on the theoretical foundation and empirical research, the study reinterprets *dialogic teaching* in the literature classroom and characterizes three points in a consideration of the effect of contextual cultures. Also, the study reveal implications for reading pedagogy from the perspective of positioning. In so doing, the study engages the literary teachers from both Danish and Chinese classes in reflection on the literary pedagogies, illuminating inspirations for other educators and researchers in both countries.

The study is built upon my interdisciplinary experience as a college student studying in literature in China, as well as a PhD student researching on pedagogy in Denmark. Opening a platform for communications, reflections, and learning is the purpose that I pursue.

The experience of studying in Denmark gives me the completely different and unforgettable life. I was deeply impressed by the clear blue sky, the green natural scenery, the warm and kind people, the "hygge"[①] lifestyle, the icy winter and cool summer, as well as the blue sparking sea and the golden coastline. Whom I miss a lot is my supervisor. She concentrated on my project and was concerned with my study and life when she was on sick leave. In spite of the serious illness and weakness, she attended my defence and gave an encouraging and impressive speech at her last stage of life! All of these are precious memories that I will cherish forever!

The publication of this book is supported by Shanghai Pujiang Talents

---

[①] "Hygge" that is a Danish word means "cosy".

Funding. Also, it is partly on the basis of Youth Project of Shanghai Philosophy and Social Science Planning①.

  This book is finally published in memory of my PhD supervisor, Professor Vibeke Hetmar, who passed away in summer that year when I got my degree.

---

① 本书出版受到"上海市浦江人才计划"资助,系上海市"浦江人才"计划资助项目(项目编号:18PJC059)研究成果,也为上海市哲学社会科学规划青年课题(项目编号:2018EYY006)部分研究成果。

Contents

Chapter 1   Introduction: Dialogue in the Literature Classroom / 1
  1.1   Overview of the Topic / 2
  1.2   Educational Contexts of Denmark and China / 4
  1.3   The State of the Art — Current Research in the Field / 7
  1.4   Research Gap and Research Questions / 14
  1.5   The Meaning of *Dialogic* in the Literature Classroom: Theoretical Framework / 15

Chapter 2   Qualitative Case-Study Research on Classroom Interactions / 48
  2.1   Research Design / 48
  2.2   Research Setting / 56
  2.3   Research Procedures and Specific Methods / 60
  2.4   Building Trustworthiness / 74
  2.5   Conclusion / 77

Chapter 3   The Case of Teacher S / 78
  3.1   Contextual Cultures / 78
  3.2   Pre-Observation: Teacher S's Perceptions of Literature Teaching / 86
  3.3   During-Observation: Three Types of Classroom Interactions / 92
  3.4   Post-Observation: Comments and Reviews / 128
  3.5   Conclusion / 133

Chapter 4   The Case of Teacher P / 136
  4.1   Contextual Cultures / 136

- 4.2 Pre-Observation: Teacher P's Perceptions of Literature Teaching / 142
- 4.3 During-Observation: Three Types of Classroom Interactions / 151
- 4.4 Post-Observation: Comments and Reviews / 169
- 4.5 Conclusion / 175

Chapter 5 The Case of Teacher X / 178
- 5.1 Contextual Cultures / 178
- 5.2 Pre-Observation: Teacher X's Perceptions of Literature Teaching / 185
- 5.3 During-Observation: Three Types of Classroom Interactions / 191
- 5.4 Post-Observation: Comments and Reviews / 213
- 5.5 Conclusion / 219

Chapter 6 The Case of Teacher Z / 222
- 6.1 Contextual Cultures / 222
- 6.2 Pre-Observation: Teacher Z's Perceptions of Literature Teaching / 226
- 6.3 During-Observation: Three Types of Classroom Interactions / 231
- 6.4 Post-Observation: Comments and Reviews / 247
- 6.5 Conclusion / 253

Chapter 7 Going Further with Comparing the Cases: Discussions and Conclusions / 255
- 7.1 Synthesis of Findings for RQ1: Summaries of the Findings / 255
- 7.2 Synthesis of Findings for RQ2: Differences and Commonalities / 267
- 7.3 Theoretical and Empirical Discussions / 276
- 7.4 Implications for Reading Pedagogy from the Perspective of Positioning / 290
- 7.5 In Closing: Contributions of the Study / 293

Bibliography / 296

Appendices / 303

Index / 314

Chapter 1
Introduction:
Dialogue in the Literature Classroom

The present study is situated in the fields of dialogic pedagogy and literature education. The purpose of this study is to explore the patterns of framing classroom interactions and the applications of the patterns in teaching literature in different upper secondary classes of two countries with a comparative view, and then to develop new understandings of *dialogic teaching* in the literature classroom theoretically and empirically, based on the explorations and comparisons.

There are five classes involved in this book, three Danish classes and two Chinese classes. In each case, the study examines the classroom interactions between the teacher and students (teacher-student), the student and the student (student-student), as well as students and the reading texts (student-text). Teacher-student and student-student interactions refer to the external oral and written classroom communications, and the student-text interaction is related to the internal communication between the reader and texts. This type is illuminated through examining how the teacher directs the student-text interaction by means of reading instructions, rather than the nature of the student-text interaction itself. This is because the internal interaction is inconspicuous in class, but embodied in the teacher's pedagogy of literature reading.

By comparison and analysis of cases, this book addresses the differences and commonalities, focusing on the possibility for substantive student engagement to dialogue through participating in activities and assignments in each class. Based on the findings of the cases, this book also discusses and modifies a pedagogical model, extends the thinking about dialogic teaching in the literature classroom, and suggests the factors that impact the development of dialogic teaching.

1.1 Overview of the Topic

This study is designed with two considerations. The first is the consideration of the gap between the ideal theory about classroom discourse and the reality of teaching practice. For more than a quarter of a century, the polemics surrounding educational reform have centred on two points of view: one favours a progressive child-centred mode of education, which focuses on the importance of student talk in the construction of knowledge, and the other prefers a return to a more structured and teacher-directed curriculum, which emphasises the transmission of basic knowledge and skills. As a matter of fact, for a long time, a conventional teacher-centred form of a pedagogical sequence of Initiation-Response-Evaluation (IRE) (Mehan 1998, p.249) has dominated the classroom. IRE represents a traditional and typical mode of classroom discourse, that is, the teacher initiates a question, and students answer, and then the teacher evaluates students' answers. This traditional pattern, which was once a prevalent instructional discourse in the classroom, has recently received much criticism from both theoretical and empirical perspectives (Reznitskaya, 2012). IRE is thought of as a *recitation* that focuses on the power of teachers (Mehan, 1979; Mroz, 2000; Nystrand & Gamoran, 1991), controls key aspects of communication, and impedes student engagement in classroom interactions (Alexander, 2008a; Galton, 2007; Nystrand, Gamoran, Kachur & Prendergast, 1997). In its place, *dialogue* has become a concept of the growing importance in discussions of learning and teaching and has been stressed by some theories and researchers (Alexander, 2008a; Bakhtin, 1981, 1984, 1986; Nystrand et al., 1997; Vygotsky, 1978). Despite many learning theories have supported the importance of dialogism in the learning process, studies have shown that student talk has a limited place in the classroom. It was found that the asymmetry of classroom discourse has not been noticed by many literary teachers even though varied reform pedagogies in American and European contexts advocate students as the active agent in the group work and class discussions (Dysthe, 1993). In a carefully executed study of more than 200 American classes, Nystrand, Gamoran, Zeiser, and Long (2003) concluded that there was "little discussion in any classes in the sense of an open and in-depth exchange" (Nystrand et al., 2003, p.178), because they found that what most teachers called "discussion" was, in fact, another version of recitation (Nystrand et al., 2003). Evidence from another study in England also demonstrated that despite national strategies to promote more interactive approaches to teaching and learning, the traditional teacher-centred practice dominated in the classroom (Lyle, 2008). The reality of typical classroom practices does not correspond to the highly advocated educational ideal of dialogic teaching (Reznitskaya, 2012). Recognizing the gap between the reality and the theoretical ideal, this study is designed to investigate the reality of teaching practice in Danish and Chinese classes, focusing on the framing of the classroom discourse in different classes and the exploration of potential dialogic discourse.

The second consideration leading to the comparative-study design arises out of the heated discussion about the teaching methods in Danish and Chinese secondary schools. Inspired by the Danish TV program *9.Z mod Kina*, the differences between Danish and Chinese classes give rise to a heated discussion in the community of professional educators and researchers. This programme not only introduces something different in the educational systems embedded in distinct social and cultural contexts but also attracts the attention of educators and researchers of two countries to reflect their teaching. Despite the programme's intent as entertainment, it indeed opens a topic of comparative education in Denmark and China, creating a platform for communication, reflection, and learning. On the basis of my educational background and study experience in Denmark and China, the present study narrows down the focus on the comparison of the literature teaching methods, exploring the particular differences in the framing of classroom interactions, and how these differences affect student engagement and in which ways.

1.2 Educational Contexts of Denmark and China

The methods and patterns of teaching are different in Chinese classes compared with Danish classes because they are embedded in distinct cultural and social contexts within different educational systems.

1.2.1 Danish Upper-Secondary Level of Education

Danish upper secondary education comprises either general education qualifying for access to higher education or vocational or technical education qualifying primarily for access to the labour market. To be specific, there are four programmes: the 3-year general upper secondary school leaving examination (STX), the 2-year higher preparatory examination (HF), the 3-year higher commercial examination (HHX), and the 3-year higher technical examination (HTX). Among them, the STX is typically offered by general upper secondary schools (Gymnasiums) and its focus is on general education and general study preparation. The academic standard is closely linked to aspects of the academic subjects, and the students are to achieve general education and study competence in the humanities, natural science, and social science with a view to being in a position to complete higher education. Therefore, normally there are multiple study fields or subject packages for students to choose from in the upper secondary schools. Apart from the compulsory subjects, each student chooses a specialized study field consisting of a package with two or three subjects. Meanwhile, each student selects a number of elective subjects as a combination of the study field. The number varies according to the study field subjects taken by the student. In this sense, there are many possible combinations of the study field. Even for the same subject, like English, its different levels can be combined with different packages.

Equally, there is also flexibility in the assessment in the upper secondary schools. Assessments in general upper secondary education in Denmark consist of the internal evaluation and the external evaluation. The internal evaluation is continuously conducted by the subject teacher as a way to adjust instruction, and the whole course of instruction is evaluated by means of tests, special assignments/reports, or conversations. The external assessment is done by means of three forms of evaluation: marks for the year's work, examination marks, and term marks and testimonials. Marks for the year's work and term marks are given by the subject teacher and reflect the subject teacher's appraisal of the student's level of attainment at the end of the year. At most of the examinations, the pupils may utilize all types of aids, including IT, while they may normally not communicate with each other or with anyone else. The student performance is weighed by the examination average of the concluding term marks and examination marks, which is crucial to the student's future opportunities in the education system as it forms part of the basis for an admission to the higher education.

1.2.2 Chinese Upper-Secondary Level of Education

The Chinese educational system has many different aspects that contrast with the Danish system. The upper secondary education in China includes the 3-year full-time general upper secondary schools qualifying for higher education and the 2 to 4-year upper secondary specialized education (technical or vocational training). Similar to Denmark, the general upper secondary education qualifies the academic standard which requires the students to achieve the general education and study competencies in three essential subjects (Chinese language and literature, English, and mathematics) and three other selected subjects (physics, chemistry, biology as one subject package called 'science', or geography, history, and politics as another package called 'arts'). In the first year of high school, students need to learn all the nine subjects plus physical education and information technology, but during the second-year students have to choose the package in which they are interested and which might be relevant to their major of interest in college. In order to make sure that the students prepare well for the national high-stake examinations, schools usually arrange term exams at the end of each term and small tests during each term. For almost all the students in the general upper secondary schools, the goal is not only to pass these exams or the graduation examination but also to achieve high scores of the National College Entrance Examination which is commonly regarded as the most important examination in the whole system in China.

A new trend evoked by the National Curriculum Reform of Basic Education[①] has been recently changing the curriculum system in secondary schools. This policy aims at changing the way of knowing — the focus should be transferred from teachers' transmission to students' initiative in the study — and changing the traditional situation that stresses knowledge from materials rather than from the practice, to fostering student learning ability as well. Corresponding to the requests of the reform, many upper secondary schools are trying to add some new changes in teaching and their curricula, as the two Chinese schools observed in this study have done.

---

① Refer to the website of Ministry of Education, China: 教育部关于印发《基础教育课程改革纲要（试行）》的通知 http://www.moe.gov.cn/srcsite/A26/jcj_kcjcgh/200106/t20010608_167343.html, 2001-06-08/2017-05-05; 教育部关于深化基础教育课程改革进一步推进素质教育的意见 http://www.moe.gov.cn/srcsite/A26/s7054/201006/t20100601_92800.html, 2010-06-01/2017-05-05.

The difference in the educational focus affects methods of teaching and framing classroom interactions, which have been considered as a cultural context during the analysis in the study.

1.3 The State of the Art — Current Research in the Field

The role of dialogue in the classroom discourse has recently been a hotspot in the field of education, and quite a few scholars have conducted a wealth of relevant studies. These provide many possibilities for researching classroom discourse from different perspectives (e.g., Applebee, Langer, Nystrand, & Gamoran, 2003; Ball & Freedman, 2004; Doecke, Grill, Van de Ven, 2009; Dressman, 2005; Dysthe, 1993, 1999; Freedman, Delp & Crawford, 2005; Freedman & Delp, 2007; Nystrand et al., 1997; Reznitskaya, 2012; Smidt, 1999; Wells, 1999). The following are the three most relevant perspectives from which this book draws inspiration and around which it is conceived.

1.3.1 Dialogic Perspective on Teaching and Learning in General

Dialogic perspective on teaching and learning emphasises the cultural situatedness of learning and sees social interaction as the fundament. A sociocultural understanding of learning has its historical roots in Vygotsky's (1978, 1987) theory about the "understanding of human cognition and learning as social and cultural rather than individual phenomena" (Kozulin et al., 2003, p.1), placing emphasis on language and co-construction of knowledge. By highlighting the social construction of meaning during the communication, Vygotsky (1978, 1987) helped many educators see the centrality of language in children's intellectual development; this, in turn, stimulated research into the impact of language on learning. Such work has laid the ground for further study on discourse, some of which can be traced back to Bakhtin (1981, 1984, 1986). His ideas were viewed as the extension of Vygotsky's ideas about the "essential links between the cultural, historical and institutional setting on the one hand and the mental functioning of the individual on the other" (Wertsch, 1991, p.48). Both stressed the significance of language as a mediated action, and further Bakhtin explicitly proposed the dialogic nature of all utterances. His overarching conception of dialogism has been widely studied and applied in research of teachers' teaching and students' learning in the classroom (e.g., Ball & Freedman, 2004; Dysthe, 1993, 1999; Freedman, Delp & Crawford, 2005; Freedman & Delp, 2007; Smidt, 1999; Wells, 1999).

Wells (1999) was strongly influenced by Vygotsky's thinking on the role of language in knowledge-building and development, and Bakhtin's perspective of discourse. He narrowed the focus on the relationship between discourse and the development of knowledge, and then addressed the concept of *dialogic inquiry* in which teachers and students co-construct knowledge mutually through learning with and from each other in joint activities (Wells, 1999). Bringing together ideas from Leont'ev's activity theory and Halliday's systemic functional linguistics, Wells focused on the role of discourse that was defined as "the collaborative behavior of two or more participants as they use the meaning potential of a shared language to mediate the establishment and achievement of their goals in social action" (p.174) in knowledge-building. With a number of investigations on transcripts from the classroom discourse recorded from Canadian primary school classrooms, Wells (1999) illustrated the possible forms of dialogic inquiry and the conditions that made dialogic inquiry possible. *Inquiry* as an approach to education in these communities, in Wells's sense of the word, indicated a stance toward experience and ideas in learning — it expressed "a willingness to wonder, to ask questions and to seek to understand by collaborating with others in the attempt to make answers to them" (Wells, 1999, p.121). Put simply, dialogic inquiry, which displayed a way of thinking, interacting, and cooperating, played a crucial role in students' learning and knowledge-building, as well as their cognitive development. This point was in line with Langer's envisioning theory (2011a, 2011b), which formed part of the theoretical foundation of this book. The theoretical chapter reviews this theory considering that it views literature understanding as a cognitive process that involves the student thinking and the subject experience when students are interacting with the text and previous knowledge in the mind.

Ball and Freedman's (2005) study on Bakhtin's concept of *ideological becoming* (p.4), and the difference between the authoritative discourse and the internally persuasive discourse guided their further study on language, literacy, and learning. Their studies on Bakhtin's ideological becoming and its application in learning focused more on how people communicated across the divides that separated them and the role that such communication played in teaching and learning. They thought today's classroom in the United States was a place filled with struggles and tensions from the linguistic and cultural divides of diverse populations, which brought a range of internally persuasive discourses. They argued the complex contact between the authoritative discourses and the internally persuasive discourses in the classroom could impact the ideological development of students. With a notion of Bakhtin's ideological becoming and the nature of struggles and tensions nowadays, they presented several implications from this perspective and the relevant cross-national projects they had undertaken. As a result, they developed the concept of *ideological becoming* in the process of writing. They offered several perspectives and possibilities of reinterpreting Bakhtin's dialogism and its application in the study of multivoicedness of current classrooms.

1.3.2 Dialogic Perspective on Literacy

Dysthe (1993, 1999) is one of the Nordic scholars who applied Bakhtin's ideas to investigate talking and writing as a dialogic way of teaching. A study by Dysthe (1993) on the pattern of writing and talking inspired the current study. With a dialogic perspective, Dysthe (1993) investigated students' talking and writing in an empirical study in three classrooms in the USA and Norway. She started with Bakhtin's ideas of monologic and dialogic utterances from his book on E. Dostoevsky, and in her study, she discussed the possibilities of the documented strategies used by teachers in schools in USA and Norway as students wrote, spoke, and discussed subject matter. In her study, she put more attention on how dialogism supported the importance of student talk in participation and deepened the understanding of writing that assisted learning, illustrating that the individual writer or speaker at school was always developing his or her learning potential in Bakhtin's way of thinking. Despite being inspired by Dysthe's concern on dialogism in classrooms, this book differs from hers in looking at the interaction between the teacher and students, the student and the student, students and the reading text in the literature classroom, and also in the detailed analysis of the pattern of teaching. The perspectives from positioning theory and literary reading theory are also combined with the dialogic perspective to examine the literature classroom in this empirical study.

Another Norwegian researcher, Smidt (1999), explored the development of students' texts and how students tried out language and genres of school writing by "discourse roles" about "the socially patterned ways of writing" (p.91). He was interested in looking at how students positioned themselves dialogical in their writings — how they positioned themselves specifically in relation to the theme or topic, norms and expectations at school and their teachers, as well as their own developing self-image when they tried out genre roles and ways of thinking and writing. By viewing students' writing in this way, he illustrated the pedagogical implications of Bakhtin's dialogism on student writing. Smidt's (1999) research on students' writing and their positioning or self-positioning in their written utterances provided a way of combining Bakhtin's dialogism with students' identity construction. The current study is similarly interested in the positioning of teachers and students, and further this book is also concerned with how the teacher improves teaching through changing their ways of positioning. In the present study, except for the concept of positioning, the ways in which literature is read and taught dialogical relates to Bakhtin's dialogism.

Freedman, Delp, and Crawford (2005) conducted a detailed investigation of the teaching method in Delp's untracked[①] English classroom. Delp, whose approach for teaching English was grounded in Vygotskian and Bakhtinian theory, did not traditionally organise small groups (as in cooperative learning or complex instruction) but relied on whole-group, multimodal activities and one-on-one teacher-student interactions during group activities. From the perspective of Vygotsky's and Bakhtin's ideas about the development of meaning mediated by social interaction, Freedman et al. (2005) assumed several underlying principles which facilitated Delp's students to develop as meaning-builders within her activity system. After analysing Delp's methods of teaching — using whole-class participant structures in combination with individual attention — they claimed that teachers must consider the way of managing the heterogeneous space with many voices, especially when teachers struggled to create opportunities for meaningful interactions for their students. In Freedman's and Delp's next reflective essay (2007), they focused their attention on the whole-class learning space which was comprised of a diverse student population. Situating their work in Vygotskian and Bakhtinian theory, Freedman and Delp (2007) further addressed the concept of *a grand dialogic zone* (GDZ) to name the whole-class learning space and re-examined key aspects of the GDZ (p.261). Their studies on Delp's whole-class activities and her teaching methods illustrated a possibility for framing the whole class dialogically by

---

[①] *Tracking* means sorting and separating students into classes by ability. It is often found in high schools which can include Advanced Placement classes, high, average, and low ability classes as well as special education classes across a range of academic subjects (Rex & Schiller, 2009, p.60).

validating multiple and complex interactions. Inspired by Delp's classroom, the present study not only examines the interactions in group work, which is usually regarded as a dialogic way of framing but also pays attention to whole-class teaching, which indicates how the teacher frames the whole-class discussions and activities. The inclusion of the teaching method also constitutes one dimension of the theoretical foundation in the study.

1.3.3 Dialogic Perspective on the Theory of Literary Reading

Bakhtin's ideas about dialogism and how understanding was created were of great importance for instruction in literature classrooms. Following Bakhtin, Rosenblatt (1978, 1985, 1993, 1995) explored the dialogic exchange between the reader and the text — in her word's *transactional relationship* (Rosenblatt, 1978, p.ix). Briefly, the transactional theory viewed the reader as a responsible reader who co-constructed the literature as the work of art with the writer, as Faust (2000) confirmed "the work of art does not exist except as a process of becoming what it is within and across the experiences of readers" (p.26). This interpretation implied the importance of the reader's active role in recalling their past experience, which was brought into the act of reading, and in calling forth the lived-through experience in the process of meaning-making. In other words, the reader's background, their vision of the world, past experience, the feelings, memories, and associations were recalled in the reading; and then the meaning of a text was built upon these things in the reader's mind. Thus, transactional theory cared about who the readers were, what they brought to the text, the expectations they had of texts, and the choices they made as they read (Probst, 1987). Hence, the same text may be read by different readers with different purposes and ways, which creates the diversity of meaning of the same text. In order to highlight the reader's subject experience in the reading event, Rosenblatt distinguished two stances of the reader — *efferent reading* and *aesthetic reading* (Rosenblatt,

1978, 1995). In *efferent reading*, the reader was primarily concerned with the information to be acquired from the text, and in *aesthetic reading*, the reader was concentrated on what happened or in other words, the actual experience he/she was living during the reading.

Based on the diversity of meaning made by different readers, Faust (2000) asserted that the transactional theory provided an efficient way of framing the literature classroom, to solve the dilemma of literary teachers that they sought "to validate students' personal responses" but were simultaneously confronted with a problem of "warranting unbridled subjectivism" (p.9). Faust termed this dilemma as *double bind* (Faust, 2000, p.22), which will be discussed further in the last chapter of this book. In Faust's view, in the classrooms framed on the basis of transactional theory, multiple readings were encouraged and respected, and students would be invited to share the reading experience with others as a dialogic interchange to develop thoughtful responses and understandings to enrich the possibilities of making meaning with literature.

However, Faust's (2000) interpretation of using the transactional theory in literature teaching was regarded as the old map of the pedagogy of literature (Dressman, 2004). Dressman (2004) argued that this old map that either described teachers "as master readers and students as apprenticed supplicants" (p.34) or described teachers "as facilitative guides and students as autonomous meaning makers" (p.34) was increasingly questioned according to the reality in current classrooms. Instead, he drew a new map based on the congruence between Dewey's transactional and aesthetic experience and Bakhtin's dialogism. Dressman (2004) asserted that this approach, grounded in a dialogue between the work of Dewey and Bakhtin, significantly extended Rosenblatt's *an individual reader* to view readers as *social subjects* (p.48) whose responses were the result of their history of experiences within the social world. Also, Rosenblatt's view of the text as "mere ink spots on the page" was extended, seeing texts as having social and cultural agency. With the comparison of Dewey and Rosenblatt, as well as Dewey and Bakhtin, Dressman (2004) pointed out that it was important for literary teachers to invite students to understand their personal responses as the result of their historical and cultural position in relation to the text. Further, Dressman (2004) reminded teachers to notice the development of students' dialogue with the text over time. Briefly, the reader's response was ever-changing, so that students could revisit the development and adjustments made in the current response compared with a previous one. This point was developed by Langer's envisioning theory (2011a, 2011b) — a part of the theoretical foundation of this book — which views the development of understanding as a fluid and ongoing process.

1.4 Research Gap and Research Questions

1.4.1 Research Gap

There have been many studies in this area with different purposes. However, these studies focus mainly on reinterpreting Bakhtin's dialogism to explore what dialogic discourse means in the classroom and how it facilitates teachers' work and students' learning. With a different approach, this book is not only grounded in Bakhtin's work, but also in other theories that can be related to Bakhtin's work but with more focus on the ways of social interactions and literary reading. Besides, there are research gaps in studying the factors impacting dialogues in the classroom, and also in the cross-national investigation of literature classrooms. To bridge these gaps, this book is conducted in a comparative view, analysing the various ways of framing classroom discourse in different contexts. Further, this study focuses on the possibilities of students' engagement in dialogic interactions with teachers, texts, and other peers. When the pattern of teaching and possibilities of engagement are investigated, barriers of dialogue in the literature classroom are also considered in different contexts.

1.4.2 Research Questions

This book is focused on two main research questions: (1) How are the interactions between the teacher and students, the interactions between students, and the interactions between students and the text framed in Danish and Chinese literature classes? (2) What are the differences and commonalities between the framing approaches in Danish and Chinese classes?

The main research questions imply four specific objectives of this book: **Firstly**, to describe interactions in different classrooms focusing on the possibilities for students' engagement including the possibility of multiple positions offered to students and the possibility of multiple readings encouraged in the classroom. **Secondly**, to compare the similarities and differences between the patterns of framing classroom interactions in Danish and Chinese classes. **Thirdly**, to develop an understanding of dialogic teaching in the literature classroom from theoretical and pedagogical perspectives. **Finally**, to illuminate the factors that impact the development of classroom interactions in Danish and Chinese literature classes.

1.5 The Meaning of *Dialogic* in the Literature Classroom: Theoretical Framework

This section presents and discusses the theories and literature the study built on, which provides a theoretical foundation for this book regarding the framing of classroom interactions in the literature classroom. It presents a review of some theoretical perspectives on dialogism and related research that most directly contribute to the development and conceptualization of the study. Generally speaking, this theoretical section includes three parts: the theoretical interpretation of Bakhtin's dialogism, the application of dialogism in the teaching practice, as well as three theories that constitute the theoretical framework of this book — positioning theory (Harré & van Langenhove, 1999), envisioning theory (Langer, 2011a, 2011b), and *Cross-model* of teaching methods (Bundsgaard, 2009). Based upon the theoretical combination, this section concludes with defining the meaning of *dialogic* in the present study.

1.5.1 Interpretation of Dialogism

Dialogism, which is a term from Bakhtin's focus and interest, has received much attention recently. According to Bakhtin, any utterance was inherently dialogic (Bakhtin, 1981). Dialogism covered all verbal communication, including the oral and the written, the internal and the external (Dysthe, 1999). The external dialogue was primarily oral, referring to the face-to-face turn-taking, while the internal dialogue was a sort of silent dialogue happening in one's mind when one responded to the utterance of others without necessarily saying something in voice (Dysthe, 1999). In Bakhtin's sense, interactions in which persons took the turn-talking were not necessarily dialogic, whereas dialogism occurred when one utterance depended on the other and when new meaning was produced in a tension between the utterances (Dysthe, 1999).

Dysthe's words indicated two meanings of dialogism. First, in Bakhtin's view, each utterance was dialogic and echoed another's utterance (Bakhtin, 1986). Bakhtin explained how an utterance was shaped and understood in an interaction with another's utterance. According to him, understanding of any utterance was established on a dialogue between a listener and a speaker who held different social and cultural backgrounds, in terms of knowledge, dialects, opinions, beliefs, and so on (different conceptual systems, in Bakhtin's words) (Bakhtin, 1981). These differences influenced the dialogue that acted as a bridge to the interaction of the struggles and disagreements of the participants. The process whereby the listener responded and participated in establishing understanding and meaning was termed "active understanding" (Bakhtin, 1981, p.282) by Bakhtin. Bakhtin further elaborated how understanding occurred out of a dialogic interchange which will be discussed later.

The second meaning of dialogism was that interaction was dialogic when it was "continually structured by tension, even conflict, between the conversants, between self and other, as one voice 'refracts' another" (Nystrand et al., 1997, p.8). This meaning explained how *heteroglossia*, another essential concept in Bakhtin's theory, occurred in a social context. *Heteroglossia* allowed tension and conflict among different types of speech and ideas and let them juxtapose and interact.

1.5.1.1 Active Understanding

In the act of reading, thinking about how understanding is constructed is usually pedagogically important for teachers. Bakhtin explained how understanding and learning happened when analysed the dialogic nature of language. As any discourse had dialogic orientation, all rhetorical discourses were oriented toward the listener and his or her answer, which was the basic feature of rhetorical discourses (Bakhtin, 1981). To be precise, for the speaker, the meaning could not come out of the monologic utterance. As Bakhtin said, "The language collective, the plurality of speakers, cannot be ignored when speaking of language, but when defining the essence of language this aspect is (was) not a necessary one that determines the nature of language" (Bakhtin, 1986, p.68). Instead, it was constructed with the consideration of the listener who "simultaneously takes (took) an active, responsive attitude toward it (the meaning of speech)" (ibid). The understanding that a listener's response participated in was termed as *active understanding*, and it was the only way to produce the actual meaning of utterance (Bakhtin, 1981, 1986, pp.280–281):

> Responsive understanding is a fundamental force, one

that participates in the formulation of discourse, and it is moreover an active understanding, one that discourse senses as resistance or support enriching the discourse. Linguistics and the philosophy of language acknowledge only a passive understanding of discourse (...) it is an understanding of an utterance's *neutral signification* and not its *actual meaning*.

For Bakhtin, "any understanding of live speech, a live utterance, is (was) inherently responsive" (Bakhtin, 1986, p.68). Understanding was based on the response, which prepared the ground for an active and engaged understanding. Thus, there was such an intimate relationship between understanding and response, "One is (was) impossible without the other" (Bakhtin, 1981, p.282). On the contrary, monologic utterance without response closed the entry of new ideas, meaning, and even knowledge. This understanding was contrarily named "passive understanding" (Bakhtin, 1981, p.281) which only mirrored the words, and reproduced the meaning of the word. As for the reader self, she/he also desired speech communication, expecting response, "agreement, sympathy, objection, execution, and so forth" (Bakhtin, 1986, p.69). In short, one-way transmission of knowledge did not produce understanding (Dsythe, 1999). Understanding which was built on the speech communication, so to speak, was a bidirectional and reciprocal interaction by which partners could meet, had dialogues, and gained new meanings that they had not met before.

But how can understanding and learning grow out of a dialogic interchange? Bakhtin explained that two conceptual systems — the speaker's and the listener's — confronted and conflicted in the conversation where something new and understanding grew, thus he argued that an active understanding was the "one that assimilates (assimilated) the word under consideration into a new conceptual system" (Bakhtin, 1981, p.282). Bakhtin's distinction of two individual conceptions also implied that the language was a social and historical becoming (Bakhtin, 1981) so that within a unitary national language, "various different points of view, conceptual horizons, systems for providing expressive accents, various social 'languages' comes (came) to interact with one another" (Bakhtin, 1981, p.282) when the dialogic interchange and active understanding happened. Briefly, Bakhtin's idea can be interpreted that in the conversation the speaker and the listeners — even if they speak the same national languages — hold different social and cultural backgrounds, knowledge, dialects, opinions, beliefs; these differences create *heteroglossia* and meanwhile make interactions between each other to negotiate and assimilate struggles and disagreements. In the context of literature classes, Bakhtin's active understanding can be seen as a way of allowing students to play an active role in working with other opinions and developing own understanding, through a process of dialogic interchange with others and assimilation of new elements from others' discourse.

1.5.1.2 Heteroglossia

When a teacher and a number of students talk in the classroom, there is the diversity of voices. If you look at the class with a lens of Bakhtin, this environment filled with multi-voices is much like the diversity of languages in the novel where all the characters utter different voices in different languages (Bakhtin, 1981). Bakhtin (1981) used *heteroglossia* to describe the juxtaposition of different types of speech in a novels — the speech of characters, the speech of narrators and the speech of the authors — which made up the composition of the novel and could "mutually supplement one another, contradict one another and be interrelated dialogically" (Bakhtin 1981, p.292). The term *heteroglossia* explained the dynamics of the relation and contradiction among these speeches (Nystrand, 1997). Despite being in different languages, these speeches were related to each other and served to express authorial intentions in a refracted way (Bakhtin, 1981), as Holquist

(1990) claimed, heteroglossia also displayed "a plurality of relations" (p.89) of related voices. Bakhtin explained how the utterances were related to each other. In Bakhtin's sense, an utterance was a hybrid construction of mixed utterance, speech manners, styles, languages, semantic, and axiological belief systems (Bakhtin, 1981). That is to say, except for the speaker's own speech, there were many other speeches from different sources incorporated in all utterances. These other words were from another speaker, utterance, language or texts, and "exits (existed) in other people's mouths, in other people's contexts, serving other people's intentions" (Bakhtin, 1981, p.294). He explained that how a speaker's speech was shaped and developed in the constant interactions with others' utterances (Bakhtin, 1986). This process was characterized by Bakhtin as a process of "assimilation" or creative work of others' words (Bakhtin, 1986, p.89). However, not all the words could fully coincide with the speaker's words, but in fact, all utterance was filled with centrifugal forces (Bakhtin, 1981). By re-accentuating others' voices, narrators and ordinary speakers could establish positions for themselves. Any utterance was, so to speak, not only "filled with echoes of the others' utterance" (Bakhtin, 1986, p.88), but also "overpopulated with the intentions of others" (Bakhtin, 1981, p.294). Hence, a speaker's utterance including the creative works needed him to "assimilate, rework and re-accentuate" (Bakhtin, 1986, p.89). In this sense, it could be argued that by re-accentuating others' voices, speakers could establish positions for themselves.

Therefore, with the notion of heteroglossia, the diversity of languages of teachers and students who are from various cultural and knowledge backgrounds and take up diverse identities and positions, creates a multi-voiced climate for dialogues in the classroom. How these languages contradict, intersect with each other, and are dialogically interrelated to each other is an interesting issue to be noticed when investigating classroom discourse. In such a classroom with *heteroglossia*, students' creative speeches that present their positions are encouraged, and new opinions are valued. Diversity of voices, points of view, and positions, which add to the heteroglossia in the classroom, constitute an enrichment of the learning environment (Dysthe, 1993). In order to explore new meanings of dialogic teaching, three types of interactions — the interaction between the teacher and students, the student and the student, and students and the text — are investigated, giving prominence to student talk in the classroom discourse. Further, in the context of literature classrooms, heteroglossia can also specifically refer to the diversity of readings and understandings from students, which will be discussed later as one part of the theoretical foundation of this book. In Bakhtin's sense of *heteroglossia*, it is worth noting that the teaching method that involves much student talk is not necessarily dialogic if there are no interactions or contradictions between one and another.

In short, Bakhtin's notions of *active understanding* and *heteroglossia* illuminates the essence of dialogism, which has been used to reflect on the teaching in class. As a result, dialogic teaching as an application of dialogism in pedagogy is attracting more attention.

1.5.2 Use of Dialogism in Pedagogy

The term *dialogic teaching* has been regularly used in recent research on classroom discourse, but it appears to have different meanings within the literature.

1.5.2.1 Monologic Discourse vs. Dialogic Discourse

Defining *dialogic teaching* usually begins with the distinction between *dialogic discourse* and *monologic discourse*, which can be traced back to Bakhtin who made an epistemological distinction between these two kinds of discourse in his book *Problem of Dostoevsky's Poetics* (1984).

> In an environment of philosophical monologism, the genuine interaction of consciousness is impossible, and thus genuine

dialogue is impossible as well. In essence idealism knows only a single mode of cognitive interaction among consciousness: someone who knows and possesses the truth instructs someone who is ignorant of it and in error; that is, it is the interaction of a teacher and a pupil, which, it follows, can only be a pedagogical dialogue.

(Bakhtin, 1984, p.81)

While Bakhtin's discussion on "monologism" and "dialogism" is mostly philosophical in nature, showing his deploring of this typical asymmetrical dialogue as a non-productive monologism, researchers have seen much pedagogical potential in the process of meaning-making in dialogues, as opposed to the conventional "monologic" instructional approach (Lyle, 2008; Nystrand et al., 2003; Skidmore, 2006). This distinction between monologic discourse and dialogic discourse is widely adopted in classroom research. According to Bakhtin's distinction, researchers usually describe the monologic approach as a one-way transmission of knowledge from the teacher to the students. In a monologic discourse, the teacher is typically the main speaker, who controls the goals, process and time of conversations. On the contrary, the dialogic approach is concerned to promote communication through authentic exchanges of voices. There is genuine concern for the views of the partners and effort is made to help participants of conversation share and build mutual meaning collaboratively (Lyle, 2008; Nystrand et al., 2003). Therefore, dialogue is not merely a mode of communication, but a way to build understanding and knowledge.

Following Bakhtin, more researchers from different parts of the world advocate dialogic discourse through summarizing features of dialogic instruction from classroom practice. Studies by Nystrand, Gamoran, Kachur, and Prendergast (1997), Alexander (2008b), and Reznitskaya (2012) are among the most notable examples. In the book *Opening Dialogue* (1997), Nystrand et al. argued that dialogic teaching favoured a different pattern of interaction characterized by the use of authentic questions on the part of the teacher and the pupils where answers were not prespecified but incorporated into subsequent dialogue so that pupils' responses modified the topic of discourse (Nystrand et al., 1997). Further, he put forward the features of *"dialogically organised instruction"* which represented a paradigm shift as compared to the traditional instruction in American classrooms (Nystrand et al., 1997, p.19). Table 1.1 was extracted from Nystrand et al.'s (1997, p.19) work.

Table 1.1 Key Features of Monologically and Dialogically Organised Instruction

	Monologically organised instruction	Dialogically organised instruction
Paradigm	Recitation	Discussion
Communication model	Transmission of knowledge	Transformation of understandings
Epistemology	Objectivism: Knowledge is given	Dialogism: Knowledge emerges from interaction of voice
Source of valued knowledge	Teachers, textbook authorities: Excludes students	Includes students' interpretations and personal experience
Texture	Choppy	Coherent

Since the early 2000s, Alexander (2008a, b) developed the term of *dialogic teaching* which was seen as a way to balance the power of classroom talk and explore students' thinking as well as improve their understandings. For him, *dialogic teaching* was distinct from the question-answer and listen-tell routines of traditional teaching and it treated students' contributions, and especially their answers to teachers' questions, as stages in an ongoing cognitive quest rather than as terminal points. It improved the quality of classroom talk as a means of increasing students' engagement, learning, and attainment. He identified essential features of dialogic teaching. They require:

(1) *interactions* which encourage students to think, and to think in different ways;

(2) *questions* which invite much more than simple recall;

(3) *answers* which are justified, followed up and built upon rather than merely received;

(4) *feedback* which informs and leads thinking forward as well as encourages;

(5) *contributions* which are extended rather than fragmented;

(6) *exchanges* which chain together into coherent and deepening lines of inquiry;

(7) *discussion and argumentation* which probe and challenge rather than unquestioningly accept;

(8) *professional engagement with subject matter* which liberates classroom discourse from the safe and conventional;

(9) *classroom organisation, climate and relationships* which make all this possible.

(Alexander, 2008 b)[①]

More clearly and specifically, Reznitskaya (2012) identified the following key verbal behaviors and practices that characterize *dialogic teaching* on the basis of many research studies (Alexander 2008a, b; Billings & Fitzgerald 2002; Nystrand et al., 1997; Nystrand et al., 2003; Soter, Wilkinson, Murphy, Rudge, Reninger & Edwards, 2008):

(1) In a dialogic classroom, power relations are flexible, and authority over the content and form of discourse is shared among group members.

[①] Retrieved from the homepage of Robin Alexander, http://www.robinalexander.org.uk/dialogic-teaching/.

(2) Dialogic teaching relies on questions that are "fundamentally open or divergent ... in terms of allowing a broader degree of uncertainty in what would constitute an adequate answer."

(3) To advance the group's inquiry further, teachers in dialogic classrooms provide students with meaningful and specific feedback.

(4) Participants in dialogic discussions consistently engage in meta-level reflection.

(5) Students in a dialogic classroom present lengthy, elaborate explanations of their ways of thinking.

(6) During dialogic discussions, students engage in the collaborative co-construction of knowledge.

(Reznitskaya, 2012, pp.447–448)

The above three approaches to dialogic classrooms evidently differed from each other. From a perspective of epistemology, Nystrand and his colleagues (1997) examined what the dialogic instruction and dialogic conversation were like through a comparison with monologic ones. Alexander (2008b) did a broader research on dialogic teaching, which extendedly explored classroom discourse, classroom setting, the relationship between the teacher and students, and students' engagement in the interaction. Drawn from the research of Nystrand et al. (1997) and Aexander (2008b), Reznitskaya (2012) synthesized the features of the dialogic classroom, dialogic teaching, and the roles of teachers and students.

Although taking up different paradigms using different terms, these studies reach a consensus that dialogic teaching is mainly characterized by the following aspects: (1) authentic exchanges of understandings; (2) quality of classroom talk such as questions, answers, interactions, discussions, and argumentations; (3) flexible relationships between the teacher and students; (4) students' collaboration with the teacher in the co-construction of knowledge. While these researchers present a broad perspective on the features of dialogic teaching, their concern for the understanding process in the literature classroom is minimal.

1.5.2.2 Dialogic IRE

Drawing comparisons with Bakhtin's dialogism and features of dialogic teaching, IRE, the conventional classroom discourse was increasingly being identified as monologic instruction/recitation (Mehan, 1979; Mroz, 2000; Nystrand & Gamoran, 1991). This recitation approach, in which students only demonstrated their ability to recall assigned information but had few opportunities to question or explore ideas to regulate their thoughts, was recognized as the opposite of the approach where open dialogues and exchanges of students' ideas were involved (Nystrand et al., 2003).

Despite these criticisms, the IRE approach can also move towards the opposite direction for use in a dialogic classroom. A number of researchers have on the one hand criticized IRE as a common pattern of all official talk in classrooms, while on the other hand, recognized several features which demonstrated that IRE discourse could be dialogically organised (Dysthe, 1993; Lyle, 2008; Nystrand et al., 1997; Nystrand et al., 2003). These features emphasised the quality of initiated questions, students' engagement, and the level of teacher's evaluation, and they all together contributed to a dialogic instruction, which was named *dialogic IRE* as opposed to the *monologic IRE* in the researcher's previous study (Liu, 2016). In the previous research, the researcher incorporated four dialogic indicators that were synthesized from studies by Collins (1982), Dysthe (1993), Nystrand and Gamoran (1991), and Nystrand et al. (1997, 2003). These four indicators were "authentic question", "uptake", "high-level evaluation", and "substantive engagement" (Liu, 2016, pp.52–53). The first three indicators borrowed from predecessors aligned with the work of Nystrand et al. (1991, 2003), Collins (1982), Nystrand et al. (1997), whereas the concept of *substantive engagement* had been modified and developed in the particular context of literature reading. The meaning of *substantive engagement* was redefined to echo Bakhtin's (1981, 1984) concept of *active understanding* and Rosenblatt's (1978, 1995) *transactional theory* both of which foregrounded the importance of dialogue in reading and understanding, and diversed readings from individual experience (Liu, 2016). The current study continues the researcher's previous work, deeming *substantive engagement* as an approach to validating students' personal readings that are based on personal lived-through experience in the process of reading. Meanwhile, the present study further extends the meaning of substantive engagement and dialogic discourse based on the theoretical foundation.

1.5.3 Extending the Thinking of Dialogic Teaching

The interpretation and application of dialogism in teaching stimulates further thinking of classroom discourse. Firstly, positioning theory and envisioning theory are incorporated into a combined lens from which the differences in ways of framing classroom interactions in different classrooms can be examined. Then the teaching-method model (*Cross-model*) functions as a point of departure from which the teaching method in each classroom is described and discussed.

Positioning theory and envisioning theory are relevant to this study for two reasons. First, increasingly, much research has been done on classroom discourse from a perspective of social interaction which enriches the complexity of the classrooms and is appropriated to using positioning theory. Positioning theory, based on social constructionist psychology, is seen as a branch of sociocultural theory (Howie & Peter, 1996). Second, Nystrand (2006) points out a number of studies that show the relationship between reading comprehension and the classroom interaction of students with their teachers and peers. Envisioning theory (Langer, 2011a, 2011b) which rethinks how literature is read and taught on the basis of Bakhtin's (1981, 1984) ideas about meaning-making and Rosenblatt's transactional theory (Rosenblatt, 1978, 1995) further examines the process of understanding when students read, write, talk, discuss, and interact with others about a piece of work.

1.5.3.1 Positioning Theory

As Harré and van Langenhove (1999) explained, the concepts of *positioning* and *position* in positioning theory stemmed from Hollway who focused on the gender differentiation in discourses and the relations among various positions in discourses (as cited in Harré & van Langenhove, 1999). Harré and van Langenhove improved Hollway's idea of positioning and developed positioning theory. From the perspective of social constructionism, positioning theory dealed with how people in society created themselves and others through ordinary conversation within a mutually determining triad: position, the social force of action, and storyline (Harré & van Langenhove, 1999). People constructed the triad of conversation by positioning others and themselves simultaneously, which was termed as interactive positioning and reflexive positioning (Davies & Harré, 1990) respectively. Besides, there were other types of positioning according to positioning theory (Harré & van Langenhove, 1999; Davies & Harré, 1990).

Locating positions and their attendant storylines in local interaction conveys the rights, duties, and responsibilities presumed to be associated with such positions relative to shared cultural repertoires (Anderson, 2009). Positioning illustrates that people position or arrange themselves and others along with storylines, related to both social responsibility and cultural ideologies. In this sense, when positioning theory is used to look at teaching and learning in a social context, it is also relevant to the socio-cultural theory of learning which claims that learning involves contextual social acts, meaning is made, and identities are constructed through these social acts.

- ***Role vs. Position***

The concept of *position* was addressed by Davies and Harré (1990) who saw *position* as a dynamic alternative to the more static, formal, and ritualistic concept of *role* (p.43). Starting from a discussion about the concept of *role* in the dramaturgical model, Davies and Harré (1990) noted that people's roles were determined by the particular play and the role models, whereas position allowed people to locate themselves in conversations according to narrative forms that people were familiar with and to bring personal lived histories to "those narratives" (p.52) because in positioning theory, the way of interacting in everyday life was compared to a metaphor of an unfolding narrative in which people occupied, refused or negotiated multiple positions. In role theory, people can always be separated from the various roles based on the way any particular conversation is interpreted and understood (Davies & Harré, 1990), but in positioning theory, people cannot be separated from the multiple positions they occupy as the actual relations between people and positions are jointly produced in the act of conversing. This is the important difference between these two concepts.

When comparing with role theory, it is important to emphasise the dynamics of positioning theory. *Position* is something that is created in and through a conversation as the interlocutors take themselves as persons (Davies & Harré, 1990). In a discursive practice, people can challenge positioning or being positioned, as Harré and Moghaddam (2003) elaborate, "people can adopt, strive to locate themselves in, be pushed into, be displaced from or be refused access, recess themselves from and so on, in a highly mobile and dynamics way" (p.6). Thus, the focus of the positioning is not to understand what people are saying but to analyse the way in which they constitute self and each other in discursive practice. The concept of *position* pays attention to the dynamic aspects of conversations (Davies & Harré, 1990).

- ***The Position/Act-Action/Story Line Triad***

From the perspective of social constructionism, positioning theory deals with how people in society position/arrange themselves and others through the ordinary conversation within a mutually determining triad — position, act-action, and storyline (Harré & van Langenhove, 1999, p.18). Harré and Moghaddam (2003) interpret the meanings of these three components of the positioning triangle:

Position is "a cluster of rights and duties to perform certain actions with a certain significance as acts, but which also may include prohibitions or denials of access to some of the local repertoire of meaningful acts" (Harré & Moghaddam, 2003, pp.5–6). In positioning, people can adopt, resist and modify the positions and reposition themselves again.

Act-action includes every socially significant action, intended movement, and speech that is interpreted as an act. Thus, the act-action is socially meaningful and significant performance. It is not significant until it is given a meaning in a social episode (ibid).

Story line is an already established pattern following which the social episodes unfold as this or that person. Each story line is expressible in a loose cluster of narrative conventions (ibid).

These three components are interwoven and closely related to one another. The shift in positions takes place when a new storyline is created by the shift of speech — acts of the positioned interlocutors. Correspondingly, when people negotiate for new positions in a conversation, they are creating a new storyline and new actions. Therefore, positioning is flexible and there is positioning and repositioning during conversations.

- **Identity, Discourse, and Position**

The term *identity* has a long history and carries many different meanings based on various literature and theories. Among the interpretations of identity, there is an approach named *discourse-based* approach that engages identity into social contexts and focuses on the central role of language and interaction in the constitution of people's identity (Benwell & Stokoe, 2006). This approach describes identity as fluid and dynamic, shifting primarily according to what the people are recognized by others and the contexts where they are (Benwell & Stokoe, 2006).

The discourse-based approach to identity can be interpreted further with Gee's (2011a) sense of *socially situated identity* (p.30) which replaces the concept of social position and relates to the different identities people take on in different practices and contexts (1999). In and through words and deeds, people seek to sustain some kind of identity (socially situated identity) in a certain way, as in Gee's words, "doing (acting out in thought, word, and deed) being some identity" (Gee, 2001, p.27). Such socio-cultural characteristic ways of being a certain kind of person in the world — such as ways of combining and integrating language, actions, interactions, ways of thinking, believing, values, and using various symbols, tools, and objects to enact a particular sort of socially recognizable identity (Gee, 1999) — is termed *Discourses with capital 'D'* (Gee, 2011a) or *identity kits* (Rex& Schiller, 2009, p.22).

Gee explained that *Discourse with capital D* helped people to recognize themselves and others who enacted a particular sort of socially recognizable identity (socially situated identities) and engaged in a social activity (social practice) (Gee, 2011a). Put simply, these multiple ways of being made people present different identities in different situations (Rex& Schiller, 2009). Therefore, by changing the contexts and the socially constructed practices, people can change the socially constructed identities flexibly, which may create new interactions and relationships among people. Rex and Schiller argued that the relationships people had with each other in different contexts affected the identities people present and vice versa (Rex & Schiller, 2009). With the discourse-based approach to identity, this study thus examines the positions (situated identities) of teachers and students and their relationships within different teaching practices and sociocultural contexts, and as well how the shift of interactions and relationships affects their situated identities/positions.

Positioning theory that investigates the dynamic positions and relationships of people in social interactions is thus seen as a discourse-based approach to analyse identity in different contexts (Benwell & Stokoe, 2006). The present study uses positioning theory to illuminate the complexities of classroom interactions by two means. One is examining the positions teachers occupied as they presented their own identity as a literary teacher embedded in different socio-cultural contexts, such as how teachers looked at being a literary teacher and their teaching of literature (through an interview before observation). The other is examining the multiple positions that teachers offered students as they constructed various situated identities in different activities during the teacher-student, student-student, and student-text interactions.

- ***Application of Positioning in the Educational Research***

Much research has adapted the concept of positioning or positioning theory to analyse classroom interactions in educational questions. Anderson (2009) applied positioning theory to analyse classroom interactions from an integrated micro-, meso-, and macro-social perspective to explicate how learning and identity were mediated by classroom participation, social and textual artifacts and discursive processes (Anderson, 2009). There were more studies on the interrelation between positioning way and teaching in classrooms. Some focused on the way in which teachers' positioning improved their teaching and facilitated students' learning (Rex & Schiller, 2009; Vetter, 2010). Rex and Schiller's (2009) study focused broadly on the question of how teachers built interactional awareness to improve teaching, while Vetter's (2010) study took a microscope view, researching how teachers navigated improvised responses to position students as engaged readers and writers to facilitate the process of literacy learning and identity construction among students. Some research focused on the effects of reflexive and interactional positioning on teachers' teaching and students' participation (Clarke, 2006; Reeves, 2009; Yoon, 2008). Reeves's (2009) study demonstrated that teachers could improve their teaching competence by positioning themselves as learners in teachers' training. In addition, Yoon's (2008) study illustrated that positioning theory could broaden teachers' perspectives on ways of teaching by showing that how teachers positioned themselves influenced English language learners' (ELLs) participation and their positioning. It was found that what teachers said and how they acted showed how they positioned the students, which over time shaped the student learning, and further how students positioned themselves and each other also contributed to learning. Clarke's (2006) study illuminated that students' positioning influenced their relationships in the class, and their participation and engagement in learning literacy. By examining how four students were positioned and positioned themselves within literature circle discussions, Clarke (2006) found the class-specific storylines brought the asymmetry of girls' power and boys' powerlessness in the literacy development and consequently suggested that teachers should create opportunities to enable girls and boys to reposition themselves in school literacy events and help them acquire new skills.

These researchers applied positioning theory in studying on the teaching and learning literacy in the classrooms, however, not many studies that have analysed classroom interactions have included the interaction between teachers and students, the student and the student, as well as students and the text in the literature classroom. In this study, positioning theory is useful in that it is interested in the influence of positioning on student engagement in the literature reading and discussion activities, and the meaning of dialogic teaching developed from the perspective of positioning theory that is incorporated in the theoretical framework of this study. Wee (2010) did conduct a similar research study which was to examine positions of students and the teacher in dialogic discussions, and the impact of positions on student learning in dialogic discussions. This study involves the application of positioning theory not only in analysing literature discussions but also in discussing other classroom discourses including lectures, presentations, and even writings. This discussion involves not only the interrelation between positioning theory and reading instructions but also the features of dialogic teaching from the perspective of positioning and reading in a broader view. Furthermore, the current study comparatively investigates the classroom interactions not only in one context but also across different contexts rooted in different cultures.

In brief, the study applied positioning theory as a discourse-based approach to identity what positions/situated identities were constructed by teachers and students in different literature reading and discussion activities (different practices) across divergent classrooms and countries (different contexts), what the relationships between teachers and students were, and how teachers' positioning influenced the possibilities for student engagement in the classroom interactions. Studying positioning in the literature classroom in this study was also seen as an examination of how teachers aware of the interactions with students facilitated students' personal reading and understanding. The following part then narrows down the focus on the literature classroom and discusses envisioning theory (Langer, 2011a, 2011b) which particularly sees the classroom as an envisioning place where thinking and reading occur together.

1.5.3.2 Envisioning Theory

Bakhtin's dialogism in the process of understanding and Rosenblatt's transactional theory (1978, 1995) have had a great influence on people's thinking on how literature is read and taught in recent years. Envisioning theory (Langer, 2011a, 2011b) on the basis of above two theories, further examines the process of understanding when we read, write, talk, discuss and interact with others about a literary text. Envisioning theory treats understanding as fluid and changing; all the cognitive activities in the listener's mind-questions, ideas, agreements, disagreements, arguments, and so on, as responses to any speech (verbal or written, oral utterance or texts), are the engine of developing understanding and enriching envisionment.

This theory is proposed by Langer (2011a) to emphasise the significance of literary experience, and the core of literature understanding. In Langer's (2011a) view, literary subject experience provides a participant's perspective to make sense and gain understanding through personal interpretation. One's experiences can be gained from different domains and they are related to each other. During every experience, people get something in the mind such as ideas, images, questions, and arguments, and this "something" is open for development in the process of reading. She argues that literature understanding can be taught and nurtured by building and developing a literary mind during every literary experience, which is predominantly an imaginative and creative act (Langer, 2011a).

- **The Concept of Envisionment**

According to Langer (2011a), Bakhtin's internal dialogue may occur simultaneously when a work of art triggers a silent dialogue between the text and the previous knowledge in one's mind. As a result, the understanding in one's mind is ever-changing and developing with the proceeding of internal dialogue. Arguing that much previous work has misrepresented the nature of understanding, Langer (2011a, 2011b) names ongoing understanding *envisionment*. Thus, *envisionments* are "dynamic sets of related ideas, questions, images, anticipations, agreements, arguments, and hunches that fill our minds during every reading, writing, discussion, technology interaction, or other experience where we gain or express thoughts and understandings" (Langer, 2011b, p.17). Langer points out, envisionments that develop all the time change as the text proceeds and understandings change (Langer, 2011a). They function based on a premise that acknowledges reading as an interpreting act and people have a number of options to develop their interpretations. With the notion of *envisionment* in the classroom, it is assumed that after reading, all readers including all students and the teacher have their own initial impressions that are ready to change in response to their own and others' ideas through the interchange.

The process of building and developing envisionment is essentially social and consistent with Bakhtin's *active understanding* (Bakhtin, 1981, 1986). Langer defines *envisionment-building* "as an activity in sense-making, where meanings change and shift and grow as a mind creates its understanding of a work" (Langer, 2011a, p.15) and even "after the last word is read [...], we are left with an envisionment that is also subject to change with additional thought, reading, discussion, writing, and living" (p.16). Envisionment-building for one person, so to speak, is a result of responsive understanding and assimilation of new elements from the constant interaction with previous understandings and other people's understandings. Echoing transactional theory (Rosenblatt, 1978), Langer also agrees that there is a constant interaction between the reader and the text, and the meaning that is made is a result of their encounter. Therefore, envisionments are built and developed during the ongoing interaction between self and text. According to Langer, envisionment-building is identified as a general phenomenon in literary reading, but she advocates that in teaching literature it is teachers' responsibility to support and develop the subject experiences and envisionments of the students. She explains further that in the envisionment-building classroom, activities and assignments are designed to invite students to engage in minds-on activities through which students not only read materials but also think about materials (Langer, 2011b).

- *Two Orientations toward Meaning*

In Langer's (2011a) view, envisionment-building always occurs in people's minds when they are making sense, but their primary purposes of making-sense are different. Langer uses the word "orientation toward meaning" to describe two main ways of making-sense-one is *exploring horizons of possibilities* (Langer, 2011a, p.28), and the other is *maintaining a point of reference* (Langer, 2011a, p.32). The purpose of maintaining a point of reference is to gain concepts or information, and in contrast, exploring horizons of possibilities aims at a reconnaissance orientation that involves an open-ended search (Langer, 2011a). Further, these two ways are related to each other and often they work together in many fields in life. Langer argues that in the process of reading, one can move from one to another, but at any point of time, one only has one primary orientation according to his/her primary goal (2011a).

- *Literary Thinking*

Langer always treats literature as a way of thinking, rather than a type of text. In the process of reading, Langer asserted that literature fostered a way of thinking that went far beyond understanding the conventions of genre and text. This way of thinking is different from mathematical reasoning or scientific thinking because it has been widely accepted as a cognitive way. In her word, she was using a "socio-cognitive approach"[①] to think about literature.

As did her predecessor Rosenblatt, Langer claimed for the personal, social, and intellectual benefits of literature. To be specific, *literary thinking* is characterized as a way people's minds work with the orientation of exploring a horizon of possibilities. In the open-ended search, readers utilize creative and imaginative acts to interpret a piece of work, therefore, through literature "students learn to explore possibilities and consider options [...] they become the type of literate, as well as creative, thinkers [...]" (Langer, 2011a, p.2). She further explained that the way of thinking literature stemmed from literary experience which was a kind of exploration by means of scenarios created by readers. The personal, social, cultural contexts, feelings, intentions, different perspectives are considered in reading and understanding so that more possibilities of interpretation and understanding of the text arise with the process of exploration based on the readers' previous reading experience and life experience and imagination. From this perspective, Langer (2011a) thought the way students reading, which could be taught and nurtured, was more important than what they read, because literary thinking empowered them to think creatively as well as critically.

Furthermore, the literary way of thinking was seen by Langer (2011a, 2011b) as a way across the curriculum. It means that students' understandings of the subject content can be enhanced through "interiorized experience" (2011a, p.144). In this sense, envisionment-building is a cognitive approach to literature understanding, and it facilitates literary thinking through literature-based instructions.

- ***Stances in Envisionment-Building***

Envisionment-building as a changing process includes that a series

---

[①] Judith Langer described her approach as "socio-cognitive" way when she was interviewed by the author of this book, at Zhejiang University on 9th, December, 2014.

of relationships readers take toward the text; the relationships are termed *stances* by Langer (2011b). Specifically, *stance* refers to ways or options in which the reader can relate to the material they are reading as they develop their interpretation (Langer, 2011a, pp.16-17; 2011b, pp.21-22). Langer defines five stances during the envisionment-building, and each one offers a different vantage point from which to gain ideas. They are not linear but can recur at any point in the reading (Langer, 2011a, 2011b).

Stances are part of the reader's envisionment-building experience (Langer 2011a), and they actually account for how the reader constantly interacts with the text at different points of reading — being out or in, being closer or distant from the text. The meaning of each stance and the interpretation of the reader's interaction with the text at each stance are listed below.

Stance 1: Being out and stepping into an envisionment — On the surface with the initial ideas of the text; the reader dialogues with superficial elements of text, such as the genre, content, structure, language.

Stance 2: Being in and moving through an envisionment — Further creation by supplementing gaps and lacunae during the process of dialogue with the narrative text; in this case, readers immerse themselves into the process, with focusing on the gaps as signs and points.

Stance 3: Stepping back and rethinking what one knows — Deep reflection on their previous understanding; in this case, it seems that readers have no direct dialogue with the text, but readers have a dialogue with their present envisionments established on the text in the first two stances.

Stance 4: Stepping out and objectifying the experience — Distance self from text to evaluate, examine and analyse the text and envisionments themselves in the perspective of literary theory, or in another word, critical dialogue with the text as an integrated literature rather than focusing on detailed elements, gaps or marks.

Stance 5: Leaving an envisionment and going beyond — This occurs less, and is more demanding for the reader who has built rich and well-developed envisionments to use in unrelated situations; in this case, the dialogue between the reader and the text shifts to the dialogue between the envisionment built in this text to another text or situation (summarised from Langer, 2011a, pp.17-21).

A process of reading experience may involve one or more stances. The recognition of these stances and its interrelation with the text helps teachers design strategies and envisage an interactive way to guide the students to change different stances when reading a piece of work.

- *Use of Envisioning Theory*

Teachers who want their students to build rich envisionments focus not only on the content to be taught but also on how their students think about the material and what they understand (Langer, 2011b, p.43). Teaching and learning envisionments legitimize students as thinkers in their classrooms and unhesitatingly invite them to further develop their understandings. Teachers and students spend class time together on developing understanding and building related and new ideas. Most importantly, in envisionment-building classrooms, the literary thinking and literary experience as a means of exploration of possibilities is supported and nurtured because multiple perspectives are used to enrich possibilities and interpretations, and then multiple readings arise and are juxtaposed. Thereafter, the responses — struggle, choice, and assimilation (Bakhtin, 1981, 1986) — occur when one listens to another's sharing of readings, opinions, and understandings, agrees or disagrees, expresses argumentation and questions, and then goes beyond.

From the perspective of envisioning theory, a literature classroom is a place where the teacher offers enabling strategies to help students envision knowledge, and reading literature is treated as a process of exploring multiple understandings and gaining literary-thinking skills. In this kind of classroom, substantive and sustained discussions and reflections are orchestrated by the teacher, and student literary experience is valued and validated through inviting students' diverse understandings in the process of reading and envisionment-building. Illuminated by envisioning theory and stance tools, this study investigates the reading instructions of divergent literature classrooms, reflecting on how teachers instruct literature reading, whether they engage students in thinking and facilitate the interaction between students and the text and in which way, and whether their instructions can be related to envisioning theory and stance tools.

1.5.3.3 Cross-Model

In the current study, positioning theory and envisioning theory are mainly combined to examine the classroom interactions and reading instructions in each case, whereas the theoretical research on the teaching-method model offers another theoretical perspective to recognize, discuss, and compare divergent teaching methods utilized in different classes.

Since 1946 when a prominent educator Edgar Dale developed the *Cone of Experience* (1946) to emphasise the importance of altering teaching methods according to student background knowledge (Lalley & Miller, 2007), there have been ubiquitous studies on the different teaching methods and their relationships with learning. Among these studies, the *Learning Pyramid* transformed from the cone has been widely discussed or modified in some studies (Lalley & Miller, 2007). These pyramids illustrated the hierarchical relationship among different instructional methods in relation to the levels of learning retention in the shape of a pyramid, indicating that different teaching methods may lead to different levels of student engagement. After reviewed several pyramids of teaching methods, Lalley and Miller (2007) finally recommended consideration of teaching methods on a continuum as opposed to thinking of them in a hierarchy, so that students could experience various teaching methods including direct instructions like lectures. It was because all the methods had advantages and disadvantages. It meant that none was consistently superior to the others and all was effective in certain contexts (Lalley & Miller, 2007). This idea was applied by Bundsgaard (2009, written in Danish) who designed a *Cross-model* of teaching methods (Figure 1.1 translated in English).

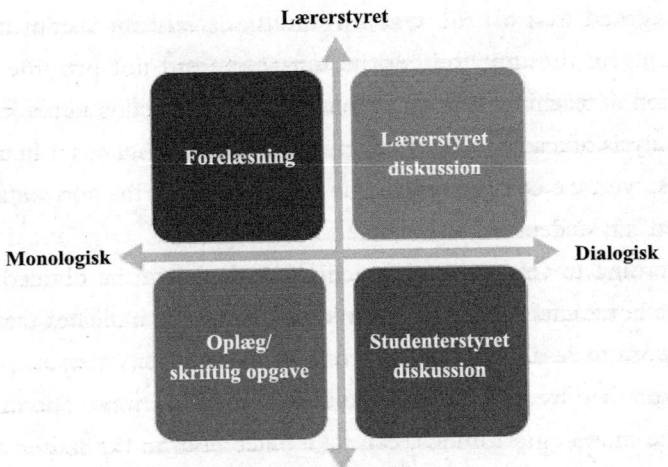

(Bundsgaards Krydsmodel over Emne-/Indholdsorienterede Undervisningsformers Organiseringstyper) (Bundsgaard, 2009, p.12)[1]

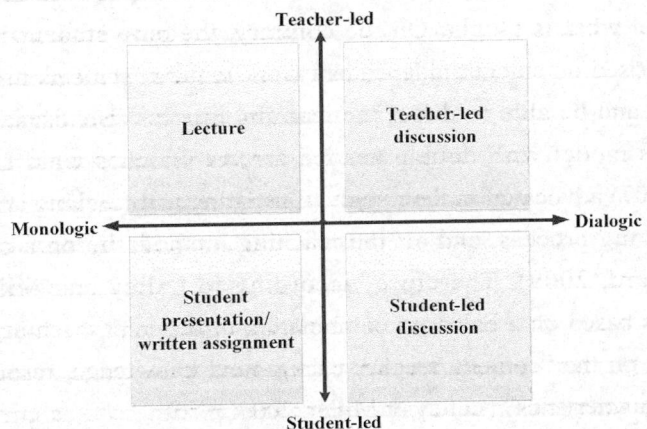

Figure 1.1　Bundsgaard's Cross-Model of Topic/Content-Oriented Teaching Methods and Framing (Bundsgaard, 2009, p.12)

---

[1] Figure 1.1 shows two figures. The first one is originally cited from the article (Bundsgaard, 2009) written in Danish, and the second figure is the English version translated from the Danish version.

He agreed that all the teaching methods laid on a continuum, but meanwhile, he thought the continuum-shape did not provide a logical organization of teaching. Aiming at changing the conception into a logic model for the analysis of teaching, he developed the model in Figure 1.1 in the form of four fields, with the contrast monologic and dialogic on the horizontal axis and teacher-led and student-led on the other.

According to Cross-model, teaching methods can be divided into four types. The horizontal axis from monologic to dialogic indicates that teaching may be more or less carried out by one person or many persons, and more or less expressed by individual behavior or mutual actions. The dialogic, as well as the monologic formats, can take place both in the larger or smaller groups. The axis from teacher-led to student-led indicates how the students have a great influence on what is going on. Pure teacher-led teaching will be completely insensitive about student assumptions, so that the teaching refers to the dissemination of prepared content, regardless of whether students understand what is taught. On the contrary, the pure student-led format which is based on student independent work requires students to have self-discipline and be able to direct the learning process (Bundsgaard, 2009). The Cross-model with double-headed arrows matches what Lalley and Miller (2007) advocated in their study, illustrating that teaching and learning is an ongoing process, and all the teaching methods lie on a continuum (Bundsgaard, 2009). Therefore, according to Lalley and Miller, good teaching is based on a balanced combination of different teaching methods, depending on the "content, teacher background knowledge, resources, and student characteristics" (Lalley & Miller, 2007, p.70).

A balanced combination of different teaching methods is not the only implication from the continuum-shape. A teacher can also shift and adjust his/her teaching methods, moving from one to another in the continuum according to students' competencies and needs. In fact, it is quite common to see the combination of teaching methods in teaching in current literature classes, but it is not common to find shifts and adjustments in teaching to meet students' needs. Instead, teachers are inclined to follow their teaching plan to organise the class. However, the dialogic classroom can be a place where shifts and adjustments are possible and the activities are open for students to join in. For instance, when talking with a teacher, if the student could not see the signals or hints points by the teacher or misunderstand what the teacher means, the adjustments should be made by the teacher in order to keep the coherence of teaching and learning. In this process, it is necessary to utilize a dialogue between the teacher and the student to negotiate an appropriate teaching method.

- **Use of Cross-Model**

The main function of the Cross-model in this book is to provide a point of departure on which this study firstly explores extra teaching methods, particularly dialogic teaching through the empirical research, to echo, supplement, or revise the Cross-model. On the basis of the Cross-model, the exploration of this book contains two aspects.

First, it explores more specific teaching methods in literature classes. Bundgaard (2009) analysed the *Cross-model* and did empirical research in university education, but the model could also explain a general situation across the school years. But of course, it is necessary to specify, supplement, or modify each field when applying it at a given time and place. For instance, the project-based learning which could belong to the student-led discussion in the Cross-model is appropriate and also becomes common for the undergraduates in the university, but obviously, it is not commonly used in the lower secondary or primary schools where the teacher-led format like whole-class discussion and group discussion occurs more often.

Further, in the context of literary teaching, there may be some special teaching methods that can be added to this model. Take *role-play* as an example. *Role-play,* which is commonly used in primary schools, was indeed supported by Vygotsky (Yandell, 2013, 2014). Vygotsky (1978) argued that the play as the major source of development was a significant contributor to the *Zone of Proximal Development* of children (p.102). In Yandell's (2013) study, the part of *role-play* of an English lesson was teacher-guided and facilitated, but the discussions and debate among groups aroused by the play were student-led. When the students played a role and gave their speech in their character roles, it appeared monologic. However, the act of reading, in this case, was more complicated. Yandell's main point was not to show this lesson as a drama lesson, but to stress that reading was a process of meaning-making socially constructed in the classroom when readers with different interests engaged with texts (Yandell, 2013). Thus, different students engaged with the text in different perspectives of roles, which made the text ("sign" in Vološinov's original word) unstable, complex, and multi-accented (Vološinov 1973; Yandell, 2013, 2014), or in Bakhtin's word heteroglot or dialogic nature of meaning-making (Bakhtin, 1981). In this sense, it seems too simple to label the *play* including both teacher-led and student-led tasks as monologic or dialogic.

The ***second*** exploration based on the Cross-model is to unfold a broader range of dialogic teaching that should not be limited at the right dialogic part of the four-fields. The reality in classrooms is more complicated than what was described in this model. On the dialogic part of the model, the teacher-led discussion is not necessarily dialogic. Indeed, it can be organised dialogically, such as dialogic IRE that has been discussed earlier. On the monologic part of the model, *lecture* is not necessarily monologic. Like IRE, *lecture* also has two sides: dialogic or monologic. Traditionally, a lecture has been considered as a teaching method in which there is only one presenter who "imparts his view on a subject" using "a slightly impersonal" style (Goffman, 1981, p.165). Rine (2009) argued that academic lecture in universities could be manipulated dialogically, namely *dialogic lecture*. The *dialogic lecture* was investigated as a particular kind of interactive lecture in Rine's study; in this kind of lecture "the teacher tries (tried) to get the students involved in the lecture through questions-and-answers, debate, etc., and attempts (attempted) to develop a rapport with the students" (Rine, 2009, p.5). Student written assignment is not necessarily monologic either. Many studies on writing have argued that writing is also an interactive way of learning, which echoes the meaning of Bakhtin's dialogism (i.e., Dysthe, 1993, 1999; Middendorf, 1992). With a notion of dialogue in a written way, it is possible to see students' written assignment as dialogic interaction between the teacher and students, and between the student and the student. For instance, the interaction in a written way between the teacher and students might be the case — the teacher corrects and comments and then students question, discuss, argue with teachers, and may revise the essay after that. The case that students revise and give feedback to each other after reading peers' written texts is an example of the interaction between the student and the student.

Summing up, it can be seen that the Cross-model on the one hand, illuminates the logical relations of teaching methods, but on the other hand it has the potential to impede other possibilities. What the model shows is not such exact and it doesn't account for different contexts. From analysing the Cross-model as a point of departure, other possibilities need to be explored further. The current study seeks to open an exploration through which more possibilities from two entirely different socio-cultural contexts are exposed.

1.5.4 Conclusion

The above three theories are composed of the theoretical perspective of this book. The positioning theory and envisioning theory are applied to observe, describe, and analyse some specific teaching methods/activities in each case study, uncovering the features of framing classroom interactions of each teacher. The Cross-model provides a general framework for classifying different teaching methods, especially distinguishing between dialogic teaching and monologic teaching. Built on this model, the present study explores and discusses diverse teaching methods embedded in different contexts, indicating the patterns of the framing in each case.

Broadly described, *dialogic teaching* refers to an interactive way of teaching by which students are offered the opportunity to participate in dialogue with the teacher and other peers both in oral and written ways. In the context of literature classrooms, *dialogic teaching* stresses the student engagement in reading and discussing, such as sharing personal reading experience, expressing diverse understandings based on reading, and discussing some points of view in a democratic climate in the classroom. Particularly in the current study, the possibility of student engagement is examined mainly by two means — firstly by discussing the possibility for students to take up multiple positions or modify the given positions, and secondly by discussing the possibility for students to read and think of a literary text diversely. **On the one hand**, from the perspective of positioning theory, in the dialogic literature classroom students' substantive engagement is validated by teacher's offering various positions for students to occupy, and it is possible for students to resist, modify, or reposition. Through investigating the positioning of the teacher and students in the class, the possibility of students' engagement in dialogue with others can be unfolded. **On the other hand**, aligned with envisioning theory and Bakhtin's sense of dialogism, the dialogic interactions in the literature classroom of this book include the oral and written external interactions between teachers and students and between students, as well as the internal dialogues between students and reading materials in the envisionment-building process. Further, from the perspective of *heteroglossia,* these interactions also contain discussions and contradictions. Thus, the possibility of student substantive engagement can be increased by validating students' subjective experience, fostering student literary thinking, valuing student personal understandings, and orchestrating discussions and argumentations. Briefly, ***dialogic teaching*** that this study defines stresses the student substantive engagement in both external and internal dialogue with the teacher, peers, and literary texts, and facilitates a dialogic learning environment by creating the possibility for students to occupy, resist, or modify different positions.

Chapter 2
Qualitative Case-Study Research on Classroom Interactions

This study applies a qualitative case-study method combined with the descriptive and interpretive approach to document specific conversations and interactions between teachers and students, readers and texts, and among students in each case study. Meanwhile, the present study also uses a comparative approach to compare and discuss the similarities and differences among the patterns of different classes with a consideration of the larger sociocultural contexts in Denmark and China. The methodological consideration is mainly based on the discourse analysis reframed by the theoretical foundation. The discourse analysis perspective provides an analytical lens to look at the classrooms in social contexts.

2.1 Research Design

2.1.1 Qualitative Case Study Research Design

This study follows a qualitative empirical research design, seeking to create evidence by argumentation and discussion based on rich descriptions of a small number of samples rather than to deliver statistical evidence. In particular, this study deals with detailed observations in the classrooms, including transcripts of conversations, observation journals of activities, interview transcripts of some participants, responses to the questionnaire, and relevant documents collected in class. Meanwhile, the present study also applies a case study methodology. As asserted by Creswell (2013), the case study is rooted in the experiences of people in their every day, uncontrolled, and un-manipulated environment, displaying the close relationship between a phenomenon and its context. The observations conducted in this study document in detail how teachers framed classroom interactions, rather than controlling what happened by measuring learning outcomes at the end or through statistically testing the effectiveness of dialogues by means of intervention. At the heart of the study is an interest in looking at what was naturally happening in five classes where the language was used to make meaning of literature. Sometimes observations in the classrooms influence and change original assumptions on which the study approaches have been planned. In general, this study combines a qualitative research method with a case study method, namely the *qualitative case study* that is defined as "an approach to research that facilitates exploration of a phenomenon within its context using a variety of data sources" (Baxter & Jack, 2008, p.544) and "allows for multiple facets of the phenomenon to be revealed and understood" (ibid). This combined research method is chosen because this study involves a "how" question based on a contemporary set of events within a real-life context, over which the researcher has little control (Yin, 2003b).

While there is a place for quantitative methods when studying classroom discourse, in many cases the combination of quantitative and qualitative methods can help allow generalization and complementation (e.g., Nystrand & Gamoran, 1991; Nystrand et al., 2010). In contrast, the current study is conducted on a small scale focusing on the literature classroom discourse within five classrooms of two countries. It investigates the classroom discourse using the qualitative research method — by describing, interpreting, and discussing some teaching methods and phenomena from selected cases to highlight the distinctions among cases and their common grounds in line with the research questions of this study. This qualitative case study design mainly adopts two approaches: the descriptive and interpretive approach and the comparative study approach.

2.1.1.1 The Descriptive and Interpretive Approach to the Case Study

This qualitative case study specifically adopts a descriptive and interpretative approaches. It involves descriptions of the setting, participants, activities, conversations, and what was going on in each class, and as well as interpretations of patterns of the framing classroom interactions and some unique phenomena of targeted footages selected from data in each case. After data analysis, the findings are summarized and further interpreted, ultimately giving rise to discussions, implications, and contributions this study suggested. Briefly, the present study is preoccupied with descriptive interpretations (Yin, 2011) as its final goal is neither to explore the advantages or disadvantages of some teaching methods nor to indicate some presumed casual links as many case studies do. The feature of description as a major type of qualitative interpretation is that most studies aim at reaching a generalizing type of conclusion (Yin, 2011). This study also seeks to achieve a broader conclusion, with the objectives to explore what the dialogic teaching in the literature classroom would be like and to generalize the differences and commonalities the case study demonstrated. Thus, the findings of this study are intentionally open rather than seeking to test hypotheses or explain the reasons behind certain phenomena.

In light of the objectives of the current study, three reasons for choosing a descriptive and interpretive approach to the case study are worth mentioning. *First*, despite the case study being more explanatory, it can also be used for the descriptive purposes (Yin, 2003a). Apart from two main research questions, this study also intends to describe teaching practices and interactions that occurred in the daily classroom, which was mentioned as the research's objectives of this study. The process and outcomes were not controlled, which made it possible to discover and describe any interesting but previously unpredictable phenomena that mainly referred to the special moments when students had a special chance to talk. *Second,* the description of the occurrence in the classroom is not enough. There is a need for documentation of concrete details of teaching practices, participant interviews, and documents collected in order to understand the features of teaching, the ways of framing classroom interactions, and the reasons for doing that, because the "knowledge of reality is gained only through social constructions such a language, consciousness, shared meanings, documents, tools, and other artifacts" (Klein & Myers, 1999, p.69). Further, the researcher's interpretations also need to be involved in this study because the researcher's interpretations play a key role in the interpretive case studies by engaging in the process of data collection and analysis (Diaz, 2009). *Third,* when the classroom observations are conducted through a comparative lens, the comparison sheds the new light on what happened in different classes. In order to compare, each setting including detailed practice is described as fully as possible. The interpretive approach allows sufficient materials to be obtained from the selected cases for subsequent analysis (Diaz, 2009), which is beneficial for a well-founded interpretive comprehension.

2.1.1.2 Multiple-Case Studies with a Comparative View

To take the method one step further, the research is based on multiple-case studies with a comparative view. The multiple-case studies (Yin, 2003a) predict similar results or contrast results for predictable reasons in Yin's sense. In this study, the cases — the English literature classes in the Danish Gymnasiums and the Chinese literature classes in the Chinese high schools — are selected at random rather than by intention. Meanwhile, the present study also wears a comparative lens to look at these classes (multiple cases) for seeking similar or contrasting results, phenomena, or patterns.

The comparative approach of this study focuses on two levels: the micro level and the macro level. The micro comparative view is on the particular details of teaching methods and classroom interactions. These details include a focus on the profile and teaching style of the teacher, how the teacher positioned the students through particular kinds of activities, and how the teacher guided students to engage in the reading experience and literary thinking. Thus, it is possible to derive similarities and distinctions through comparing and contrasting these comparative aspects. The macro comparative view is to take the social and cultural contexts into account when compared the above aspects. The social and cultural contexts of each case are indeed defined as the contextual cultures (Cheong, 2000) that will be elaborated as an influential aspect of comparison.

2.1.1.3 The Concept of Contextual Culture

Grounded in the sociocultural theory of learning, the current study places the importance on the social and cultural contexts of cases. In particular, this comparative study on the framing of classroom interactions was conducted in a western country and an eastern country and so it needs to consider the macro societal cultural factors of both countries and the micro school and classroom cultures of each class. The study of culture and its influence on teaching and learning in the field of educational research and comparative study can be traced back to the 1980s (Cheong, 2000). Especially, in the past decades, there has been a growing concern with the cultural differences between the East and the West and how the cultural forces shape the features of schooling processes and dominate the effectiveness of education in students' academic achievements (ibid). But different scholars defined culture differently for various intentions. Cheong (2000) defined this concept built on several other definitions: "Culture is a system of shared assumptions, beliefs, values, and behaviors in a given group, community, or nation" (Cheong, 2000, p.209). Further, Cheong (2000) described a model of four levels of cultures — classroom culture, school culture, community culture, and societal culture. In particular, Cheong argued that societal culture was regarded as the common patterns of social norms, values, and assumptions shared at the macro level, and similarly, community, school, and classroom cultures were seen as common patterns of social norms, values, and assumptions shared by local people or members in a community, a school, or a classroom (Cheong, 2000). They were all involved in the contextual culture which was the "critical sources of ambient and discretionary stimuli" affecting and shaping school members' behavior and performance (Cheong, 2000, p.210). Cheong's (2000) study also suggested the relationship of four contextual cultures to educational effectiveness with a detailed figure (p.211), showing a process of the macro-level of cultures penetrating into the school level or classroom level to affect teaching and learning. As Cheong (2000) pointed out, the classroom culture had a more direct and closer effect on students' educational performance and academic achievements than other three contextual cultures, and meanwhile, the school culture which is directly related to the classroom culture also plays an important part in teachers' teaching performance and student learning performance. The conception of contextual culture, therefore, offers a framework for carrying out a comparative research or a cross-culture study within different contexts.

While the present study does not aim to research on the cultural factors in the learning effectiveness, it is necessary to integrate the classroom cultures, the school cultures, and the societal cultures when carrying out a comparative study on the classroom interactions rooted in different social and cultural contexts. Thus, each classroom in this study is viewed as an occasion where teaching and learning involved were highly context-specific and affected by multiple levels of contextual cultures. The first introductive chapter has described the differences of the educational system that indicated part of the societal cultures, setting up a broader cultural backdrop that each case of this book was situated in. During the process of data collection and data analysis, the micro-level of cultures — the school culture and the classroom culture — were also considered. Consequently, the school cultures are described respectively at the beginning of each case study in this book, relating to the societal cultures of two countries and reflecting on what they brought to the classroom cultures.

2.1.2 Viewing Classroom from a Language-in-Use Perspective

When conducting the empirical research including the data reduction and analysis, this study applies discourse analysis from a language-in-use perspective. Applying discourse analysis in classroom interactions is commonly referred as a study of language-in-use (Rex & Green, 2008; Rex & Schiller, 2009). According to Schiffrin (1994), there have been many approaches to discourse analysis in the last few years. Among them, the present study uses an interactional sociolinguistic approach that views discourse as a social interaction, and the situated meaning is facilitated in the interactions (Schiffrin, 1994). Gee (2011a, 2011b) who wore a sociolinguistic lens explained that discourse analysis was to study "language at use" (Gee, 2011b, p.ix). Gee asserted that language-in-use was about saying (informing), doing (action), and being (identity), and they had important connections among them when making meanings (Gee, 2011a). Further, Gee argued that discourse not only meant language-in-use but also involved non-language factors. The language-in-use discourse was termed by Gee (2011a, 2011b) as *discourse with "little d"* and the integrated discourse that melded with non-language stuff was called *Discourse with capital "D"*. With a notion of *Discourse* in looking at the classroom, it was illuminated by Gee (2011a) that the teacher and students could take on different situated identities, different from each other and different within different activities, within the classroom Discourse created by the recognition work of the teacher and his/her students.

The present study on classroom interactions also took identities, relationships, teaching activities, and social contexts into account. From the perspective of discourse analysis, this study treats the classroom as a place where the ways of positioning and instructing can be viewed by looking at their interactions. Although this study is mainly interested in looking at the classroom interactions, teachers' and students' ways of positioning self and each other (situated identities), the reading instructions (social activities), and various teaching methods (social activities) are presented through the classroom interactions. Therefore, this study applies discourse analysis as an analytical lens for looking back at the interactions through which teachers and students built different social identities and social activities within different contexts. Three theories that constitute the theoretical foundation frame analysis of the data: positioning theory sheds light on the discursive construction of social identities and relationships of participants (Davies & Harré, 1990; Gee, 2000/2001; Harré & van Langenhove, 1999), envisioning theory is related to the social activity of pedagogy in the literature classroom (Langer, 2011a, 2011b), and the Cross-model also illuminates the social activities-various teaching methods situated in different sociocultural contexts. Figure 2.1 shows a general model, relating positioning theory, envisioning theory, the perspective of discourse analysis.

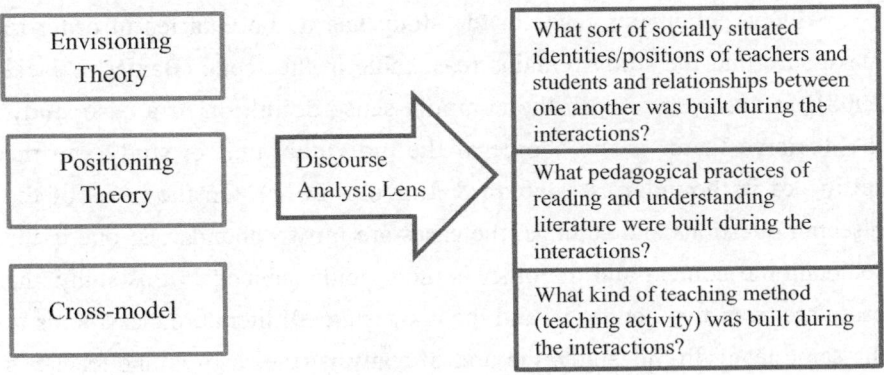

Figure 2.1   The General Model of Using Discourse-Analysis Lens

The above model of using the discourse-analysis lens is developed to manifest how the language (both oral and written) was used by the teacher and students in the classroom to enact practices (teaching practices), identities, and relationships between one another. To be specific, positioning theory is used to examine how the teacher and students built situated identities and relationships between one another through the interactions between the teacher and students and among students as well. Envisioning theory looks through how students were instructed to read a piece of work, relating to the interaction between students and the texts. The Cross-model examines all three types of interactions (teacher-student, student-student, and student-text) to shed light on what kind of teaching method was built in each case.

2.2 Research Setting

This section consists of the setting of the empirical research, with respect to the sample, the participants of the sample, and the researcher's positioning in the classroom investigation.

2.2.1 Sample Choosing and Accessibility

Always, choosing cases in the study has its boundaries in order to make sure that the study remains reasonable in the scope (Baxter & Jack, 2008). In accordance with the common-sense definition of a case study, the decisive factor is the choice of the individual unit of study and the setting of its boundaries (Denzin & Lincoln, 2011). On the basis of the research questions and settings, the cases are in two boundaries: one is the sociocultural context and the other is the specific subject. In this study, the cases are from two countries, and the classes are all literature classrooms at the same level. In this study, the unit of analysis (the case) is one teacher's one or two classrooms. In total, this study investigates five classes taught by four teachers (one teacher taught two classrooms) as cases and analyses their differences and similarities. Among them, three are from Denmark and two are from China.

Generally speaking, the empirical research in four schools with four teachers was divided into two stages. In Denmark, the first stage of the empirical research work was conducted in two general upper secondary classrooms (Gymnasium, STX) from August to October, 2014. During the 8-week investigation, both Teacher S's second and third-year English classes in R Gymnasium were observed, as was Teacher P's second-year English classes in B Gymnasium. During the first stage, there were two obstacles confronted. *First* was the inability of the researcher to speak Danish. Considering the language challenge, this study only focused on how the literary texts were read and taught regardless of the linguistic aspect of language. Teacher S and Teacher P's Danish classes were selected because English class in Danish Gymnasiums involves both the linguistic knowledge of the language and the knowledge and understanding of literature in English as well, as the English classes of two Danish teachers did. These English classes where teachers and students spent much time on the literary text reading and analysing thus became the Danish cases in this study. The *second* obstacle was to gain accessibility into Danish classrooms. As a beginning, the researcher selected possible Gymnasiums and contacted their administrative staffs by emails. After a rough self-selection, there were nine emails sent to nine upper secondary schools. Nevertheless, finally there was only one positive reply received from B Gymnasium which was visited by the researcher afterward. Then the coordinator of the school suggested which specific teacher and which class would be the sample. Teacher S's classes in R Gymnasium were recommended by a colleague because Teacher S was an experienced teacher in teaching both English and Danish literature. This suggested that she followed the same teaching methods both in English and Danish classes, so the effect of a second language on the teaching pattern was likely to be minimized.

In China, during another period from November to December, 2014, similar field research was conducted in two upper secondary classes as the second stage of the empirical research. The data were collected from two Chinese language and literature classes: one was Teacher X's first-year class in the Z High School, and the other was Teacher Z's second-year in the E High School. During the three-year high school education, Chinese language and literature is one of the three essential subjects. Literary texts including national and foreign works of art that include poems, novels, prose, drama are the main content of teaching in the Chinese classrooms. Also, Chinese classes are the places where it is possible to find the typical teaching in literature as opposed to English classes where learning and using English as a second language is more important. Therefore, the decision to conduct the empirical research in the Chinese classes allowed a focus on literature teaching, instead of English classes in China.

2.2.2 Participants of the Sample

The participants of the study are comprised of teachers and their students.

2.2.2.1 Teacher Participants

The selection procedure and criteria for choosing teacher participants are the same as those for choosing classes. Although the procedures of sampling were different from each other, the principles were the same. The criteria were:

(1) The classes must be either English classes in the Danish Gymnasium or Chinese literature classes in the Chinese high schools.

(2) Teachers should be literary teachers who taught not only language but also literature.

(3) There should be literature reading activities and discussions about reading in these classrooms.

(4) The period of observation should be no less than three weeks. In reality, the number of observed lessons varied from one to another, depending on the teacher's planning and schedule.

(5) The schedule of visiting, observing, interviewing, camera shooting, conducting questionnaire was determined based on the agreement with the targeted teacher, and as well as teachers' willingness to participate in the project.

While the teachers were selected at random, they were expected with different teaching experiences, backgrounds, styles, and ideas about teaching literature.

2.2.2.2 Student Participants

Student participants refer to student interviewees. They were chosen by the teacher in that classroom, according to the following principles:

(1) The teacher in each class selected five students to attend interviews as requested by the researcher.

(2) There should be a distribution of both male and female student participants.

(3) There should also be a distribution of above average, average, and below average students, talkative and quiet students.

5 students with different academic levels and personalities were selected in each class because different experiences enabled them to express ideas from different perspectives which increased the complexity of the reality in the classroom.

2.2.3 Researcher Positioning

The role of the researcher in this study had a dual purpose: first to observe the participants, activities, and context of the situation, and second to actively collect multiple sources of data, take notes, reflect on what happened, and record these in the research journal. Both teachers and their students supported the researcher's role. Teachers legitimized my presence in each classroom without explicitly mentioning to the students about my research questions and purpose. More often, the researcher tried to be invisible to students, being separated from them and leaving a voice recorder on their desk when they were discussing or doing group work.

2.3 Research Procedures and Specific Methods

This section introduces the specific procedures, tools, and qualitative methods for data collection and data analysis in empirical research.

2.3.1 Data Collection

A camera and audio recorders were used in the classroom research to collect primary data during the observations and interviews. Thus, the data of this book are mainly in the form of video and audio recordings and transcripts, which marks this study as a "constitutive ethnography" (Mehan, 1979, p.18). Constitutive ethnography emphasises that objective social facts like students' academic achievements, or classroom organizational arrangements were achieved in the interaction between teachers and students, and the constitutive ethnographer is not merely a participant observation study, but studies the structuring activities and the social facts they constitute (Mehan, 1979). In the process of data collection, four specific qualitative methods constituted the methodological *triangulation* (Mason, 2002), that is, the multiple sources of data and the multiple methods of collection. The specific methods of data collection were direct observations, document collection, interviews with teachers and selected students, and issuing anonymous questionnaires.

2.3.1.1 Direct Observations

Classroom observation is usually used as a method that can make the commonplace become problematic and the invisible visible (Dysthe, 1993). What was going on in the classrooms was videotaped and audiotaped, generating some sources of data: extensive field notes, transcripts of video files, and as well as reflections and generative thoughts in the field notes. Using video and audio files together, it is possible to come back to the data now and then in order to enrich the observation and capture all the occurrence and settings of classrooms, behaviors and even the expressions and tones of speakers with focusing on their interactions.

2.3.1.2 Document Collection

During observations in the classroom, as many relevant documents as possible were also collected from schools and classrooms. These include the basic information of the schools (e.g., the school policies and aims), handouts, copies of some students' written work, and teachers' lesson plans. Besides, some relevant official documents with respect to the educational system and curriculum of the subject were also gathered from the website of the ministry of education.

2.3.1.3 Interviews with Teachers

Each teacher had two one-on-one interviews. Thus, there were eight interviews with four teachers totally. All the interviews were semi-structured (Harrell & Bradley, 2009), which means that the interviews included both structured and unstructured elements. Some topics and interview questions were planned before each interview started; however, the order was flexible according to the respondents' answers and some of the questions were changed as appropriate.

The teacher in each classroom was interviewed before and after observing to determine their intentions of teaching, their thoughts, and comments about the lesson and students' performance. At the first teacher interview, general questions were used to gain a first impression of their conception of the ideal situation of the literature classroom, and specific questions focused on the special methods the teachers used to achieve this ideal situation. In general, the questions were almost the same and revolved around the following points:

(1) Perceptions of an ideal literary teacher/teaching situation;
(2) The intention, teaching content, and teaching plan;
(3) Methods to achieve the intention and plan;
(4) Methods to engage students in the interaction.

For each teacher, the order of questions was slightly different, and for some, an additional question or questions were used based on their responses and reflections. Through these questions, teachers' self-positioning of being a literary teacher, their aim of teaching, and conceptions of teaching methods and the classroom interactions were uncovered. Further, during observations, it was interesting to find something consistent or contrasting with what teachers described in the pre-observation interview.

For the second teacher interview, specific questions were used that focused on the particular teaching approach and student performances that were noticed during the observations. This focus provided information about the intentions behind some of the teachers' behaviors, and how they understood students' behaviors and responses. For each teacher, different sets of questions were prepared. These questions followed a general guide, which included the following common points:

(1) Comments on students' performance and contributions;
(2) To what extent the intention and plan were fulfilled;
(3) Something that did not predict happened;
(4) Interpretations of some activities and actions in class;

(5) Characterize selected students interviewed.

Guided by these questions, teachers looked back at their teaching practices and reflected on what they had done in class. Their comments on student performance and contributions implied their expectations for students and their interactive positioning toward students. Their reviews of teaching practices were compared with what they said in the pre-observation interview and what they did during observations.

2.3.1.4 Interviews with Selected Students

Student interviews were conducted once during the observations. The teachers helped to select five students in each classroom with different genders and competencies. Five students were divided into two groups when being interviewed, thus in each group, there were more than one student interviewee. in total, there were 10 student interviews involved. During the interviews with students, a set of general questions were used, following some common themes:

(1) Describe the experience of engaging in the classroom interactions;

(2) Characterize themselves as students in class;

(3) Describe the most interesting moment;

(4) Expectations/aims of attending the course;

(5) The approach to reading literature;

(6) Preparation before the class and homework after the class;

(7) Suggestions for changes in class.

These questions were designed because they might reflect students' conceptions of literature reading (in class and after class), their attitudes toward literary class, and their comments on some activities. Student comments were used to compare with teachers' comments and purposes, showing the consistency or the conflict of them. On the basis of general questions, several different questions were added relevant to students from different classes.

2.3.1.5 Issuing Critical Instant Questionnaire (CIQ)

At the end of the observations, a short-condensed questionnaire was designed to explore all the students' common experiences in learning. The questionnaire was based on the concept of *Critical Instant Questionnaire (CIQ)* proposed by Stephen Brookfield. The idea of CIQ is to provide students with a quick way to give anonymous feedback to the instructor on course content and presentation. The primary purpose of this instrument is to assess student critical thinking and subsequently reflect on these findings as a source of professional development by teachers (Brookfield, 1995). The reason that CIQ is employed in the present study is that the instant answer can reflect students' real and critical responses after a short reflection on the teacher's teaching practice. CIQ is used as a window to explore what kind of activities was the most interesting and helpful for the students and whether they were engaged in these activities or not. Therefore, the questions of the original CIQ were adapted in order to be appropriate to this study (Appendix 2.1). Built on the original CIQ questions that reflect five moments/actions in class, the adapted CIQ questions are comprised of five similar questions and one additional question. They focus on:

(1) The most engaged moment;
(2) The most distanced moment;
(3) The most affirming action;
(4) The most puzzling action;
(5) What surprises students most;
(6) The fulfillment of students' expectations.

There were students' comments that indicated their interests and confusions, which were compared with teachers' comments and purposes. The results implied students' engagement in the classroom interaction and teachers' means of engaging them. The specific data collected by the above four methods are described in Table 2.1.

Table 2.1 Data Collected by Type

Data types	Data collected
Direct observations (38 observations)	■ Transcripts of video and audio tapes ■ Written field note (on-the-spot observation and post-observation) data
Document collections	■ Information of the schools, the educational system, and the curriculum ■ Hand-Outs Teacher S: worksheets of three topics, copies of three literary texts, three written guidance for reading; one written task for students Teacher P: worksheets of the big topic, copies of four literary texts, two written guidance for reading Teacher X: copies of two texts in the textbook; copy of the homework in the exercise book; copy of the answer key in the exercise book Teacher Z: copy of two texts; one written task for students
	■ Teachers' lesson plans written in "Lectio"[①] and recorded in the observation notes
	■ Student written assignments Teacher S: two group written presentations; three student written exam essays (and three revised essays) with the teacher's comments Teacher P: three students' written assignments with the teacher's comments Teacher X: three student written homework in their exercise books Teacher Z: eight student written assignments
Interviews with teachers and students	■ Two formal interviews with teachers (before and after observations) (eight interviews) ■ Formal interviews with 25 selected students after observations (10 interviews) ■ Informal interviews with teachers and students during lesson break or group work
CIQ	■ Sent out 171 and received 152 responses

Field notes including on-the-spot observation notes and post-observation notes: These field notes were written in the form *Observations Notes*. Thus,

---

[①] "Lectio" system is a prototype app of the Danish school portal. Teachers can share any documents and resources about what they are learning in advance, and also assign tasks through this app.

the field notes that reflected the real situations of classrooms constituted the main basis for analysing what had happened in the classroom moment by moment.

Transcripts of video and audio tapes: During observations, all the lessons of a whole unit of each classroom were video recorded, including group work and student presentations. After reviewing these tapes, some footage was transcribed for analysis.

Information of the schools, the educational system, and the curriculum: Through visiting schools and their websites, some relevant documents regarding to the basic information of schools were gathered, as the information collection of the educational system and the curriculum.

Hand-outs: All the hand-outs that teachers gave to the students were collected during observations, including worksheets, some literary texts for reading, written tasks, and student written assignments.

Teachers' lesson plan: Teachers' explanations of their lesson plan were recorded and written down in the observation notes. Danish teachers made their plan of each lesson available on a common online system "Lectio".

Copies of students written work: The principles of selection of students' written work were — there was a distribution of above average, average, and below average students in reading and writing competence.

Transcripts of interview with teachers and selected students: Each teacher was formally interviewed twice and five selected students were interviewed once in each classroom. In addition, several students were informally interviewed in groups during observation of their group discussions in the group work.

Responses of CIQ: A short instant questionnaire was conducted in each classroom, which resulted in 152 response documents in total.

The intent of collecting multiple types of data is to increase the reliability of the data. Diverse types of data made it possible to describe from different angles and sources, depicting a full picture of the reality in the classrooms. Further, different data could be compared and contrasted with one another, supporting the interpretations.

2.3.2 Data Analysis

Data analysis began with organizing the data and the research journal to summarize and catalogue data. Formal interviews of teachers and students were fully transcribed, and video and audio recordings were transcribed at points of interest determined by the research questions and recurring themes. Table 2.2 includes the number of minutes of video and audio data used. Repeated readings of the research journal and content of transcriptions identified some features of framing class interactions.

Table 2.2 Video and Audio Data Matrix (minutes)

Teacher participants	Interviews with teachers	Interviews with students	Video and audio tapes
Teacher S	45 mins 46 mins	78 mins (2nd-year class) 67 mins (3rd-year class)	720 mins 720 mins
Teacher P	38 mins 45 mins	68 mins	540 mins
Teacher X	33 mins 38 mins	65 mins	360 mins
Teacher Z	30 mins 43 mins	70 mins	280 mins

Data analysis involved two steps. First, data were selected and analysed in terms of the content of textual data. Second, when investigating and analysing the classroom interactions, Gee's (2011a) approach to discourse analysis was used for transcribing discourses and examining the transcripts from language-in-use perspective (Gee, 2011a; Rex & Schiller, 2009).

2.3.2.1 Qualitative Content Analysis of Text Data

Qualitative content analysis is a widely used method to analyse text data in qualitative research. It was defined as a research method for the subjective interpretation of the content of text data through the systematic classification process of coding and identifying themes or patterns (Hsieh & Shannon, 2005). This step is necessary for that it is useful to collect and read through documentation as much as possible, and to find out features of the educational system, the teaching content and plan, and the curriculum through searching and reading relevant text documents. The analysis focused on the content of transcriptions from target episodes to identify the features of classroom interactions. During the process of data collection, reflective, explanatory, and interpretative remarks were recorded alongside the field notes after each observation. After data collection, the data were read again and again to identify portions to be further analysed or used as cases in this book.

2.3.2.2 Discourse Analysis of Speech Transcripts

In discourse analysis, any speech can be transcribed in more detailed (narrow) or less detailed (broad) ways (Gee, 2011b). Reflecting Gee's approaches (Gee, 2011b), this study applies broad transcripts, because its focus is on the content and themes of the speech rather than on the tone and intonation. Discourse analysis, in Gee's sense of the word, looks at "meaning as an integration of ways of saying (informing), doing (action) and being (identity)" (Gee, 2011a, p.8). In order to indicate the speakers' ways of speaking, acting, interacting, gesturing, listening, moving, and sometimes even writing and reading except for specific content of conversations and contextual notes, transcripts in this book also include pause, overlaps, emphasis, markers of final intonation. Table 2.3 shows the conventions for transcribing. The situated identities of teachers and students constructed in the interactions and the social activities that occurred in the process of reading literature can be recognized through what they said and did.

Some interesting interactions that presented the feature of framing interactions or student engagement in the interactions were selected and transcribed. Specifically, these were episodes when students had possibilities or barriers to engage in the classroom interactions, or when teachers showed their "interactional awareness" (Rex & Schiller, 2009, p.ix) in teaching.

Table 2.3 Defined Conventions of Transcribing

Sign	Definition
T	teacher
Uppercase letter	abbreviation of teachers' or students' names
(text)	description of contexts and non-verbal behaviors
text	stressed or emphasised speech
text	quoted text
<text>	overlapping speech
(number)	pauses in second
text ↑	sharply rising intonation
text ↓	sharply falling intonation
te: xt	elongated syllable
(...)	missing words which can not be heard clearly or omitted words

Those moments were examined and reread, and the interpretations of their meanings were made during the process of data analysis. This method of capturing a moment in the interactions is called *freeze-frame* (Rex & Schiller, 2009, p.9) from a language-in-use perspective, just like a projector might do with a piece of film. Freezing a moment can help the investigator to move the film back and forward so as to recognize the identities and activities involved in it and to make the frozen moment meaningful. Also, the freeze-frame over extended periods of time was seen as a way to allow participants to see how the interactions reoccurred in patterns (Rex & Schiller, 2009), in particular, to allow teachers and educators to reflect on their discursive choices that were made in patterns, and reconsider other possibilities. It is also what this study intended to do — focused on capturing and recognizing the repeated patterns of classroom interactions, comparing different patterns, and then unfolding the features. Using *freeze-frame*, some interesting excerpts, actions, and activities observed were frozen during the initial data reduction, so in the interview with teachers and students after observations, they were guided to look back at their saying and doing in class. The description of each case in the following chapters (Chapters 3–6) was divided into three parts, pre-observation, during observation, and post-observation. The post-observation part contains the comments and reviews from the teachers and students when they were guided to look back at their actions in class.

2.3.3 Frameworks for Analysis and Discussion

Built on the theoretical foundation, two coding frameworks (Table 2.4 and Table 2.5) drawn from positioning theory and envisioning theory are used to analyse specific phenomena and conversations. There are many types of positioning according to positioning theory (Harré & van Langenhove, 1999; Davies & Harré, 1990). Table 2.5 lists some types of positioning defined according to positioning theory (Harré & van Langenhove, 1999; Davies & Harré, 1990).

Table 2.4 Types of Positioning Defined (Harré & van Langenhove, 1999; Davies & Harré, 1990)

Positioning	Definition
Interactive	Positioning of oneself in a conversation (which implies the position of other)
Reflexive	Positioning of others in a conversation (which implies the position of self)

(continued)

Positioning	Definition
Moral (role-based)	Positioning with regard to the moral orders in which people perform social actions or based on established roles within institutional aspects of social life (e.g., a teacher, a student)
Performative	Positioned by actions, either with or against the storyline
Tacit	Unintentional positioning: most positioning is tacit. The people involved will not position themselves or others in an intentional or even conscious way
Intentional	Purposeful positioning based on a goal: people intend to position themselves or others in an intentional way Four forms: deliberate self-positioning, forced self-positioning, deliberate positioning of others, and forced positioning of others

Table 2.4 is used to look through the positioning ways of teachers and students, and analyse the relationships between the teacher and students, the student and the student when they interacted with each other. In the institutional context, positioning always occurs during the teacher-student, student-student, and student-text interactions. They are morally positioned related to their social roles. Meanwhile, they can be positioned by their actions, which is performative positioning. These positions can also be resisted or modified by their actions. Mostly, tacit or unconscious positioning takes place in an ongoing storyline, but sometimes intentional positioning occurs forcedly or deliberately. Deliberate self-positioning occurs when the speaker wants to express personal identity to achieve a specific goal, such as a teacher who deliberately expresses his/her identity as a literary teacher with the purpose of teaching literature. In contrast, forced self-positioning is requested by a person or an institution other than the persons involved, such as a teacher/school that requires students to participate in some activities or assigns tasks for students. Similarly, a teacher's deliberately positioning of students occurs when the teacher wants students to express a certain identity (e.g., being a student teacher who is requested to give a presentation to peers). Forced positioning of others

comes from someone else, such as schools that force teachers to position students as receivers or the co-constructors of the knowledge according to the policies. Situated in different contextual cultures, this study attempted to explore diverse positions/situated identities that teachers performed and that were intentionally offered to students, discussing the possibility for students to occupy, resist or modify various positions through their "act-actions" (Harré & Moghaddam, 2003).

Another framework drawn from envisioning theory is designed for analysing the interaction between students and the text in this study. Langer (2011b) not only addressed the concept of *stance* but also applied the five stances into the classroom as instructional tools in teaching as shown in Table 2.5.

Table 2.5 Stances as Instructional Tools (Langer, 2011b, pp.21–27)

Types of stances during envisionment-building	Stances in the classroom as instructional tools
Being out and stepping into an envisionment	*Stance1: Getting started with the material —* using questions to tap their background knowledge
Being in and moving through an envisionment	*Stance2: Developing understanding of the material —* connect relevant details to make a more cohesive envisionment
Stepping out and rethinking what you know	*Stance 3: Leaving from the material —* examine any new ideas it may offer or any existing ideas it may change
Stepping out and objectifying the experience	*Stance 4: Thinking critically about the material —* objectively examine the events, issues, data, concepts, and related social occurrences and effects; make comparisons and offer critiques
Leaving an envsionment and going beyond	*Stance 5: Going beyond the material —* leave their thoughts behind and use ideas to create new uses

Through examining teachers' different questions and activities, the stances that the activities or questions related to and teachers' instructions are unfolded. At Stance 1, the teacher uses some questions to tap students' background knowledge and helps them to enter into an initial envisionment of the text. Using Stance 2, students are guided to connect relevant details in the text and build upon them to make a more cohesive envisionment. In accordance with Stance 3, the teacher directs students to step out of the envisionment and reflect on any new ideas the envisionment can offer or change, showing that there is a change in their understandings. With Stance 4, students have the chance to critically reflect on their understandings, make comparisons between what they have learnt with other knowledge, offer critiques, and evaluate sources in terms of reliability or bias. Utilizing Stance 5, the teacher asked students to leave their thoughts behind and use the ideas they have gained to create new adaptations. Put simply, using five stance tools to orchestrate questions or activities, the teacher can instruct students to read and think of the text from different perspectives. The present study applied stance tools as an analytical lens of literature pedagogy, looking at how teachers' instructions of reading facilitated the student-text interaction, despite that teacher participants had no consciousness to apply stance tools in their teaching.

When analysing a particular activity in the classroom and some segments of classroom interactions, two frameworks are applied together to investigate how teachers' interactional awareness can improve literature teaching. They were individually applied to the data and then the analysis across frameworks was conducted to search for patterns and features within each case, relating to RQ1 (*"How are the interactions between the teacher and students, the interactions between the student and the student, and the interactions between students and the text framed in Danish and Chinese literature classes?"*). After each case was individually analysed, the cross-case analysis occurred, dealing with RQ2 (*"What are the differences and* commonalities between the framing approaches in Danish classes and Chinese classes?") (Table 2.6).

Table 2.6　The Integrated Framework for Data Analysis

Data analysis		Themes
Pre-observation (First interview with the teacher)		■ Reflexive positioning of the teacher ■ Purpose of teaching literature ■ Perceptions of how to engage students
During-observation (Direct observation and documents collected)	Teacher-student interaction	■ Positions of teachers and students in the three types of interactions ■ Stance tools that the teaching practice can be related to
	Student-student interaction	
	Student-text interaction	
Post-observation (Second interview with the teacher; interview with selected students, CIQ)		■ The teacher's comments ■ Students' comments ■ Reviews of the teaching practices (Both the teacher and students)
Analysis within each case		■ Patterns of the framing of classroom interactions ■ Features of positioning and reading instruction → RQ 1
Cross-case analysis		■ Commonalities and differences among cases → RQ2
Analysis within each case and cross-case analysis (Research journal involving reflections and generative thoughts)		Discussions ■ Modification of *Cross-model* ■ New understanding of dialogic teaching ■ Factors in engaging students in dialogue

2.4　Building Trustworthiness

The trustworthiness and credibility of the present study are ensured by being methodical, using methodical triangulation, and considering ethics.

2.4.1 Being Methodical

As Yin (2011) suggested, descriptions of what was going on in the classrooms were written objectively, avoiding bias or deliberation. Interesting findings were discussed with different colleagues. In this way, researcher bias or blindness could be minimized by comparing different opinions about the same data. After observations, the field descriptions were checked again and again to make sure they were sufficiently detailed. Reading and revision of interpretations of data were repeated to ensure that they were answering the research questions.

2.4.2 Methodical Triangulation

Triangulation was defined as the use of multiple methods of data collection and regarded as a powerful way to demonstrate validity in qualitative research (Cohen, Manion & Morrison, 2011). Using triangulation allowed the research questions to be approached from different angles and to be explored in a rounded and multi-faced way (Mason, 2002). The primary sources of the data were transcripts of discourses and descriptions of observations in literature classrooms. Throughout the analysis, other data sources, such as interviews, field notes, documents, and audio and videotapes were revisited to confirm the interpretations and to make the findings more explicit, showing a full map of the complexity of the classroom interactions. Examining data across multiple sources established triangulation of the data and these multiple data sources that were connected to each other supported interpretations and strengthened the findings.

2.4.3 Ethical Considerations

This study abides by *the Act on Processing Personal Data* in Denmark that is monitored by *the Danish Data Protection Agency*[1]. Before conducting

---

[1] See *Datatilsynet* homepage: https://www.datatilsynet.dk.

the empirical research, approval was obtained from the Danish Data Protection Agency for researching on young students in the classrooms. In addition, this study follows a set of general ethical considerations in educational and social research, including obtaining informed consent, gaining access to and acceptance in the research setting, matters of anonymity and confidentiality, and codes of practice for research (Cohen et al., 2011).

In this book, all the findings are de-identified when used in public, and schools, teachers, and students are represented by the acronyms of their names. Also, participants were informed about the background, purpose, focus, and empirical methods of the research, and the nature of the participants' roles in the study. At the first contact, an introductory document about the research was sent together with the researcher's CV to the coordinators or the teachers of the targeted schools. For each school, after this initial contact, an appointment was made with the teacher for a face-to-face meeting. During the first meeting, the teacher was presented with the focus and procedures of the investigation in her classroom. Meanwhile, the teacher was also showed an information letter that outlined the focus of the study, when and how the observations in her classroom would be conducted, what tools would be used (camera or sound recorder, or both), what the possible participation would involve, how the data would be used and in which way, and as well as the assurance of maintaining confidentiality. Before the observations in the classrooms, a letter to each student's parents was also sent with information and a request for student parents' consent considering these students were under 18 years of age. On the first day of the investigation in the classroom, the researcher was introduced, and the students were given general information about the project, the purpose and the procedures of the fieldwork, and their roles in the participation. During the period of fieldwork, dialogue occurred with each teacher participant periodically, especially after each lesson when something interesting or relevant to this study was found, or when it was time to conduct the next step of the research. Every effort was made to gain acceptance in the research setting, obtain informed consent, and negotiate with participants.

2.5 Conclusion

This research design is integrated with descriptive, interpretative, and comparative approaches, looking for the differences and commonalities in the framing of classroom interactions across multiple cases. The descriptions, interpretations, and comparisons are built on the theoretical foundation with an analytical lens of discourse analysis. Through this analytical lens, analyses and discussions are directed to the social activities and social identities built in the classroom discourse, and the effects of social contexts/ contextual cultures as well. As a result of these methodological choices, the data illustrates the positioning of teachers and students and teachers' reading instructions. The research also involves analyses of data that demonstrates teachers' patterns and features of framing classroom interactions embedded in divergent contextual cultures. Built on the empirical data, the findings are used to discuss a modified *Cross-model*, new meanings of *dialogic teaching* in the literature classroom, and the factors influencing the classroom interactions.

Chapter 3
The Case of Teacher S

This chapter presenting the case of Teacher S starts with an introduction of contextual cultures of this case, including profiles of the school and classes. From a perspective of discourse analysis, Teacher S's case is then examined through some excerpts frozen-frame in three phases: pre-observation, during-observation, and post-observation. In the pre-observation interview, Teacher S mainly talked about her perceptions of teaching literature, indicating her reflexive positioning, the purpose of teaching, and general features of teaching style. During the observation, the investigation focused on how Teacher S framed three types of classroom interactions. After observation the teacher was guided to look back at what she said and did before and during observation, to see if what she did in class matched what she intended. Students' comments reflect their responses to the teaching methods, as a supplement of on-the-spot observations. Finally, the findings of this case are concluded based on the inter-comparison of three-phase descriptions.

3.1 Contextual Cultures

Describing contextual cultures of each case is the first step which establishes a basis for the further interpretation of the influence of the contextual cultures on the ways of teaching and framing classroom interactions. This section mainly describes the school cultures and classroom cultures including profiles of the school and Teacher S's two classes, with some reflections on how these cultures might penetrate daily teaching and learning.

3.1.1 Profile of the School

R Gymnasium is located in a county in Denmark. This Gymnasium was created in 1969 and has 1,000 students including STX and HF of which there are 18 STX study fields/subject packages for students to select. The school offers ICT (Information and Communication Technology) equipment and Wi-Fi in the classrooms, and also other study facilities, sports facilities, and a varied selection of after-school activities. The school describes itself as a school where students use the school as a study camp for homework assignments and thus the leadership supports teachers for guidance after school. It claims that the main values are learning, community spirit, and diversity, and its main task is to offer top-quality teaching that will prepare the students for further studies and their life in general. Besides, its policy is to involve students in a democratic process of decision — making through listening to what students say on what happens in the classrooms and the school[①].

The above principles of the school mainly indicate two aspects of the school culture. One is the focus on the democratic atmosphere of the school and classes. Thus, the Gymnasium claims to consider students' ideas when teachers make decisions on the ways and content. It indicates that the school puts democracy, which is embedded in the cultures of the society and the whole country, at an important place of the school cultures. The other aspect of the school cultures is the installation of ICT equipment and Wi-Fi in classrooms, which supports teachers and students to use electronic media and computers in class. Moreover, Danish schools described in this book shared

---

① The information, principles, and values of the school were summarized from its website.

an online system "Lectio" which is a prototype app of the school portal. Through this app, students could know about teachers' plans, the tasks for them, and the requirements in advance. Sometimes students could also send a message to teachers through this app to interact with teachers in advance.

The above school cultures are closely related to societal cultures. In this case, the societal cultures mainly refer to the sense of democracy of the society and the curriculum of English of Danish Gymnasiums. The curriculum declares that the ministry of education aims to give students greater independence and responsibilities to gradually replace teacher-centred teaching, and hence the teaching methods and techniques are expected to adapt to professional goals, and written and should be varied to develop nuanced and flexible fluency in both spoken and written oral assignments modes. Besides, the curriculum of English explains the goal of using ICT in class, which is to strengthen students' ability to search, select, and disseminate relevant learning material, to acquire knowledge of different electronic media's impact on communications, and well as to help them to experience the language in varied, authentic and current contexts (Appendix 3.1 Curriculum of English A).

In summary, the democracy that constitutes part of the societal cultures was mainly embodied in two aspects of the school cultures. One was the proposition of student-centred organization and the other was the use of computers and electronic media. With these cultural effects, there is a question raised: Under the influence of the school cultures how did Teacher S frame the classroom interaction in a democratic way and meanwhile carry out her teaching plan? This question was considered during the investigation of Teacher S's classes.

3.1.2 Profile of Teacher S's Two Classes

Teacher S was teaching two classes among which one was a second-year class with 28 students and the other was a third-year class with 25 students. Table 3.1 shows an overview of Teacher S's two classes, including the number of students, seating arrangement, time duration of each lesson, the number of lessons observed, and the curriculum of each class.

Table 3.1 Profile of Teacher S's Classes

Grade of class	Number of Students	Seating	Lesson length	Lessons per week	Number of lessons observed	Curriculum
2nd-year	28	vertical rows with students sitting face to face	90 minutes	2-3	8	■ Horror stories ■ Gothic stories ■ songs and lyrics of a British singer ■ WW1 poetry
3rd-year	25	vertical rows with students sitting face to face	90 minutes	2	8	Literary periods and representative texts of each period

In each 90-minute lesson there was a short break after 40 minutes. In the second-year class, Teacher S planned the teaching content of the whole class, including different genres of literature, whereas in the third-year class, students in groups worked with different literary periods and literary texts.

3.1.2.1 Seating Arrangement

Usually, Teacher S organised the seats in both classes into two or three vertical rows with students sitting face-to-face around the long tables as shown in Figure 3.1[①]. The uppercase letter S represents students, and the lowercase letters (a to h) represent the number of rows. The numerals are the number of students. This arrangement was of benefit for students nearby for talking and discussing, and also the teacher could walk around between

---

① In order to protect the rights of teachers and students, all the pictures taken in different classrooms and homework of students are not attached in this book.

the two rows and offer help during group work. The students' seats were not fixed but changeable, which means that students might have different seats in different lessons. It also means that the teacher and students could rearrange the seats for the different requirements of activities, such as group work and group presentation.

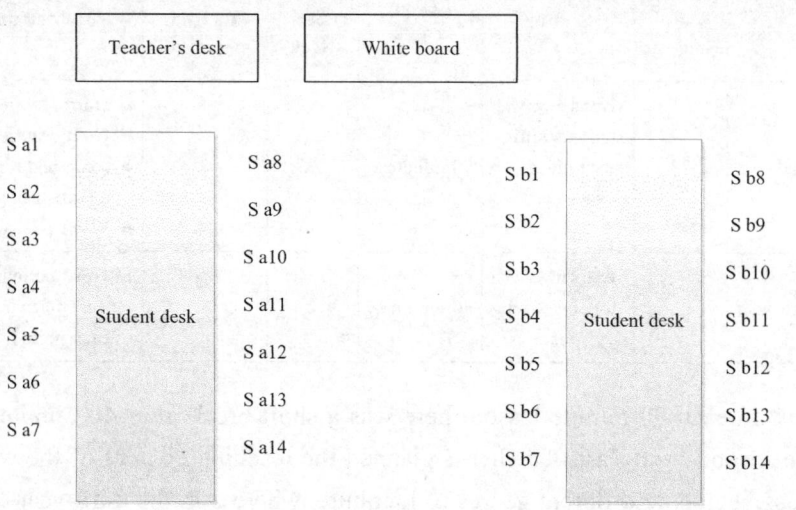

Figure 3.1   Seating Arrangement of Teacher S's Classes (2nd-year and 3rd-year classes)

3.1.2.2   Syllabus and Specific Learning Contents

In this study English classes were observed with the focus of the investigation on interactive ways to improve literature reading. Thus, the teaching language was not so important. Rather, the literature curriculum was more relevant. In Denmark, the upper secondary students need to pass English B, which is compulsory for all the students. English A is more demanding, with students required to manage complex oral and written English, as well as various types of English texts. The Ministry of Education lists specific requirements of English level A. The English and Danish versions are shown in Appendix 3.1.

The English A curriculum contains the professional goals and the core fabric of the course. Specifically, students being A level should be able to talk about a topic or an issue in complex English, discuss English-language texts and media materials, and analyse English materials historically, culturally, and socially. The core fabric of the curriculum involves linguistic aspects such as grammar, vocabulary, and communication strategies, and as well as a wide range of selection of literary texts in different periods, non-literary texts, and media materials.

The requirements of the English A curriculum indicate that English A level classes in Danish Gymnasiums should involve a wealth of English-language materials so students can get language skills by reading, interpreting, analysing, discussing, arguing, and presenting. The specific learning content and texts are not specified in the curriculum; instead, merely some basic topics are included, such as the works of Shakespeare. It is worth mentioning that Danish teachers have autonomous rights in choosing texts and topics of learning. In other words, Danish teachers are not strictly required to use authoritative textbooks, instead, they are given a general curriculum including course goals, basic content, organization, and evaluation. Within the scope of basic content, teachers have choices to decide which texts and what topics or issues they want students to study. Teachers' flexible choices make it possible to create a diversity of course content in the classroom.

In this case, Teacher S's classes were English A level. As requested by the ministry, they spent more time analysing literary themes, topics, and genres than practicing linguistic knowledge, such as grammar. Consecutive lessons were not observed; instead, lessons were observed when they were relevant to the focus of this book. Thus, the 16 English lessons described here focused on literature reading and discussion rather than learning English as a second language. Table 3.2 lists the specific curriculum with detailed content of each class and the teaching method used.

Table 3.2 Curricular Units and Activities in Teacher S's Classes

Classroom observed	Curricular units observed	Characteristic teaching method
2nd-year English A (8 lessons)	A short story *A Good Night's Sleep* (from Brian McCabe: *Dark Room with a Stranger,1993*)	Group discussion (1 lesson)
	Horror story: the first part of *The Squaw* (Bram stoker, 1897)	Short teacher's lecture (0.5 lesson) group discussion (0.5 lesson)
	The second part of *The Squaw;* gothic story	Group work and whole-class discussion (0.5 lesson) The teacher's lecture (0.5 lesson)
	Songs and lyrics of a British singer (4 lessons)	Group work (3 lessons) Group written presentation (1 lesson)
	First World War (WW1) poem: *Dulce et Decorum Est*	Student comments on the work of a British singer; Group discussion and the whole class discussion (1 lesson)
3rd-year English A (8 lessons)	Literary periods and representative work of art of each period (The Renaissance, Enlightenment, Romanticism, Victorian, Modernism, Postmodernism)	Group work (4 lessons) and group oral presentation/student lecture as a way to teach other peers (one lesson for each group)

Teacher S applied different methods and these methods mainly involved lecture, whole-class discussion, group work including oral and written group presentations, and student written assignments. These approaches are defined as follows:

- *Lecture*

The teacher's lecture is defined here as a teaching method by which the teacher gave a prepared monologue on a professional subject for the whole class as Teacher S did in her second-year class. But in Teacher S's third-year class, lectures did not only mean the teacher's lectures but also might mean student group presentation by means of student lectures. In this way, each student group was given the responsibility to teach other groups and peers, after reading and studying the history and representative texts of a certain literary period. This student teaching sometimes contained lectures from students and sometimes combined student lectures with discussions or other activities designed by each group.

- *Whole-class discussion*

As a whole-class activity, this approach refers to a teacher-led discussion on the subject-related issues or literary texts between the teacher and more than one student in the class. Teachers usually framed the whole-class discussion starting with a form of IRE that can be framed in a dialogic or monologic way. Any conversation where a teacher only asked questions and students only answered was not considered as a substantive discussion in this book. Conversely, whole-class discussion may be substantive when it was conducted in a way of dialogic IRE.

- *Group work*

Group work here means students worked with literary texts in groups independently, without the participation of the teacher in a formal way. Instead, the teacher was like a consultant whose assistance was available when needed by some groups. In Teacher S's classrooms, group work also involved group discussions and group presentations including oral and written forms.

- *Student written assignment*

Student written assignment includes student essays, written presentations during the learning process, or exams. In Teacher S's second-year class, student written assignments were given in the form of the exam after the first academic year. Each student was requested to write an essay based on his or her reading of a short fictional piece. In the third-year class, students were asked to write essays based on what they had studied and discussed during group work and what they had taught to their peers during the student lectures.

In both Teacher S's second-year and third-year classes, students spent the majority of lesson time on group work. During observation, second-year class students spent four whole lessons on group work with a British singer including group presentation, three lessons on group discussion and whole-class discussion, and one lesson on teacher's lecture. In the third-year class, students spent all their eight lessons on group work including group discussion and oral presentation. The time distribution in the two classes showed Teacher S's intention of gradually fostering students' independent learning ability.

3.2 Pre-Observation: Teacher S's Perceptions of Literature Teaching

Before observation, in the first interview with Teacher S, she generally talked about how she thought of herself in the class (namely, deliberately self-positioning of Teacher S), what her purpose was, and how she usually engaged students in reading literature.

3.2.1 Reflexive Positioning

Teacher S is a veteran in teaching both English and Danish, especially in teaching literature. Until then when being visited, she had been teaching for 32 years. She came to R Gymnasium more than 10 years ago. Her extensive teaching experience had given her rich experience of teaching language and literature, and as well as in interacting with her students. In her own words, she characterized herself as below:

Excerpt 3.1

TS[1]: I think of myself as one who likes what she is doing. Perhaps not very innovative, I would say that. I do many things in an old-fashion

---

[1] In order to distinguish from students' names, teachers' names in transcripts are represented by T+ the acronyms of their names. For instance, TS refers to Teacher S.

way. But of course, I use computers much more than I used to (...) I want to do things in dialogue with my students. I like to push them but I don't like to force them too much. When I was young, I sometimes got annoyed with them because young people can sometimes be rude (...) but I tried to be not annoyed even if they were annoying. I tried to ignore them when they spat me, sort of, to break through the hard surface that some students have.

I: So, can I say you are an experienced teacher?

TS: You can say that, but that doesn't mean I know everything. I am still learning.

In this excerpt, Teacher S positioned herself as a person who was working on her chosen career, and who continued to learn about teaching and adolescents during her teaching life. At the beginning of her teaching experience, she noticed the characteristics of adolescents' behavior, so gradually she developed ways to cope with them and how to talk with them, and how to push them without forcing them to do something. She was not young but still kept learning and tried to keep up with trends and times. Supported by the school, Teacher S did use the computer much more than she used before, and she was becoming good at using "Lectio" to manage the schedule and teaching plan. In short, Teacher S wanted to keep herself energetic and being closer to her adolescent students — despite that she was in her fifties. Thus, she deliberately positioned herself as a literary teacher who also was a learner in some aspects that she did not know rather than an omniscient.

3.2.2 Purpose of Teaching Literature

Teacher S had enthusiasm for teaching literature because she had interest in working with literature. She had a clear purpose and high expectation for her students.

Excerpt 3.2

I: What are your intentions, content, or plans for the course?

TS: I have diverse expectations. Because some of the students would like to study literature later, most of them don't. I think all the students can benefit from reading text, from the practices to see the spiritual essence, not the surface value, because I think that it's useful in life in general. And also, through seeing spiritual essence in people talking, they can learn from reading literature. They can reflect on weak subjects in life, problems, and feelings.

I: What's your expectation for the students?

TS: For instance, second-year class students are not very independent. As I said I tried to push them because they did actually independently in their exam this summer. I wasn't content with that (exam) so I am trying to push them to go deeper with it (...) So of course, they are expected to become more and more independent. But they still need guides obviously (...) I will just sort of be there as a consultant, to be consulted.

In general, her purpose in teaching literature was to have students benefit from reading diverse literature throughout their lives. Working with diverse literature, she had diverse expectations, but she also had a general demand and expectation for students in learning literature — she expected her students to be independent learners in working with literature, with her assistance. Hence, group work was used as a typical form of interaction in Teacher S's class. Teacher S, so to speak, aimed to facilitate the shift from the teacher-centred teaching to the student-centred teaching as the ministry aims to do.

3.2.3 Perceptions of How to Engage Students

In order to achieve her main purpose, Teacher S tried to motivate students and trained them to become independent readers who were able to read and understand literary texts deeply. In the pre-observation interview, she explained her ways of motivating and engaging students in the activities of learning literature as shown in Excerpt 3.3.

Excerpt 3.3

TS: I think that it (an ideal teacher) would be a teacher who can make the students to be curious in the study, to make the students interested obviously (...) I try to give them texts that can surprise them (...)

I: Usually how do you do to achieve this ideal situation?

TS: I did many different things. Sometimes I cut the text into pieces so that the students can reflect on what comes next. Sometimes I choose the text that will be interesting to them. Sometimes they are allowed to choose their own texts because some of them do read some books or songs on their own.

I: Can students choose their own texts?

TS: Not always, no. There is a curriculum for them since I have to present for them. But sometimes they are allowed to choose. It is a way of appealing to how they bring in their own interests. We try to have a dialogue, not as much as students would like because they have not enough time.

I: What is the intention, content, and plan of this lesson/course?

TS: My plan is very flexible. Sometimes I leave things more open, at least I do. I know some of my colleagues have better plans (...)

The above transcripts of the teacher's pre-interview demonstrated three features of Teacher S' teaching style.

- *Pay More Attention to Students' Interests and Curiosity*

As a way to motivate students, Teacher S cared greatly about students' interests and curiosity. She introduced two strategies that she usually used in her classes. One strategy was to give choices for the students to propose texts that they were interested in, as many Danish teachers were doing. As she said when she introduced her purpose of teaching, she tried to make a dialogue with students when she planned content, but not as much as students would like, considering the limited school time. When she created the limited choice for the students, she also noticed there was a balance in between — on the one hand, allowing students to bring their experience into the classroom, and on the other hand, selecting some texts that students would not choose on their own but which were useful and representative of the teacher's aim. For instance, the topic of a British singer in her second-year class was suggested by one student during a whole-class visit to an exhibition in Germany. The student's idea was approved by Teacher S who thought the songs and texts of a British singer were popular and influential. In short, Teacher S would like students to be able to work with some topics when they wanted to because she thought of this as a helpful strategy to accommodate students' interests. Also, it indicates that Teacher S considered integrating a democratic way of interacting with students into the process of planning teaching.

The other strategy of attracting students was to give texts that surprised them. For instance, sometimes she cut a text into pieces and gave them to students in turns so that students could reflect on what came next using their prejudices or hints they found in the text. She explained that sometimes she gave them a keyword on the title of the text, so students could reflect on that and discuss what could be expected in the text. It was not merely a way to attract students, but also a way to foster their ability of independent working with literature, to illustrate how important it was that they read the text properly through hints that sometimes were overlooked by them.

- *Plan Teaching with Something Open*

Teacher S described her style of planning teaching as flexible because sometimes she left things open, leaving some space for students' suggestions. When Teacher S was firstly contacted by the researcher, she sketched out the first version of her teaching plan. Later during the next contact through email, Teacher S changed her plan a little bit, adding WW1 (First World War) poems into the second version, but still, she did not confirm that. Later when she was firstly interviewed before observation, she added something new in her plan again, especially she decided to add the texts of a British singer after students suggested when to do with that. Thus, students' voices had some influence on the formation of teaching plans in Teacher S's classes.

Not only making a general plan but also working with a specific topic, Teacher S selected specific texts of that topic with some flexibility. The class used a textbook of horror stories that was selected by Teacher S. In her class, some boys who liked to read fantasy books or played computer games had certain knowledge of some writers of horror stories, so they knew Lovecraft, for example. Thus, Teacher S allowed them to choose a text written by Lovecraft instead of what was written in the textbook. When Teacher S planned literary texts for a topic, students' background knowledge of that topic was also considered as a way of appealing to students. It was an example of how Teacher S put the school policy "involve them [students] in the democratic process of decision making" into practice.

- *Adjust Ways in accordance to Students' Levels*

Indeed, Teacher S's flexible style was consistent with her purpose of teaching literature — to foster the abilities of students' independent learning. From the first year to the third year, students were increasingly expected to become more capable of analysing the literary texts independently through many group activities. Teacher S's purpose and demands became clearer with the growth of students' levels. Demands on students varied according to their different levels when they worked with texts. Further, their assignments were dependent on their levels. For instance, second-year students worked with different genres that were decided by the teacher, and the assignment of student group work was group presentation in a written way. But the third-year students had to work with histories and texts of different literary periods together in groups from the beginning of the semester. Each student group was required to start studying a certain literary period and then choose a representative literary text for analysing; as a result, they needed to address questions and prepared a lecture to teach other students the knowledge of that particular period and text they chose. Obviously, the tasks for the third-year students were more demanding and students consequently took on more responsibilities during the process.

Summing up, the above three features she described demonstrated that Teacher S expected to treat her students in a dialogic, open, and democratic way, with an aim to improve their independent learning competence. It followed that she employed different strategies to motivate and engage students, with her awareness of democracy and her awareness of facilitating student-centred teaching advocated by the school culture and societal culture.

3.3 During-Observation: Three Types of Classroom Interactions

This section presents how three types of classroom interactions in Teacher S's classes were framed with a focus on the teacher's positioning and reading instructions, to see if what she really did echoed what she aimed to do or not and how she transformed her intentions into practice.

3.3.1 The Interaction between the Teacher and Students

The interaction between the teacher and students existed in both oral and written communication, such as a lecture combined with whole-class discussion, and the student written assignment with back-and-forth reactions between the teacher and students. These two methods were typical in Teacher S's classrooms.

3.3.1.1 The Teacher's Lecture Combined with Whole-Class Discussion

Commonly, a teacher's lecture is considered as one teacher's speech about his/her views on a subject, using a typically and slightly impersonal style (Goffman, 1981). In Teacher S's classrooms, the teacher's lecture time only occupied one eighth of total time during observation, just like she said, "I don't like to directly give lectures." Even if she gave a lecture, she combined it with whole-class discussion or group discussion. It means that usually, the lesson started with a short lecture after which the teacher invited students to respond or discuss some points in the lecture or in the texts. The next is an example of her combining two methods in order to open the dialogue with students. They were working with a horror story, *The Squaw* by Bram Stoker. Teacher S planned two lessons on this text. At first, they started with an introduction of the concept "the first narrator" and then discussed in groups around the teacher's guiding points relevant to the texts, and after that, the whole class discussed what students had done in groups previously.

The lecture in the first lesson was very short, and during the lecture Teacher S often invited students to give their contributions. The following excerpt was extracted from a conversation in the first lesson between Teacher S and Student K in the pattern of IRE, about "the first narrator" as an introduction to learning *The Squaw*.

Excerpt 3.4
TS: What do you know about the **first personal narrators**?
K: They told the story as if from their own perspective.
TS: Yes.
K: And the stories are usually about themselves.
TS: Not always. ↓
K: But usually. ↓
TS: Not necessary. But it sometimes depends on the title, which is what? We call it the genre ↑...
K: Horror? Or short stories (...) ↑
TS: Um, yes↑, you can say that, but (...) (as if she was thinking of something) . You can write short stories and you can have first personal

narrator; they are completely different.

This short excerpt illustrates how a short lecture was merged with the whole-class discussion. It was obvious that Student K was relaxed to talk with the teacher, arguing with the teacher although his idea was not affirmed by the teacher. Teacher S was good at persuading students to think along with her thinking, as she did not directly decline what Student K said. Instead, in a mild way she gave her explanations and guided students to continue thinking. In this way, students' contributions were merged into the teacher's lecture.

After the short lecture about "the first narrator", students were asked to do group work with the teacher's four guiding points. In the second lesson, after the students finished discussing the second part of *The Squaw*, the whole class discussed the guiding points in a pattern of IRE. There were seven students who joined in whole-class discussion. Some talked on behalf of their groups, and some spoke about their own ideas. The following is an extract from the discussion between Teacher S and three students who were talking about the characteristics of a cat in the story.

Excerpt 3.5

K: I mean it can figure out if he (the cat) attacks the custodian then.

TS: Yes. So, this cat is very special. It seems to be able to have actually, sort of, deductive knowledge, and have sort of logical cause of thought that normal cat wouldn't have.

G: It seems like almost human way. Because it is so upset about its child that is killed. It seems it gets revenge.

TS: Exactly. So, the cat is special. So, we must somehow see the cat as a principal of, I don't know of what? Of justice, of revenge, of anger, of motherhood? What do you think? What would the cat present at the end? What happens to the cat after it kills Elias P.?

A: The narrator kills the cat.

TS: Yes.

A: I personally think, well, the cat is not the symbol of justice. It is not real justice.

TS: No? ↑no. ↓

A: Of course not. ↓ But I think she is the symbol of motherhood, something like that.

TS: Yeah. Sort of very instinct in the way. It is very like a principal that has rational thoughts; it is feeling something wild.

A: And of course, the cat marries; (it is) the squaw.

TS: It does. Maybe there is more than that (...)

Teacher S could have some direction to certain information in the text, but she did not do that in an obvious way. Rather, Teacher S kept some possibilities for students' personal thinking and participation in discussion, through listening to and sharing with them. The teacher and speaking students listened to one another in the extended back-and-forth conversation as they built on what others said, got inspiration, and added new explanations. This produced a kind of *active understanding* in a Bakhtinian sense (Bakhtin,1981). For instance, Teacher S listened to Student A's personal opinion, "motherhood," which was to some extent against what Student G said, "revenge". That means students listened to each other and expressed their personal thinking. But Teacher S did not deny any of them; instead, she followed up their thinking in a responsive way and then also shared her own ideas.

On the whole, Teacher S was playing the role of teacher and instructor, as the institution authorized. In the two excerpts above, Teacher S occupied a position of a teacher who guided students deeply into the text analysis step by step. She controlled the steps and pace of learning, the process of discussion, and the questions for discussing because at first students were morally positioned as learners and they were expected to learn more deeply.

Then, sometimes students were also deliberately given chance to take up other positions when some of them expressed their readings from the perspective of the reader (like students K, G, A) and could argue with others and the teacher. At that time, Teacher S's position of supporter was achieved by her way of speaking, and the students' position of the personal reader was supported by the teacher's guiding words.

In the process of working with the fictional piece, Teacher S gradually guided students to change stances from lecture to group work, and then to whole-class discussion. In the first lesson Teacher S tapped student knowledge of "first narrator" by asking a question about this meaning from the perspective of stances (Stance 1 Getting started with the material). The guiding questions for group discussion were proposed by using Stance 2 (Developing understanding of the material). Among these questions, the last question (*What can we make of that in a Gothic story?*) can be related to Stance 3 (Leaving from the material) to think on a broader issue of the Gothic story. From whole-class discussion (Excerpt 3.5), it also can be seen that their interpretation about the cat in the fiction became richer with the process of discussion among the teacher and three students. Their individual thinking about the cat was guided by the teacher step by step.

3.3.1.2   Student Written Assignment

Some research claims that dialogue is both oral and written (Dysthe, 1999). Inspired by that, student written assignment is seen as a way of dialogic teaching rather than a monologic way according to the definition of *dialogic* in this book. In Teacher S's classrooms, students had different kinds of written assignments. Some were written presentations based on group work, some were student essays based on group work and presentations, and others were essays analysing a literary text as an exam at the end of the academic year. No matter in which way, they were products of interactions either among the teacher and students or between the student and the student.

The student individual essay that analysed a literary text in Teacher S's classroom demonstrated the interaction between the teacher and students clearly.

Excerpt 3.6 includes a part of Student M's essay that was part of a written exam on her analysis of a short story *A Good Night's Sleep* by Brian McCabe for the end of their first academic year. Each student wrote this essay twice because Teacher S was not pleased with their first version; most of them did it in a superficial way. In the first class of their second year, students, therefore, were asked to work in groups with the literary text again, thinking and discussing in a step further with the guiding bullet points given by the teacher. Then they were asked to take the task home and finish writing the second version. Teacher S commented on the first essays on the paper, with revisions, comments next to sentences, and grades at the bottom. In the second version, Teacher S did the evaluation on the computer. By comparison, students did revise their first essays when they wrote the second ones according to Teacher S's evaluations. Take Student M's essay as an example. She was described by the teacher as an average student who also had great potential.

Excerpt 3.6   Student M's Essays
Engelsk Delprøve2-Årsprøve (English Subtest2- Annual Test)
1. First version: *A Good Night's Sleep — Student M*
(...) Both Lockhart and the homeless woman is (are)[①] in a place with a need for love (...) They have each other and do not see the homeless girl's needs, the same way Lockhart do (does).
The Teacher's comments: *A very good and significant observation! But have you noticed that George Lockhart actually teaches social studies?*

---

① The words in the parenthesis are the correct words revised by Teacher S.

2. Second version: *A Good Night's Sleep — Student M*

(...) From Lockhart's job as a professor in social studies, he has a lot of theoretically (theoretical) knowledge about people in the same situation as the girl outside his door. He knows the numbers and statistics behind disadvantaged people like the girl, but he has never had a relationship, not even a conversation, with one (someone) like her. This is also a reason why he helps this girl, when no one else does. He has some kind of affiliation to the girl, in the way that he works with cases like her every day (...)

<u>The Teacher's comments:</u> *Very good work. You know how to use your own language in a comment on the text.*

Comparing Teacher S's first comments and Student M's second essay, it can be seen that the student tried to analyse further based on the teacher's comments. Student M added the above paragraph in the second version as her response to Teacher S's question in the first comments. The second comments from the teacher could be seen as the teacher's reaction to the student's response. Here, the IRE pattern was formed in a written way, but the student written assignment with the teacher's comments in this case was not necessarily dialogic.

In the above written assignment, the students' personal points were allowed and encouraged to be included in the essay. For instance, Teacher S often commented, "good point/good observation, using source to argue and reason" when she read students' new points that she had not mentioned before. This means that Teacher S had her interpretation of the text, but was still open to another possibility from students. She asked students to notice that George Lockhart actually taught social studies, because as she said: "I want students not to say that he (George Lockhart) doesn't know anything about the problem of society, of course, he does as a teacher, but that he knows on a different level." In fact, Student M gave her response in their own words (*"He knows the numbers and statistics behind disadvantaged people like the girl, but he has never had a relationship, not even a conversation, with someone like her")* that were supported by the following quotation from the text based on her reading. This also means that Student M understood the teacher's question and assimilated the teacher's comments into her understanding. In other words, Student M took an active and responsive attitude toward the teacher's comments. This active and responsive "assimilation" produced *active understanding* in the Bakhtinian sense (Bakhtin, 1981). From this perspective, students' second-version essays in this case were dialogic utterances with assimilation of the teacher's responses.

In the written interaction, the teacher and students still played their intuitional identities because the teacher had rights and responsibilities to evaluate students' written assignments, and students were expected to revise, taking these comments seriously. Meanwhile, students had a different performance in their writing and sometimes talked about their different viewpoints. The teacher's attitudes towards their performance and different viewpoints indicated her positioning strategy — by and large, the teacher positioned students by reference to their institutional roles, but sometimes they could be positioned as readers who might understand the text in a different way if they could support their readings by using relevant source.

- ***Summing Up: Teacher S as a Supporter of Student Thinking and Reading***

During the teacher-student interaction, Teacher S morally positioned herself as a teacher who controlled the content of learning, the pace of studying, the form of interaction, and even the grade of students' written assignments, but meanwhile she tried to motivate students to engage in thinking about literature in a way of supporting students' personal reading and discussing with them, thus she deliberately express her situated identity as a supporter of learning in the communications in order to push students to think deeper and acquire literary experience. The teacher-student interaction including oral and written ways facilitated *active understanding* (Bakhtin, 1981) of the students through back-

and-forth exchanging and assimilation of voices.

3.3.2 The Interaction between Students and the Text

Excerpt 3.6 can also serve as an example of the interaction between students and the text. The investigation on this type of interaction is actually to examine how the teacher directed students to read a literary text. Excerpt 3.7 shows the full version of the written task that was set up as an exam for the first academic year. As introduced above, students did the writing twice because Teacher S was not pleased with what students had written at the first time, so she gave a worksheet (Text 2) *"Taking a literary analysis a step further"* to guide students.

Excerpt 3.7
Text 1: Engelsk Delprøve2-Årsprøve[①] *(English Subtest2- Annual Test)*
A Good Night's Sleep
Write an essay (600–800 words) about the text in which you include the points listed below. You may include further points you find relevant. Your essay must also include a couple of quotations that are relevant to your analysis/interpretation. (Your essay should not include a summary of the text).

- Characterize George Lockhart.
- Characterize the girl and discuss her function in the text.
- The setting.
- The ending.
- The themes.

Text 2: Taking a literary analysis a step further
Use the bullet points from your exam paper task sheet:
1. Characterize George Lockhart

[①] Danish words. These danish words mean "English Subtest 2 — Annual Test".

As many details as possible. Note his name. Observe his situation his job, the relationship between his job and his life. Consider whether he is a very special individual or a representative of people/men in his time and age. Why does he suffer from insomnia?

2. Characterize the girl, and discuss her function in the text

Your teacher has given you a hint that the girl has a **function** i.e., she must reflect/illustrate something other than just an individual homeless girl who has failed in her life.

(...)

5. The themes

Go deeper than just mentioning the themes and do not say: "The themes could be ..." If you do not know what the themes are, you have not read the text properly! (...)

Other advice:

Remember:
— The title may give you a hint at the interpretation and is almost always worth a reflection.
— The text is always more complex than you may see at the first glance.
— If there are two main characters, you should look at their differences as well as their similarities.
— Characters in stories don't always know themselves very well.

Text 1 is extracted from the written task sheet and Text 2 *"Taking a literary analysis a step further"* is from the worksheet. By comparison of the bullets in the above two texts, Text 2 included many details of ways of reading and analysing a text, such as how to characterize a person and compare characters in stories, how to examine the setting of stories, how to read a text thoroughly and properly, and how to deal with the title. These detailed guiding bullets can be related to a method of literary instruction that has been used in America for the past several decades, namely "close reading", which is a concept from New Criticism (Tyson, 2015, p.129). This approach advocates using concrete, specific examples from the text to validate a reader's interpretation (Tyson, 2015). New criticism was opposed by reader-response criticism because it regards the literary text as a "timeless, autonomous (self-sufficient) verbal object" (ibid, p.131), which is to say that a reader's interpretation depends on the objectivity of the text itself, rather than the subjectivity of the reader. In this sense, there is a best or good interpretation of a particular text in New Criticism's view; this point of view is also opposed to the main point of the reader-response theory including envisioning theory, which sees the reader's reading as neither good nor bad.

Today, many literary teachers are doing close reading, but maybe some of them use it in an "open" way as Teacher S did in this case. On the one hand, she thought there were hints in the texts and thus adopted close reading when she designed the bullets points for student analysis based on the hints she found in the text; but on the other hand, when she was confronted with other views from students, she did not deny them but was open to them and discussed with students in a dialogic way. In this sense, Teacher S combined an objective concept of text with a reader-response inspired pedagogy and ways of framing interaction.

The next excerpt is an example of how the teacher managed other views from students, indicting her combining of two pedagogy strategies. It was an extract from a conversation when Teacher S joined in a group discussion. At that time, students were discussing in groups about how to rewrite their essays. Before writing the second essay, students discussed further about the bullet points one by one.

Excerpt 3.8

① S1: We talked about the title, "A Good Night's Sleep" could be like, he has trouble with good night sleep because maybe his conscious is not clean, because somehow, he knows that he is, um, very materialistic and only interested in himself.

② TS: I don't know where he is materialistic↑.

③ S1: Maybe that is a wrong word, but (1.0), but he doesn't care about other people.

④ TS: Well, he is not really offered by the people to care for, is he?

⑤ S1: No, he is just annoyed by someone like his neighbour.

⑥ S2: Is that called "alienation"?

⑦ TS: I think "alienation" could be a word.

⑧ S2: He has all these people in his own belief, never really contact with them. He has students, but I don't think he will talk to them, but teach them. He doesn't really care about it. He is worried about his wife but he has also never seen her. So, the word, "alienation".

⑨ S3: He just observed but doesn't do anything.

⑩ S2: So of course, it is hard to care about other people if you are alienated, because (...)

⑪ TS: Because his contact with other people is just like the environment. He can hear them, he can see them, but doesn't talk to them. <S2: exactly>

And it is obvious that he misses his wife. He misses the life they had. So, he misses the closeness. (...)

⑫ S2: Do you think it is in purpose to mention the difficulties of George Lockhart. It did actually I think impart mercifully.

⑬ TS: I think so. Are you the one that mentioned it?

⑭ S2: Yes, I did.

⑮ TS: I think only one person did but I did not remember who. But you are a good text reader. Share with your classmates like you used to do. I think that is no coincidence. It is hard to note.

It can be seen that this group seriously discussed the meaning of the title and the representativeness of the main character with the guidance of bullet points. As usual, Teacher S did not directly decline students' responses when they shared with her; instead, she asked as if she really did not know something, for instance, in turn ② she said, "I don't know where he is materialistic." This sentence indicated that she was asking students to find the evidence in the text to support their ideas, and also implied that she might already have her understanding based on some hints in the texts. But meanwhile, this approach also appeared to encourage students to think further and find a proper word to express their ideas that might not be in the teacher's mind when S2 said the word "alienation" (e.g., the teacher used words "*could be*" in turn ⑦). Then S2 gave his interpretation that inspired S3, and also Teacher S joined and thought along with his (S2) thinking. Even finally Teacher S asked S2 to share his (S2) unique idea with other peers, it was probably because the teacher might not see the point either, as she said it was hard to note in the turn ⑮. Thus, a dialogue that affected each other's understandings was established by the teacher's encouragement-leaving space for students' engagement in talking and contributing based on their readings. In this process, Teacher S did not perform as omniscience, but a cooperator of the students, which aligned with her deliberately self-positioning in the pre-observation interview.

As a result, students' second essays indicated that group discussions with the teacher's guiding bullet points did help students to go further. From the perspective of envisioning theory, guiding bullet points functioned as instructions from Stance 2 (Developing understanding of the material). When the teacher and students talked about the text as a whole, they stepped out and rethought their understandings at a deeper level, indicating the usage of Stance 3 (Leaving from the material).

- ***Summing Up: Teacher S as a Guide of Deep Reading***

Teacher S in this case was mostly intentionally playing a teacher's role, using her power to ask students to rewrite the essay. But during the discussion time, she deliberately positioned herself as a guide who gave the guiding bullet points and joined the group discussion to help students go deeper. Sometimes, when she was listening to some students' ideas, she interactively positioned them as individual readers who could help and inspire each other. The student-text interaction indicated a combination of two pedagogy strategies of Teacher S when she guided students to see the hints in the text and meanwhile opened for other possibilities during the interaction with students. As a whole, the above example also demonstrated Teacher S's teaching in reading can be interpreted as the envisioning-theory based pedagogy combined with the dialogic way of interaction.

3.3.3 The Interaction between the Student and the Student

The majority of the time observed in Teacher S's lessons was occupied by group work, including group discussions and group presentations in both second-year and third-year classes. Eight lessons were observed in the second-year class, with four lessons of group work and four lessons consisting partly of group discussions. In the third-year class, all eight lessons observed were group work including group discussions and presentations. The group work gave the opportunity for close interactions between the student and the student, creating a chance for student cooperative learning.

Teacher S stated that she orchestrated group work differently according to students' levels in different grades, intentionally offering various positions for students through assigning tasks and responsibilities to them. The typical group work in both second-year and third-year classes was framed in a form of a miniature project that functioned as a practice of some potential formal projects in their future study. In particular, the second-year students did a miniature project about a British singer and the third-year class students did a bigger project about literary history and the representative literary text analysis. In this kind of group work, the positions that participants occupied were changing now and then; the roles of the teacher and students in the group work were not stable. The following analysis of two projects shows how students performed different positions offered by the teacher, and how they read literary texts by using these positions.

3.3.3.1 Second-Year Class: A Project on a British Singer

The second-year class spent four lessons on the group work of a British singer. For most of the working time, the interaction between the student and the student dominated. They worked together when they chose and read a text, analysed and discussed the text, as well as when they wrote and presented a written PowerPoint. In this process, students were performing different positions intentionally offered by the teacher somehow so that they read and discussed texts of a British singer from different stances.

- ***General Positioning throughout the Project — Student as an Independent Learner***

Teacher S had a general view of how to position students and how to position herself. First of all, Teacher S had a general positioning method toward students in learning something. Work with a British singer was designed as a miniature project to engage students because they were interested in it, and also as an experiment to practice students' independence in working with literature. In this sense, Teacher S regarded this small project as a strategy for engaging students, showing a positioning way that the teacher had in general — that is, students were expected to be independent learners, and the teacher positioned herself as a trainer and guide of students. This general positioning way indicates most teachers' identities authorized by institutions and related to their roles. It is therefore a moral positioning, which is inevitable for both teacher and student in schools. In this project, the general positioning is also connected to the interactive positioning of Teacher S from the beginning to the end. In particular, in this project, Teacher S also positioned students as participants of project organization from the outset (planning of the project) to the end (evaluating the project).

Before the teacher decided on the topic, Teacher S had a loose teaching plan with something open for students to fill in. Teacher S agreed that the texts of the British singer were chosen because these texts were popular, and contained some special themes, which had some cultural impact on poems and influence on later singers, actors, and songwriters. Therefore, after agreement with the teacher, songs and lyrics were brought into Teacher S's English class as a result of an interaction and negotiation between the teacher and students who contributed together to the textual choice.

In the end, students were encouraged to perform commentaries of the whole project. The class spent half a lesson for students' comments and advice on the miniature project about the singer, paying much attention to feedback that might be helpful for their future study or useful when the teacher designed another project later. Correspondingly, Teacher S was performing as a listener who expected suggestions based on the personal experience of students, treating them as responders respectfully. Five students gave comments and Excerpt 3.9 contains part of the conversation among Teacher S and two students.

Excerpt 3.9

TS: (...) I'd like to hear a few comments on the project things, all the whole project. I would like to jot down a few comments that we can use later on. And one comment that I've got yesterday was that maybe we spent too much time on it. Is that the general (0.5) question?

(...)

A: Well. I do think that we spent too much time on teamwork. But you could have more about this British singer in a different way.

TS: So, a kind of introduction?

A: Maybe, yes.

(...)

TS: OK. Would you think it is more efficient if (0.5) Er (0.5) if there had been a general introduction?

K: (coughed and cleared his throat)

TS: (had a look at him) Karl.

K: Yes, definitely. Because I knew least about the British singer before we studied on this.

TS: No? ↑

K: So, it surpasses most of my knowledge, <TS: Yeah> so that I have to look both things. <TS: Yeah>

TS: Er, and that is too much to ask? <K: Er> if we have only a couple of weeks.

K: If you had more time, it wouldn't be. But since we don't have a long time, and we wouldn't get any words, so a bit, a bit too much that.

TS: Yeah↑. Would you say perhaps that (0.5) maybe you learn a little bit from it for a future project works. Er, because that is a way to find new materials yourself and find an angle to work on, so it could be a miniature perhaps.

K: OK.

TS: Not to, er (0.5) take away your criticism, you may be right. But you know, just maybe a little better prepared for that <K: Yeah>, until you try this.

K: Yes.

TS: Who else? Christian.

C: I do think it is nice that we can choose the subject to work with.

TS: You like the free choice? ↑

C: Yeah. ↓

TS: What is good about that?

C: Em ... (0.5) It's just that (1.0) I don't know. It's a ... (0.5)

TS: It motivated you better? ↑

C: Yeah.

TS: Em (2.0) that's ... (0.5)
C: I just think it is nice. They have somewhat we are working with.
TS: You like the freedom? ↑
C: Yeah. <TS: Yeah> Although it was Maya, Jepper (other two peer's names) <TS: they> they were choosing, there was something all of us could relate to. Yeah.
TS: The ideas came up from ... (2)
C: From the students. <TS: you > Yeah.
TS: Em (0.5) I think that's a very relevant comment (...) Only I am hoping, of course, sometimes you enjoy, em, being introduced to something that you couldn't find yourselves. I am hoping that, would be the case when you are forced to do literary history next year and the (0.5) Shakespeare, that sort of thing, because there would be a free choice there. Sometimes myself I find it, I enjoy, having other people could say something to me (...)

From the above extract, it can be seen that Teacher S noticed her speaking manner and treated students' comments seriously (e.g., she jotted down a few comments from students) so that her tone was intended to negotiate with the student rather than strongly forcing him/her (e.g., the teacher confirmed what the student said by repeating "yeah" now and then). Instead of absolute rejection of what Student K said, Teacher S persuaded him in a mild way and retained his ideas ("you may be right"). In this process, Teacher S maintained her goal to foster student independent learning as she repeated it (a miniature for future project work) to the students. It means that Teacher S expected students to recognize a general position that they occupied in the project as independent learners. This general position requested students not only to participate in curricular planning and evaluating but also to work cooperatively in groups with some choices and responsibilities.

However, it is worth mentioning that some students like Student A and Student K seemed not to recognize the teacher's purpose. They thought Teacher S should have an introductive lecture on the topic. In Teacher S's view, Student A was an excellent student and Student K was a serious student who would be good at reading in a long run. Their comments to some extent represented some students' thoughts on the group work, which indicated that students usually enjoyed being introduced as an efficient way of learning something, so they had not prepared to work independently from the beginning — such as starting with choosing the topic, materials, and the angle. Thus, a tension between the teacher's expectations and students' realities was established.

- ***More Possibilities of Positions Achieved by Free Choice during Group Work***

In the process of working, there were many opportunities for students to choose on their own, without the teacher's formal participation. Free choices started with choosing group members. When organizing groups, students chose members who sat nearby, or on the basis of friendships with each other. Apart from this, there were three kinds of choices that opened more possibilities for students to join in the interaction with peers.

The first choice for each group was choosing a particular song of a British singer with its lyrics, pictures, or videos. Teacher S provided a worksheet that contained all the links of relevant texts and materials: songs, lyrics, pictures, and videos. There were dozens of songs online so that students' choices could be pluralistic. After knowing about an overview of songs via searching for the life of the singer, the background, and themes of the song, each group discussed and made a choice. In this process, the teacher did not control the choice, instead, she made some room for students to discuss and decide on their own. That is to say, she deliberately positioned herself as a facilitator who would provide some help when needed, and also kept students working alone if she was not needed. Accordingly, students were expected to perform as active participants in group work. They were allowed to use computers to search for information, play music in the classroom, and even move out of the classroom to find a quiet place to do their group work. The atmosphere looked so energetic and relaxed that there could have many possibilities of choice, but the fact was that the choices of six groups were mainly on three popular songs which were the most famous songs of this singer and told stories about that era the singer lived in. Through the internet, much information about these three songs could be easily found because of their popularity. If Teacher S did some controlling on the choosing of songs such as asking different groups to choose different songs, students in different groups might analyse at least six texts and share their products with other groups. But when Teacher S offered open choices, students might tend to choose similar texts that were easier to understand and interpret. In this sense, it is tricky for the literature teacher to foster student initiatives on some challenging work if students are given free choices.

The second choice for students was the way in which they worked together with texts. The teacher expected them to work independently and cooperatively. This means that each group finished the task on the basis of members' cooperation. Teacher S neither formally joined in each group's work, nor assigned specific responsibility to each member of the group; again, she positioned herself as a facilitator and walked around to see if anyone needed help. Hence, it was primarily the student-led group work; students themselves in a group were responsible for apportioning mutual tasks. In the process of cooperation, for student members, each had different opportunities to occupy different positions, such as performing as a leader, an organizer, or a speaker, and had corresponding responsibilities of analysing content, pictures, or videos. In this way, students collaborated with each other in the teamwork. These possibilities were open and flexible so that in the process of assigning, there was resistance, modification, and negotiation among them. Excerpt 3.10 shows a process of assigning in one group which consisted of four girls.

Excerpt 3.10

(Laughing)

① S1: Could we move on?

② S2: I think if we have to analyse the picture, why don't we split up? You know, you could discuss the picture, and we could move on to the lyrics.

③ S3: I think I want to discuss the picture.

④ S2: OK, Signe, I will (...) (music started, another group was playing song) analyse the song. We need to move, move on, OK? Because right now, we are wasting time. We need to discuss that.

⑤ S3: How can we see his finger? That is not his finger! (She was talking about the picture again)

⑥ S4: Yes, it looks like the shadow of his finger.

⑦ S2: You do what? You do the picture; you do the song?

⑧ S3: Yeah.

⑨ S2: OK, Signe and I, we will move over there.

⑩ S4: No, no, no! I want to do the picture.

⑪ S2: No? ↑ Maybe it is a good idea that you don't do the picture.

⑫ S4: But, but ... (2)

⑬ S1: Actually, I don't care.

⑭ S4: I am not the song.

⑮ S2: What about you? Do you want to be together or (...)?

⑯ S4: I want to do the picture. What do you want to do?

⑰ S1: It is OK.

⑱ S2: So, let them discuss.

⑲ S1: OK, we move.

Working cooperatively was a challenge for the students. As some students interviewed mentioned, it was so easy for them to become distracted from the work by talking about other things outside the classroom. Especially in student-led group discussions, students did not know how to share the work and meanwhile to cooperate with each other. At that time, sometimes there would be a student who occupied a position of a leader in the group work like S2 did in the above excerpt. She seemed to have a strong sense of responsibility to finish the task on time. It was tacit and performative positioning in which students were positioned by their actions with or against the storyline. At first, her position was resisted by some members (S3, S4) — either they did not accept her arrangement or did not care what she said. But then, when S1 performed as a coordinator who firstly prevented chatting to push the discussion forward (turn ①) and then adopted the position S2 offered (turn ⑰, ⑲), an agreement was finally achieved. Apparently, the four students performed differently: S1 and S2 actively occupied two positions and took the responsibilities. Simultaneously they also interactively positioned other peers as cooperators of the teamwork. However, S3 and S4 resisted or modified the positions offered by S2 and wanted to do other parts of the work. This short excerpt, to some extent, demonstrates the negotiation of different positions in the student-led group work.

The third choice was about how to present group work. The main task of the whole project was to make a written PowerPoint, in which students would present the picture and the text to peers in other groups (Excerpt 3.11). The teacher did not say how to design and prepare the PowerPoint in the worksheet; so, students could decide how to show their working results, in which way, how to design the style, how to present texts, pictures, and sound. There were many choices and decisions that needed to discuss and consider.

Excerpt 3.11

    All groups must choose one song + one picture (record cover) or video.

Task: Make a PowerPoint, in which you present the picture and the text — preferably with sound. The PowerPoint must include a full analysis of the text and the picture/video. Use the plan for an analysis of poetry that I have given you.

Two written presentations collected from the classroom showed that the type of PowerPoint was diverse. One group used "Prezi", online software, to achieve dynamic effects in images and make the presentation attractive — as they analysed the structure, themes, era, and author's life in four mobile pictures. The other group used traditional PowerPoint, which was written in a textual style, in terms of four themes that they interpreted. The difference depended on the group interests and techniques they liked to use.

Before handing in the final written presentations to the teacher, students had the opportunity to get feedback from other groups. They reorganised six new presentation groups where each student presented their working results in a PowerPoint. Thus, students in a new group could share different works with the texts of the same singer. Obviously, each student occupied new positions in a new group: each of them presented, representing his or her working group and asking for or giving feedback. The following is an excerpt from a new presentation group. The four girls were presenting one by one. Two of them were discussing a poster about a song after S1 finished her presentation on this song.

Excerpt 3.12

① S1: What's the first thing that you thought when you saw this picture?

② S2: ... I saw actually they had two sides of his face that one is <S1: true!> very dark and evil, and the other is ... (2)

③ S1: Pure, somehow.

④ S2: Yes. More front and (...)

⑤ S1: You can completely write that↑.
⑥ S2: Yeah.
⑦ S1: ↓Really, that's great! Cause on this side, he looks runnable, and on another side, it is much darker, and here has the green contrast, it's happier <S2: yeah>but on the other side, you have the reading contrast.
⑧ S2: Exactly. So ... (0.5)
⑨ S1: True, it could be actually about two sides of them ...

In presentation groups, students were given room to participate in conversations with others. Teacher S still positioned herself as a facilitator and made it possible for students to interact in new groups. In Excerpt 3.12, S1 and S2 worked with the same song, but used different pictures. S1 positioned S2 as a potential responder who could say something different. S2 did adopt that position and further, what she said was agreed and also supported by S1. Gradually, they reached an agreement on the meaning of the picture. In the final presentation of the S1's group, it can be seen that S1 assimilated S2's ideas into her group's working product, which can be seen as a result of constantly *active understanding* (Bakhtin, 1981) and assimilation of new elements from others. In this sense, there was an interactive and reciprocal dialogue between these two girls. During that period, Teacher S always performed a facilitator role so as to create an interactive and dynamic atmosphere, thus students could occupy multiple positions that were open and flexible when working in groups. This openness also made the student-student interaction substantial and diverse.

- *Different Reading Stances Related to Different Positions*

According to positioning theory, positioning is a way of examining the relationship between teachers and students. In this book, positioning can also be related to the instruction in literature teaching. In the case of Teacher S's second-year class, the changing of positions could be seen as the shifting of stances from the perspective of envisioning theory (Langer, 2011b). This group work was led by students, but usually the process followed the teacher's written guidance — *how to describe a painting* and *how to read a poem* (Excerpt 3.13), which included the procedures of reading and interpretation, and general questions for analysing poems and pictures, like "how" and "what" questions.

Excerpt 3.13
How to read a poem:
FIRST: read the poem sentence by sentence.
THEN: read the poem stanza by stanza to build up a general idea about the poem as a whole.
FINALLY: read the whole poem in one go.
- Who is the speaker in the poem?
- What is this person's background?
  (...)

How to describe a painting:
Three strategies in picture analysis.
I. Description
- Who or what is in the picture?
(...)
II. Analysis
- What do you notice first?
(...)
III. Interpretation
- Look back on what you have already noted and try to reach a conclusion: what does the picture actually mean? What is it communicating?
(...)

These questions guided students to think and go deeper step by step from the perspective of envisioning theory (Langer, 2011b). When a group chose a particular song and text of a British singer students started to step into an initial envisionment of the song with the guidance to build up a general idea about the text as a whole, which was using Stance 1(Getting started with the material). It can be seen that the above guiding questions are general, not specific for a particular text. In Langer's view, this way of providing guiding questions that included ways of doing and thinking is the teacher *offering enabling strategies* in envisionment-building classrooms (Langer, 2011b). With the guidance of these questions, students could develop understanding, especially in the discussion with peers. As mentioned above, in the group work, Teacher S always took the role of a facilitator, but in fact, that is only one aspect. Meanwhile, Teacher S also performed as a coach who enabled students to do the analysis and interpretation on their own rather than as a facilitator who just helped them in analysing some specific sentences as she characterized herself as below:

> They (students) work more or less independently. Sometimes they came and asked me to have a look, I would read through the poem or the passage of the poem they were reading, and then I would ask them what they were thinking, and they said they had certain dilemmas. Some of the songs they found difficult to analyse, and then I asked them to look for support for the different ideas they had. So, I did a bit of coaching actually, rather than just helping them.

This statement clearly indicated Teacher S's position in project-based learning. The role of the coach implies the general positioning way that Teacher S had — encouraging students to work independently. She used questions to tap their related knowledge and asked them to connect relevant details in texts to support their ideas, instead of giving them meanings of texts directly. From the perspective of envisioning theory, she was using a kind of Stance 1 (Getting started with the material) and Stance 2 (Developing understanding of the material). In presentation groups, students stepped out of their working texts, presented what they had worked out, and reflected on what they had based on the feedback from other working groups (Stance 3 Leaving from the material). Meanwhile, they were performing as cooperators, namely, they read the texts personally and also collaboratively. Finally, when performing as commenters, the teacher and students all stepped out of the texts and the presentations for a while, critically thinking about the whole project in the long run. The teacher asked students to examine the effects, hoping to find something meaningful that could be used in their future study (Stance 4 Think critically about the material). Step by step, with the change of positions they occupied, students also shifted stances of reading. They moved from the inside of the text to the outside of the text, from the details to a whole. This example seemed to bridge the gap between the envisioning theory as a pedagogy of literature and the positioning theory as a way to investigate interactions.

However, it is a pity that written presentations showed that students did not really engage themselves in the text personally. From students' written presentations, it can be seen that they were a bit stereotypical and superficial rather than novel or personal. While they adopted different types of presentation, the texts and pictures were interpreted in a way that supported a common understanding of the texts. And their interpretations were mainly about the introduction of the singer's life and era, as well as the main themes that were shared by most of his songs. Instead of exploring different understandings, they tended to summarize facts about the texts and the artist. While Teacher S changed stances in the learning process to help students to build up a rich envisionment of texts, it was still difficult for students to recognize that reading literature was a way of thinking.

In summary, on the whole Teacher S controlled the entire project — when to start, when to finish, which task students had to finish, but meanwhile she intentionally opened room for students to have some free choices and offered students chances to take up different positions during the group work. Again, this example indicated how Teacher S implemented her aim of fostering student independent learning that also refers to the ability to negotiate different positions in the group work. By shifting positions, students read specific texts and then rethought the whole project with different stances in Langer's sense (Langer, 2011b). In this sense, this case illustrated a possibility of combining two kinds of pedagogy — one was based on the positioning theory and the other was based on envisioning theory.

3.3.3.2 Third-Year Class: A Project of Literary Periods with Students as the Teacher of Peers

The third-year class started the project from the first lesson of the semester in which these senior students had to work different literary periods and representative texts through group work. During the time of group work, there were also multiple interactions between the teacher and students, among students, and between students and texts. Correspondingly, there were multi-positions for both the teacher and students to take on. But in general, both the teacher and students read and understand literary texts from double positions throughout the project.

- *General Positioning — Double Positions (Being Student and Teacher) of Students*

At the beginning of the third academic year, Teacher S assigned independent work for the students who worked in groups with different literary periods and representative texts. There were four lessons of group work and four presentations were observed. A worksheet including the specific tasks and goals, as well as the representative text of each period

(Appendix 3.2) was given at the first lesson. The task for each group was to grasp the knowledge of the period they chose and analysed the particular representative texts, and then to teach other students through oral group presentation. From the beginning, choosing an interesting literary period, the students had many choices, as the second-year students did in the miniature project of a British singer. But in contrast, this time Teacher S controlled the choice and told students that each period must be covered and then students put themselves into different groups working with different periods and topics. As a result, students organised six groups working with six literary periods: Renaissance, Enlightenment, Romanticism, Victorian Age, Modernism, and Postmodernism — mainly on the basis of their interests. They chose the particular texts on their own or as suggested by the teacher and then designed their teaching (group presentation) style. Each presentation needed to be 45-60 minutes in length based on students' cooperative work.

Compared with the second-year miniature project, the third-year project was more demanding, without the teacher's general guiding points, or ways of doing and thinking. Teacher S positioned each group of students as literature teachers of a particular lesson. These "student teachers" framed a presentation as a lesson through which they presented what they had learnt in the group work to other peers. With this position being a "student teacher", each group was requested to assign relevant homework to other groups in advance, and then discussed the homework together during the lesson, as a way to engage all the students in class. Evidently, these senior students had more responsibilities than the second-year students as they were ascribed the identity as "a teacher" in this project. As a result, these senior students had two identities integrated at the same time: one was identity authorized by the institution (student), the other was *situated identity* (Gee,2011a) ascribed by the action of teaching (teacher). When students needed Teacher S's guides, their identity of student dominated, and when presented in a lesson and taught others, their situated identity (Gee,2011a) of "a teacher" was obvious. It was the teacher's general positioning, a deliberately positioning of students — a combination of two positions.

- **Multi-Positions of Students Offered in Group Work**

As the second-year students had in the miniature project, within each group, members had to take different responsibilities for the mutual work. Some were responsible for the text analysis, some for the picture analysis, and others were responsible for searching for materials. The same as other group work, when analysing a particular text on the basis of literary history, each member in a group had a chance to occupy different positions, such as a leader of the whole work, a collector of materials, an analyser of the text, and a designer of the presentation. Their positions were open and flexible, depending on how the assignment was allotted. There were also resistance, modification, and negotiation during the working time, but students thought preparing for a lesson gave them the responsibility and motivation to learn the text better. In this process, they racked their brains to design a lesson, making it attractive and informative. It was interesting and helpful for both students who gave a lesson and other students who were listening to it because the presentation group learnt on their own in a group and also helped others to learn something from their "lesson." In this sense, there was cooperative learning within a group as well as in the whole class. The following example of the Postmodernism group reflects a way of framing the presentation/lesson, indicating how they taught and how other classmates cooperated with them.

The Postmodernism group gave a presentation including a 25-minute lecture on the text and Postmodernism, and a 30-minute game with group discussion and small presentations based on text analysis *(The Red Line)* that engaged the other students in thinking and discussing. In particular, the lecture with PowerPoint contained the definition of Postmodernism, its influence on the art, music, and architecture, and characteristics of postmodern literature. Then the game was organised with tasks for each group. The rest of the students were divided into four small discussion groups. Each of them was given a list of questions on the characters, themes, settings of *The Red Line* as shown in Excerpt 3.14. A small discussion group needed to discuss one list of questions and after a 20-minute discussion, each group delegated a speaker to give a speech about their understandings based on the group discussion.

Excerpt 3.14
The Postmodernism group homework:
Look for Post Modern traits on your part!

Berto+Cathy — Group 1
Describe Berto's physical appearance.
What effect does Cathy have on Berto?
What is their relationship? What does this represent?
What kind of human feeling does Berto represent? Elaborate.

Nameless Man (NM) — Group2
What movie character does NM remind you of?
Why is he nameless?
Why does NM remove all public hair?
Where does NM's hatred come from?
What kind of human feeling does NM represent? Elaborate.

Denise — Group 3
Do you think mentally unstable?
How does Denise view Nameless Man and Berto?
Is she deceived?
What kind of human feeling does Denise represent?

Describe the environment and London in general — Group 4

Compare London and Venice.

Describe the tube, what does it represent?

Investigate "The real red line".

It is obvious that this group of students was learning how to make questions and how to assign tasks, from a teacher's perspective. During the lesson, each member of the presentation group occupied two positions: one was the position within the group, the other was a shared position, together acting as a teacher. Within the presentation group, each member positioned themselves differently and was responsible for different parts of the mutual work. There were three boys in that group — one (Student A) was the main speaker of the lesson, one was playing the PowerPoint (Student J), while the other (Student H) was responsible for supplementing some points if there were questions or confusion. Meanwhile, the Postmodernism group together occupied a position of a teacher, controlling the structure of the lesson, the content that others were learning, and the discussion time. As Teacher S usually did, during the discussion time, they walked around when discussions were going on, trying to explain some confusing points in the text or questions. In Excerpt 3.15, the main speaker Student A started to play his position as a shared teacher in group discussions and then in the next small group presentations.

Excerpt 3.15

A: Well, let's get the play where we have tasks for small groups. If you just moved to the groups, that will be lovely. We have four groups here, two groups on the left and two on the right. So, Group 1,2,3,4 (pointed to location)

(Students moved to their new small groups)

Well. Is every group aware of the points and find out something? No? ↑ All right. You can find the document on the Lectio (online system of the school). We have one more thing. There must be much doubt about this, so please ask us if you doubt or if you need some help or guides of anything, and you have to present this when you will finish.

(...) (20 minutes later)

A: All right, all right, all right! We get to pick a group now. Please qui:et! (Shouting loudly)

<The electronic turning plate was running and then stopped, showing Student P's name on the screen>

P: Yes. (Walked to the platform) Yes. We have to describe Berto's physical appearance. And he looks like an Italian boy because he is from Venice. So, he has dark skin and thick dark hair, and dark eyes. And em, it just describes that he looks a little bit like a model.

Next question. Er, what effect does Cathy have on Berto? (Looked at the screen and read). Berto loves Cathy, so he comes from London, just to see her. And love makes him blind, love is blind, em and he will do a lot for her.

And how is their relationship? What does this represent? (Repeated the questions) Er, Berto is traditional and Cathy is an untraditional woman with an open relationship. And she is like a symbol of postmodernism and he's not, and they are sheer contradictions.

Yeah. The last question: what kind of human feeling does Berto represent? Er, we have read that he has love but is a traditional man and he is very conservative at the way he looks at things and he is faithful and brave people. Yeah, that is. (Other students applauded)

A: They have finished. There may be questions (put his hand out and invite), I don't know.

J: Any opinions, different opinions.

(Teacher S raised her hand, showing questions)

J: TS (Student A called Teacher S's name)

Student A spoke in a teacher's voice, deliberately positioning himself as a teacher, kept the lesson going, and tried to engage everyone into the task; even when the teacher performed like a student and raised her hand, Student A and his partner adopted the teacher's intentional self-positioning and asked her name like a peer. Other students also cooperated well with their teaching work, doing as they were requested. It could be seen that Student P, a presenter of Small Group 1, fully answered the first list of questions one by one. No matter whether Student P's responses were superficial or not, she deliberately performed like a cooperator with her new "teacher". In the above excerpt, students were the centre of the presentation/lesson with the teacher acting as a student. To be simple, performing a student indicated the teacher's trial to shift the teacher-centred teaching to the student-centred teaching which was embedded in the societal culture.

- ***Double Positions of Teacher S during Student Presentations***

During the time of group work, Teacher S also performed two positions as a way to engage students and guided them to deep reading. From the homework assigned by the Postmodernism group (Excerpt 3.14), it can be seen that these questions were designed in a sequence, from specific to abstract, from detailed information to a general meaning behind the text. By using these questions, they tried to develop an understanding of the materials and connect characters and some phenomena to the characteristics of Postmodernism. As envisioning theory defines, they were using Stance 2 (Developing understanding of the material) as an instructional tool, building upon the details to make a more cohesive envisionment (Stance 2) about the text and period. But the answers of Student P (Excerpt 3.15) show that she seemed not to well engage herself in literary thinking because her interpretations were a bit simplified and superficial (e.g., "Berto is traditional and Cathy is untraditional; Cathy is a symbol of the postmodernism and Berto is not."). Thus, sitting together with other students, Teacher S asked questions and discussed with her student "teacher" as Excerpt 3.16 shows below, which illustrates how she pushed students by performing double positions-student and teacher.

Excerpt 3.16

① H: I try to talk about the relationship between men and women. In postmodernism, the family pattern has changed, and there are a lot of divorces. Also, children are more socialized individually, because women work outside the home.

② TS: Can you explain that please? "Children are more socialized individually", because (...)

③ H: Em, because they are taking care of by professionals.

④ TS: Why there is more individual being in the family? I don't understand what you are saying. <H: OK> I need some really good teaching here, to make notes of that.

⑤ A: It's like, you have a child and put it in the institution.

⑥ TS: Is that more individual than being in the home?

⑦ H: Yes <A: No>

⑧ H: Yes?

⑨ A: No! Because you meet other children but you can say (...) they are less together with their parents.

⑩ TS: But they are more in the large group?

⑪ A: Yeah, they are. But the individual refers more to their family pattern than to the child self.

⑫ TS: Socialized less <A: in the family> in the family.

⑬ A: And that is what we referred to.

⑭ TS: But not more individually? Secondary socialization! (Nodding)

⑮ A: Yes. Exactly.

(After Student P in Small Group 1 responded to the first list of questions)

⑯ TS: Then I have another question. (Raised her hand)

⑰ A: Yes, please.

⑱ TS: Er, you said that human feeling that he had was, he was in love, <P: Yes>or what Cathy makes him feel. Why, why? Can we have a question on those? No disagreement? ↑ Em, don't you think she makes him feel confused? Lost <P: Yeah>left behind, abandoned, <P: Yes.> alienated. So, that is a lot more than that. It is not just a question of being left by your loved one; it is also the question of her having driven the motorway to London on a forced pretext, isn't it?

(...)

⑲ So, so what I am trying to gather is I want you to go deeper. I want <Ss: Yeah.> you to go deeper↑, I want you to go deeper↓. It's, it's a lot more. Don't just give me a general type. Go into it.

From the first part of the above excerpt, it can be seen Teacher S created the opportunity for students to discuss with her by positioning herself as a student, like the discussion with Student A and Student H who were performing as teachers. Teacher S seemed not to understand the point they addressed, so she expected they could elaborate it like a teacher. Obviously, at first, there was disagreement and incomprehension among the three boys (turn ⑦, ⑧, ⑨). But after elaborating to Teacher S, they understood better and achieved agreement. The double-position of students created the chance for them to discuss each other and also with the teacher to a greater depth. At that time, Teacher S's position of being a student was obvious. But in the other part of the above excerpt (after Student P in Small Group 1 responded to the first list of questions), Teacher S's position of being a teacher dominated. After Student P's short response, no students followed up or commented on, whereas Teacher S did. But her question indicated that she was not satisfied with student interpretation, so then she pointed out what she wanted students to see in the text ("Lost, left behind, abandoned, alienated."). Thus, her performance as a student was merged with her position as a teacher. The double-position of Teacher S was established at that time when she raised her hand and showed her respect to these three temporary "teachers," and meanwhile repeated her request of going deeper from a teacher's position.

- ***Summing Up: Teacher as a Coach to Train the Student to Be an Independent Reader***

During the student-student interactions, especially when students worked with a project in groups, the teacher often had a deliberately positioning of students, offering students general positions, and then in the process of doing group work, students' positions that were available to be multiple and flexible in accordance to their different responsibilities in groups. In Teacher S's second class, changing positions of students can also be seen as a way to engage students in reading from varied stances, and in the third-year class, Teacher S guided students into deep reading through performing double positions herself and as well as offering students' double positions. No matter in which way, in general Teacher S was like a coach who guided students to read and understand a text from different angles (positions and stances), and most importantly to train students to study literary texts independently from the beginning (searching for materials) to the final products (giving a presentation) through cooperative group work.

3.4 Post-Observation: Comments and Reviews

This section contains comments and reviews from the teacher and students after observation. These comments and reviews are used to compare with what was intended to do before the observation and what was really done during the observation, showing a full map of the classes.

3.4.1 The Teacher's Comments

During the second interview with Teacher S after observation, she commented on students' performance and checked if her plan had been fulfilled. She said:

Excerpt 3.17

TS: Basically, I am quite content with what they do, because they really do try to contribute (...) they tried and did involve themselves in the text in my opinion, so I really quite happy, even if I did tease them a little bit and I ended up saying go away because the time is up. We had a bit of fun as we went along. So, I am happy with that.

I: How much the extent of your intention and plan is fulfilled?

TS: Basically, I have rather realistic expectations. Generally, I am not really unhappy, but I always like to better them than what we do. Sometimes I get frustrated because they don't seem to learn (...) basically, I adjust my expectations to work, can realistically expect (...) For instance, I asked student comments on the miniature project of a British singer. I made notes, and I will bring them up again when we do something similar, try to adjust for next time and ask them to what degree they would like to work with the same way, and to what degree they would like to change a little bit. That is what I try to do.

The above general statement shows the basic perception of Teacher S on students' contributions, which again indicated that she was a teacher with high expectations as she described in her first interview before observation. But she admitted that sometimes she had to adjust expectations according to students' realities, such as by listening to students' comments as shown in the group work of a British singer. Listening to student comments in Teacher S's classes can be seen as a way to cope with the tension between teachers' expectations and students' realities. Here Teacher S's way of coping with student comments also indicated her democratic awareness in the process of teaching and interacting.

3.4.2 Students' Comments

In the interview with selected students, the students in both second-year and third-year classes thought of the interactions in the class with the teacher and other peers as good. They had a lot of conversations with the teacher and each other during class time. In particular, they had more group discussions than whole-class discussions. All five second-year students in the second-year class responded that they preferred group discussion to whole-class discussion because everyone had the chance to say something during group work and sometimes one might be inspired by the others. Students' thoughts indicate that they also noticed the teacher's purpose that was to create chances for students to talk, and especially to learn independently through group work. According to the results of the Critical Instant Questionnaire (CIQ) (Brookfield, 1995) in third-year class as shown in Table 3.3, about one third of respondents felt most interested when they analysed a text, made a lot of discussions and prepared a presentation in the group. One senior student regarded group work as a good way to work, in that for some of them who had difficulty reading the text alone, if they discussed it in the group work, it was much quicker for them to get understanding inspired by others.

Table 3.3 Third-Year Students' Responses of CIQ (Brookfield, 1995)

Q1: At what moment in class during these two weeks did you feel most interested in what was happening? Why?	
Type of response	**Number of responders**
1. Classmates' presentation (teaching a lesson)	6
2. Freedom of choosing text	2
3. Preparing presentation	3
4. Group work	6(both group work and presentation:1)

(continued)

Q1: At what moment in class during these two weeks did you feel most interested in what was happening? Why?	
Type of response	Number of responders
5. Analysis of text	2 (both group work and analysis of text :1)
6. Learning about literary periods	1
7. Have no idea or blank	1
In total	21

The CIQ also shows that another one third of respondents liked "teaching" others. From the presentations they taught senior students felt they could learn better. They thought preparing for a lesson gave them the responsibility and motivation to learn the literary texts better. A student in the group of Postmodernism described his experience in group work:

> In my group, some of the boys attempt to have fun as well. So, we delegated the responsibilities, and so everyone had something that they had to do. We make sure everything was done (...) It is not all the time I do my homework, but when we have group work, I always do it because I think it is very disrespectful to watch other people in the group because you are damaging their occasion as well.

From the above statement, it can be seen that for some undisciplined students, doing group work could foster their cooperative spirit and sense of responsibility. In this sense, the completion of group work required each member to perform as a responsible cooperator in the teamwork. But there were some students felt struggled in this process. Two below-average senior students that were interviewed thought of Teacher S as a little bit strict. But they added that when they knew better of her ways and intentions, they gradually felt that Teacher S was demanding because she cared for them and wanted them to be better at reading literature: "she does it for the best of us, not like to be mean or anything. I think she really cares about her students." Students gradually became comfortable with the ways of interacting and teaching in Teacher S's classrooms. From students' views, Teacher S was a professional teacher who esteemed her students and meanwhile often joked with them after the class. And from Teacher S's view, students were growing and changing, so she needed to know better of her students, know when she needed to push, and how to push them. In this way, the teacher and her students together constituted an open and democratic atmosphere in class.

3.4.3 Review of What Had Been Done

During observation, Teacher S tried to engage students in various activities with different topics and content, especially in the second-year class, indicating her different framing ways of classroom interaction. For instance, with a British singer's songs, she framed the student-student interaction through group work, whereas with horror stories she framed both the teacher-student and the student-student interactions through a combination of whole-class discussion and group discussion. When being asked about her reasons for changing ways, she said:

> (With a British singer) they work more or less independently. So, I did a bit of coaching actually, and the guiding questions were not that specific. But sometimes with WW1 poems and horror stories, because I wanted them to understand exactly, I took up my role as a teacher (...) There are certain texts that I like and I like to share with them. And when we have texts like that, I tried to guide them into understanding that is basically my understanding. Of course, sometimes, they found other things or add something to my understanding that I found interesting. I try

to give them my understanding, but also be open to other ideas.

It is evident from the above statement that with different framing ways, Teacher S also changed her positions — during group work being a coach and during whole-class discussion being a teacher. When Teacher S played the role of teacher, she tried to push students to be closer to her interpretation that was presented on behalf of the text, but sometimes if needed she still notice to left the possibility for others' readings and ideas. This statement was consistent with her combining of two pedagogy strategies for reading-one the one hand, based on the guiding points about the text, her interpretation was presented on behalf of the text, but on the other hand, she expected and opened for other interpretations from students based on their understandings. The shift of position also demonstrated how Teacher S trained student independent learning and facilitated the student-centred teaching. That is, she knew when to give students more independence and when to help them more.

3.5 Conclusion

Teacher S was a literary teacher, who had rich experience of teaching literature and knew of her students. She had a clear goal of training students to develop their independent learning competence, which fits the main values of the school: offering top-quality teaching to prepare students for their future study and their life. The observation in the classes illustrated that Teacher S's classroom was a loose and relaxed learning environment where Teacher S did not deny students' responses directly, and also the teacher and students often communicated in whole-class discussion, during group work, and in students' written papers. Affected by the school cultures, Teacher S was not forced to position students as receivers of the information transmitted from the teacher but was encouraged and supported by the school to deliberately position them as co-constructors of the knowledge and the democratic climate.

Correspondingly, students had the chance to occupy different positions in different activities and also had the opportunity to reposition themselves and others during the group discussions. The specific positions of the teacher and students, and the instructional tools used in the three types of classroom interaction are summarized in Table 3.4.

Table 3.4　Positioning and Envisioning in Teacher S's Classes
(According to Table 2.4, Table 2.5)

Type of interaction	The Teacher's positioning	Students' positioning	Stance tools
Teacher-Student	1. *Moral positioning:* A teacher assigned by the institutional role 2. *Deliberately self-positioning:* A supporter (e.g., in the whole-class discussion, student written essays)	1. *Moral positioning:* Students assigned by the institutional role 2. *Performative positioning:* Potential readers who actively engaged in discussing	Stance 1,2,3
Student-Text	*Deliberately self-positioning:* A guide of deep reading	*The teacher's deliberately positioning of students:* Potential readers who went deep reading with the teacher's guiding	Stance 1,2
Student-Student	*Deliberately self-positioning:* 1. A coach of training 2. A consultant during group work	1. *The teacher's deliberately positioning of students:* Independent readers 2. *Performative positioning:* Multi-positions in group work	Stance 3,4

As Table 3.4 shows, there were three types of positioning occurring during the interactions in Teacher S's class: moral positioning, intentional positioning (deliberately self-positioning and deliberately positioning of others), and performative positioning (Harré & van Langenhove, 1999; Davies & Harré, 1990).

Moral positioning that was not evident was related to the social roles of the teacher and students in the institutional context. Teacher S's positioning was often intentionally arranged, especially when facilitating student-text and student-student interactions. Students' positions in the group work were usually ascribed by their actions and responsibilities, which was related to the performative positioning. To put simply, Teacher S put her purpose into teaching practice and push students to read deeply through positioning students deliberately and diversely. Correspondingly, students had the chance to adopt, resist or modify various positions in the group work.

While sometimes Teacher S's teaching ways can be related to stance tools, guiding students to step further into texts and engage in the literary experience, some products of students (e.g., student presentations or essays) showed that students were not really engaged in literary thinking individually; instead, they tended to follow a stereotyped interpretation that might be easily found on the internet. Thus, a tension between the teacher/school's expectation and students' realities was established. For the teacher, she expected to train students to be an independent reader, which echoed an aspect of societal culture (student-centred teaching), and she tried to create a democratic atmosphere by creating the chance for students to engage in dialogue with the teacher and peers, as the school aimed to do. But for students, it seemed that they had not been well prepared for independent group work in which they needed to do many choices. Also, the usage of computers and electronic media which was double-sided increased the chance for students to loaf on the job during group work.

Chapter 4
The Case of Teacher P

This chapter presents the findings from the case of Teacher P, which includes profiles of the school, class, and curriculum, analyses of the positioning and reading instructions respectively in three types of classroom interactions, and the teacher and students' comments and reviews of the teaching methods used.

4.1 Contextual Cultures

4.1.1 Profile of the School

The other Danish case study school is B Gymnasium, located in another county in Denmark. B Gymnasium is a mixed school that offers two national programs (STX and HF) and an International Baccalaureate (IB) diploma program. The school was founded privately in 1868, but in 1920 it was taken over by the state. In total, the school accommodates approximately 1,100 students in these three programs and one of the STX classes was observed during the study. Similar to R Gymnasium, STX students in B Gymnasium have 20 study fields/subject packages to select, and its principles are based on the democratic climate with the emphasis on active student participation, influence, and responsibility. The school claims to aim to set up a school where argumentation and dialogue prevail over authority.[1]

---

[1] The information, principles, and values of the school were summarized from its website.

The principles of B Gymnasium indicate that this school emphasises student engagement and the democratic environment of learning in the school and classrooms. Broadly described, these two Danish schools (R and B Gymnasiums) share the same basic idea, namely democracy in teaching and learning. As R Gymnasium which claims to involve students' opinions in decision making, B Gymnasium also aims to dialogue with students in the process of teaching and learning. In B Gymnasium, teachers' schedules and teaching plans are also available to students in the "Lectio" system. Through Lectio, sometimes students sent a message to teachers as an interacting method, before and after class. In Teacher P's class in B Gymnasium, the usage of IT and electronic media (e.g., computers, iPads videos, pictures, and the powerpoint) was encouraged in class for both the teacher and students.

4.1.2 Profile of Teacher P's Class

There were 28 students in the Teacher P's second-year class.

Table 4.1 Profile of Teacher P's Class

Grade of class	Number of Students	Seating	Lesson length	Lessons per week	Number of lessons observed	Curriculum
2nd-year	28	horizontal rows	90 minutes	2	7	■ The topic of "Heroes" ■ WW1 poems (two sets) ■ Hemingway's short story ■ *Lost Paradise*

Table 4.1 shows an overview of Teacher P's second-year class. In Teacher P's classes, seven lessons in total were observed. The lesson time and lesson number in each week were the same as Teacher S's classes. In contrast, Teacher P planned fewer long literary texts, but more short texts, such as poems and short fiction.

4.1.2.1 Seating Arrangement

In contrast to Teacher S, Teacher P organised the seats in horizontal rows with students facing the whiteboard and the teacher's platform as shown in Figure 4.1. This arrangement was helpful for students who sat next to each other for talking and discussing in pairs. Indeed, Teacher P often utilized the seating arrangement to frame student discussions in pairs instead of in groups, involving students in different exercises, such as describing-terms exercise and drawing exercise.

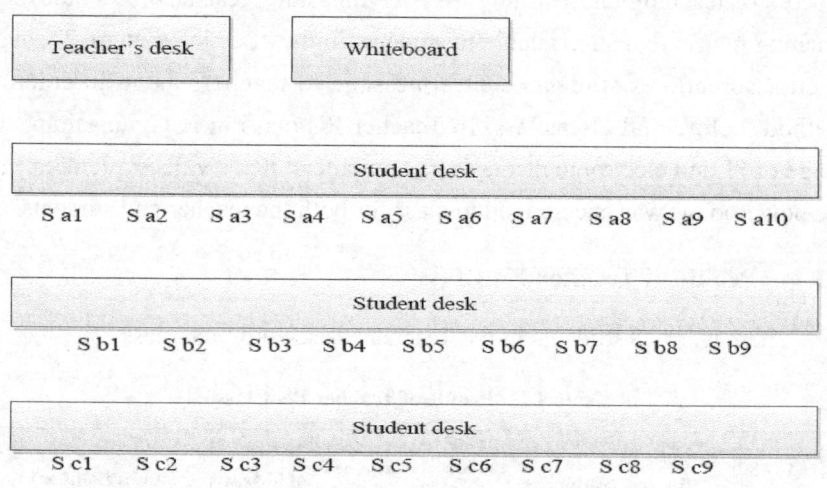

Figure 4.1   Seating Arrangement of Teacher P's Second-Year Class

4.1.2.2 Syllabus and Specific Learning Content

Teacher P's class was English-B level, which is the compulsory level for students in the Danish Gymnasium. The same as English A curriculum, English B curriculum also contains the professional goals and the core fabric of the course. It aims to foster students oral and written English, as well as the competencies of reading and analysing literary texts, non-literary texts, and media materials despite not being as demanding as English-A level. To be specific, students at being English-B level should be able to speak and write in English about a general and professional topic and master a varied vocabulary. This ability enables them to join in a conversation or discussion in English, explain the content and views in the English-language texts and media materials, and analyse and interpret literary texts, non-literary texts, and media materials taking the cultural, social, and historical perspectives into account. The core fabric of the curriculum also comprises linguistic aspects, communication strategies, and a wealth of modern literary texts, non-literary texts, and media materials (Appendix 4.1 Curriculum of English B).

Compared with the curriculum of English A-level, the curriculum of English-B level does not involve "a wide range of literary texts from different periods" and "excerpts from the works of Shakespeare". It follows that students at English-A level work with more difficult texts and varied literary periods than students being at English-B level. In reality, Teacher P's class usually read and analysed short stories and poems (Table 4.2), whereas Teacher S's second-year class worked with various genres of literature including short and long texts.

Table 4.2 Curricular Units and Activities in Teacher P's Class

Classroom observed	Curricular units observed	Characteristic teaching methods
2nd-year English B (5 lessons)	Topic about "Heroes"; War superhero (Lesson 1, 2)	Lecture; Student group presentation; Describing-terms (of poems) exercise
	Poetry terminology; WW1 poems from Siegfried Sassoon (*Suicide in the Trenches*, *Base Details*); propaganda posters (Lesson 3, 4)	Whole-class discussion; Double-circle exercise and whole-class discussion
	two sonnets, Rupert Brooke's *The Soldier* (1914) and Siegfried Sassoon's *Glory of Women* (1918) (Lesson 5, 6)	Discussion of questions in the worksheet in pairs, whole-class discussion
	Anti-hero: Milton, extract from *Paradise Lost* (Lesson 6)	Discussion in pairs and whole-class discussion
	Code hero: Hemingway *The Short Happy Life of Francis Macomber* (1936) (Lesson 7)	Circle exercise

Usually, Danish teachers have an autonomous right to choose texts and topics of learning, as these two Danish teachers did according to the disciplinary requirements of English. Teacher S focused more on literature reading and analysis, so the topics were based on literary periods or genres, like horror stories, gothic stories, and WW1 poems. Teacher P organised the whole curriculum by using a topic connecting some small subtopics and representative texts. For instance, she chose "Heroes" as a broad topic, and then her class studied subtopics and representative texts about "heroes", such as superheroes, war heroes, anti-heroes (*Paradise Lost*) and code heroes (a short story by Hemingway). Despite ICT and electronic media being equipped by Danish Gymnasiums to align with the curriculum of English, different teachers treated the electronic media differently. Around the topic "Heroes", Teacher P who was much younger than Teacher S often utilized multiple media to search for proper materials, such as electronic and paper literary texts, movies, and pictures, whereas Teacher S spent most of the time on reading literary texts and some time on analysing pictures with little time on movies.

It is also worth mentioning that both Teacher S and Teacher P showed their respect for their students' ideas when they planned the learning content at the beginning of the academic year. But the extent to which students could join in the negotiation with the teacher differed. As working with a British singer's texts in Teacher S's second-year class, the topic "Heroes" in Teacher P's class was also the outcome of students' voting from some topics that were originally chosen and provided by the teacher. Obviously, this kind of choice was restricted by the teacher's selection and interest. The difference in the extent of student choice in two Danish teachers' classes also reflects their difference in the ways of interacting with students.

Comparing Table 4.2 with Table 3.2 in Chapter 3, it can be seen that both teachers put poems of WW1 into the planned learning content although they chose different pieces This is an example of the influence of the societal culture and historical context on the learning content-under the backdrop of the 100th anniversary of the First World War (WW1). Except for the WW1 content, these two teaches planned divergent learning content for their second-year class. In both teachers' second-year classes, students worked with both fiction and non-fiction, but Teacher S oriented her students to focus on reading long fiction, while Teacher P and her students worked much more on short texts. The reason for this difference rested with the different levels of students' English. Teacher P explained that she had to consider their level of English when she chose texts because she wanted students to read thoroughly and understand what they read. Other than common activities introduced in the previous chapter, such as lecture, whole-class discussion, student group presentation, there were other new exercises designed by Teacher P, such as the describing-terms exercise, drawing exercise, double-circle exercise, and circle exercise, which created multiple forms of communications in class. The describing-terms exercise and drawing exercise were pair work, and double-circle and circle exercises were whole-class work.

- ***Describing-Terms Exercise***

This was an exercise in pairs with the main purpose for students to practice English as much as possible. Two students had two lists of words. Student A had one list and Student B had another. They took turns in explaining and guessing the words and wrote them down as they went along so that two students ended up having two full lists of words.

- ***Drawing Exercise***

This was also an exercise for students in pairs. The teacher had an image on the whiteboard. One student was looking at it and the other student was not. The person looking at the image had to describe it, and the other person had to draw it.

- ***Double-Circle Exercise***

This was an exercise for student-student interaction. When completing this exercise, students stood in two circles face-to-face, so they had partners and discussed something. Following this, one student in the inner circle moved on so the students in the outer circle got a new partner all the time. With each move, each student had a new partner to discuss a new question.

- *Circle Exercise*

This was an exercise for the teacher-student interaction. During this exercise, all the students sat in a circle with the teacher sitting in the middle of the circle. Each time the teacher asked one student to come into the circle, responding to the teacher's questions based on their reading of a text.

Indeed, what she said and what she did demonstrated that Teacher P was an energetic teacher who liked to attempt new teaching methods/forms of interactions creatively in class.

4.2 Pre-Observation: Teacher P's Perceptions of Literature Teaching

4.2.1 Reflexive Positioning

Compared with Teacher S, Teacher P was a quite young English teacher who had only been teaching for five years, but she thought of herself as a learning teacher who was learning to improve the way of teaching with the accumulation of teaching experience.

Excerpt 4.1

TP: When I was a new teacher, I thought that I was a good teacher when I was well prepared and I had a lot to say. But the longer I teach them the more I feel that students need to be active because they learn when they are active. So, when I talk, they are passive in a way. Of course, they need some knowledge from me, I need to give them information sometimes, but it is more helpful for them to learn, helping them to learn about the topic. So, I am like a guide to help them open a text, for instance.

As with many new teachers, Teacher P was energetic and enthusiastic about learning how to be an ideal teacher who did not just talk and talk but tried to activate students. She further explained her ideas of an ideal teacher. At first when she started to teach, she thought that the more the teacher talked, the more students learnt from the teacher. But during her five-year teaching life, she became more and more aware of a reality that teachers' responsibility was not only transmitting information to students but also facilitating students to learn on their own. Thus, she was conscious of being a guide instead of an authoritative speaker in the class, which was her main purpose of attracting students to learn actively. Briefly, Teacher P positioned herself in the pre-observation interview as a learner of teaching from which she knew better of her students and thus adjusted her position (as she said "like a guide") in the class. Teacher P's reflexive positioning implied her awareness of democracy in the class, reflecting the aims of the school as part of school cultures.

4.2.2 Purpose of Teaching

Compared with Teacher S who positioned herself as a literature teacher, Teacher P thought of herself more as an English teacher than as a literature teacher. She explained her purpose of teaching English as follows:

Excerpt 4.2

TP: I think the ideal teaching situation for me is when I can see that the students are enthusiastic about what we are doing because they are really interested in what they are doing that I can see they want to talk about whatever we will talk about (...) Students are constantly developing, so it is like I have a purpose that they should become better in their English, both spoken and written English. But also, just understanding different cultures and the ability to analyse texts and be critical, and they should be critical of the information they get. But it is more probably with the article non-fiction. When we teach literature, it is more about focus on close reading, the new answers like going into the texts seeing a small difference, and so on. But also, it depends on the class, sometimes, with the really good class, you can do a close reading, it is not so good class, and then it is more superficial sometimes ...

The above statement indicated that Teacher P focused more on learning English as a language embedded in various speaking cultures than on learning English literature as a work of art. Similar to Teacher S, Teacher P thought of an ideal literary teacher should keep students interests during class time. Different from Teacher S, Teacher P further aimed to improve students' English level both in spoken and written ways, to develop their academic understanding of something (a topic) as a part of culture through reading relevant texts, and to foster student critical reading. For instance, in that semester Teacher P planned to work with a topic on "Heroes, Superheroes, Heroines, and Anti-heroes" across different cultures by means of reading diverse sources as Excerpt 4.3 shows below.

Excerpt 4.3 (Appendix 4.2)
HEROES, SUPERHEROES, ANTI-HEROES, AND HEROINES
"Studieplan"[①]: This course on Heroes, Superheroes, Heroines and Anti-heroes will introduce you to new heroes and heroines as well as deepen your understanding of the iconic figures that you already know. We will look at how we define a hero as well as the cultural influence of these figures in different periods and discuss the very idea of the hero — why do we need and invent heroes? What makes someone a hero? And what is the negative effect of elevating someone to the status of hero? Also, where does the anti-hero come in and what type of hero is he or

---

① "studie" (Danish) means "study" (English).

she?

We will read texts, comic books, and graphic novels as well as watch films and look at visual material:
- Introduction: Bel Kaufmann: *Sunday in the Park* (1985).
- The superhero: group presentations.
- War heroes: S. Sassoon and the poetry of WWI. Propaganda posters.
- The anti-hero: Milton, extract from *Paradise Lost*.
- Code hero: Hemingway *The Short Happy Life of Francis Macomber* (1936).
- American soldiers in Iraq: *The Hurt Locker* (2008)

[...]

Lesson 5+6:
- The poetry of World War 1: Wilfred Owen and Siegfried Sassoon. Propaganda Posters. Students practice poetry analysis through various in class exercises and we discuss the poems.

Lesson 6:
- **Milton: extract from** *Paradise Lost*. Satan as an anti-hero. Drawing exercise to open up the topic.

[...]

Lesson 7:
- **Code hero: Hemingway** *The Short Happy Life of Francis Macomber* (1936). Discussion of language and characterization.

Apparently, in line with the school cultures, there was multi-modal in text choosing in Teacher P's class — a short story by Bel Kaufmann, *Paradise Lost*, a short story of Hemmingway, WW1 poetry, and a movie about American soldiers in Iraq. Hence, in order to enrich the materials of a topic, she selected different texts and even films that related to the cultures of the topic when she made a teaching plan, not only literary texts. Specifically, working with the "heroes" topic, she aimed to encourage students to deepen their understandings of the iconic figures, look at the cultural influence of these figures in different periods, and discuss some ideas of the hero. Her consideration of the cultural context of materials indeed was required by the curriculum of English-B level (Appendix 4.1), which implied the influence of the societal cultures. The above teaching plan that constituted part of the classroom cultures, therefore, was the result of the influences of both school cultures and societal cultures.

4.2.3 Perceptions of How to Engage Students

Around the purpose of teaching English, Teacher P formed perceptions of the method of engaging students. She had a similar view to Teacher S on what was an ideal teaching situation-that is, keeping students' interests. But these two teachers used totally different methods to attract students. According to the pre-observation interview, Teacher P's perceptions of teaching can be synthesized as follows.

4.2.3.1 Make Variations in Teaching Activities as a Strategy to Activate Students

In order to interest students in learning something, she applied various teaching methods and designed different exercises (activities) in a class, in her words to "create variation in teaching". She regarded variety as a strategy to activate students because students were different from person to person, she explained:

Excerpt 4.4

TP: (...) again as I said there are 28 students, it is almost impossible to force them to be interested, but one way is to create variation in teaching. We will do this for 10 min, do that for 10 min, it is very seldom that I just stand there and talk, talk, talk. It is most about activating them. So, they are active and work. So that is how I try to make a lot of diffident types of exercises. Also, because some students are good at some types of exercises, some students like to sit and write alone, some students like to do group work, some students like to do go out and talk and come back, so I try to create variation.

She planned a lot of diffident types of exercises about one topic and even in one lesson in order to push them to speak English as much as possible. The specific activities used depending on the purposes of the lesson. She thought for English learning, one of the purposes was to let students speak English to become better at the language, thus she described a kind of activity, drawing exercise, to activate students in speaking English. The drawing exercise is an example of one exercise about speaking English and making variations. Teacher P's planning of each lesson also indicated what she described as creating variations. Following is an example of the written plan for her one lesson.

Excerpt 4.5
Lesson 1:
- Introduction to the course.
- Pupils discuss the concept based on my introduction and come up with keywords that they write on the whiteboard. Class discussion of a number of them.
- Reading in class: *Sunday in the Park*. Focus on the characterization of the main character and his wife, narration and the theme. Look up the words you do not understand.
- Discussion of the short story and its connection to the "heroes" topic and comparison with keywords on the whiteboard.
- Pupils write for 15 minutes: "My hero is xxx because …"/"I don't have a hero because …"

- Reading aloud in pairs and a couple in class.

In the above lesson plan, Teacher P planned six different activities with specific processes, procedures, and time duration, indicating the variety of her teaching methods and her detailed and structured style of planning teaching.

4.2.3.2 Control Teaching Plan

On the one hand, Teacher P planned the teaching content freely. She did not usually follow an anthology, but only copied and scanned texts that she wanted for her students, or combined the anthology with her texts that she found, in her words, "I make my own course. There is a lot of freedom." It sounds as though there should have been many possibilities of the texts that students could learn in Teacher P's class. But on the other hand, she cut down the possibilities by closing the student participation in planning the content as she said in the first interview:

Excerpt 4.6

(I: Can students choose what they will learn?)

TP: No! At the beginning of the year, I said I don't know which topic we should start with and I said I had considered it and I wrote what I had thought of then I said OK, what do you think, then they made some suggestions. A lot of them, I cannot use (...) at the end, I said OK, you can choose between heroes, another topic is man nature and city, so it is like romantic poetry. Then it ended being 50:50, so I said OK, we will do heroes. Maybe they feel they had influence, but only to a small extent. They can vote for all the topics.

The observations in Teacher S class demonstrated that her class students' suggestions and interests had been considered and some of them were accepted as part of their learning texts. It means that Teacher S brought in the more varied corpus of texts and themes in the class, compared with Teacher P. In contrast, Teacher P's students had little effect on the choosing texts despite also having the choice at the beginning of the school year. Thus, on the one hand, Teacher P cared about student participation in the class, but on the other hand, she controlled the lesson in a structured way — she had a very clear goal, content, and structure for each lesson. The above Excerpt 4.3 that shows the specific teaching plan of working with "Heroes, Superheroes, Heroines, and Anti-heroes" contained the detailed aim of the topic, materials used, the procedure of working with the topic, and the plan of each lesson (Appendix 4.2). Evidently, compared with Teacher S's flexibility of planning, Teacher P followed a more stable, detailed, structured, and goal-oriented teaching plan, as she said she preferred following a structured plan with detailed points. In other words, there was little possibility for students to change or add in Teacher P's plan.

4.2.3.3 Try New Creative Ways of Teaching

As for reading literary texts, Teacher P also planned some exercises to attract students' interests. She introduced her ways of engaging students in the following excerpt.

Excerpt 4.7

TP: Sometimes I do something called matrix group work. So, we read the story, and in groups they have the responsibility for different types of, for instance, setting, characters, and symbols ... But it could also be, one time I ask one student to bring crayons with colours. And then I ask them to focus on different things in the text and using different colours to underlie them to open the text to the students (...) Then when we read poetry sometimes, I have split the poem into different lines and I cut it out (...) or sometimes maybe just take out just last two lines ...

or taking out of the title... so a kind of activating in a creative way. But sometimes I just talk. You know I stand at the whiteboard. They sit and put up their hands. And I read and say "do you have any ideas with this mean", so it is not like I am creating all the time. I try to change.

It is evident that Teacher P focused on how to create variation in teaching literary texts. But in teaching literature she noticed how to open texts for students, to let students become familiar with the text and notice the details and some points of the text. For instance, sometimes she asked students to focus on different things in a particular text and using different colours to underline these things as features of this text. When they read poetry, sometimes she split the poem into different lines and then asked students to compose the poem again, or sometimes took out the last two lines and students had to invent what the end would be, or she took out the title and her class imagined what the title would be. According to Teacher P's statements, many motivating activities were designed in a creative way in her classroom. For example, when asked about her way of engaging students who did not care about her teaching, Teacher P described the *double-circle exercise* for engaging all students. Students in *double circles* kept discussing with different partners, which was seen by Teacher P as an approach to cooperative learning and keep everyone active in the class. In this sense, the exercises were designed and orchestrated within the context of school cultures that advocates student active participation in class.

Summing up, Teacher P positioned herself as a young teacher who kept learning how to improve teaching English and how to engage students through designing some creative activities during class time. However, her perceptions of teaching demonstrated that sometimes she paid attention to teaching English as a foreign language, not to teaching English as a language of literature. Thus, she used multiple exercises and electronic media to engage students in practicing English. She thought she treated her students in a dialogic and democratic way that was one of the essential school cultures of B Gymnasium. But in effect, she cared so much about her teaching plan that sometimes she was still quite controlling.

4.3 During-Observation: Three Types of Classroom Interactions

In this section, three types of classroom interactions in Teacher P's class will be analysed one by one, with a focus on several new activities/teaching methods designed by the teacher.

4.3.1 The Interaction between the Teacher and Students: Whole-Class Discussion in a Way of *Circle Exercise*

Whole-class discussion was common in Teacher P's class, which was opposite to Teacher S's classes. In each lesson that was observed, Teacher P always applied whole-class discussion in working with texts. Usually, she firstly asked some questions for students in pairs to discuss, and then she asked the whole class to respond to these questions in the pattern of IRE. The following Excerpt 4.8 was a short example of a whole-class discussion, but it illustrated the general approach of framing the whole-class discussions in Teacher P's class.

Excerpt 4.8
T: And serving in heaven, sitting on the bench, does it give any sense of it?
G: I actually heard **the exact opposite**. <T: Aha, yes. ↑ >
This week I follow with (0.5) a TV or something, <T: Em. > where they interviewed an African coming to Denmark <T: Ja. (Nodding head)> and he was a big, er, ja, a big man in Africa, but here he was just, I mean, he was just the bottom of the society. <T: Ja. Ahà> Then he said that was better to serve heaven.

T: So, what was the heaven, and what was hell?

G: He thought Africa was hell, and Denmark was heaven. <T: heaven>

T: So, he (0.5) Ja. So that is interesting. So, the opposite perspective. Ja. Em, **but Satan is an anti-hero**, so this is his perspective.

This short exchange occurred when the class was discussing the meaning of one sentence in *Paradise Lost* ("To reign is worth ambition, though in hell: Better to reign in hell than serve in heaven") after pair discussions. In fact, as Excerpt 4.3 (teaching plan) showed above, *Paradise Lost* was classified by the teacher as an anti-hero, which had been acknowledged by the teacher and students. Student G expected to join in the discussion with the teacher through addressing an opposite example, but Teacher P closed this discussion by her evaluation ("*So that is interesting. So, the opposite perspective.*"). She neither followed the student's thinking nor asked a follow-up question built on Student G's response. Instead, she went back to her thinking and the particular information they have already known ("*Satan is an anti-hero*"). Briefly, Teacher P was following the pattern of IRE in this example.

As was discussed in Chapter 1, it is too simple to think of IRE as monologic, and its quality depends on how the teacher frames the conversation. As Chapter 3 discussed, Teacher S framed IRE in a dialogic way by offering the possibility for students to engage in talking and discussing. Similarly, in Teacher P's class, there was also a characteristic type of IRE that was framed in a way of *circle exercise* as depicted in Figure 4.2.

Teacher P designed this exercise as an experiment, which means she firstly used this in her class as an activity where students had the chance to talk with the teacher one by one about Hemingway's short story *The Short Happy Life of Francis Macomber* (1936) they had read and prepared at home previously. Excerpt 4.9 is their homework assigned in the school system "Lectio" before whole-class discussion.

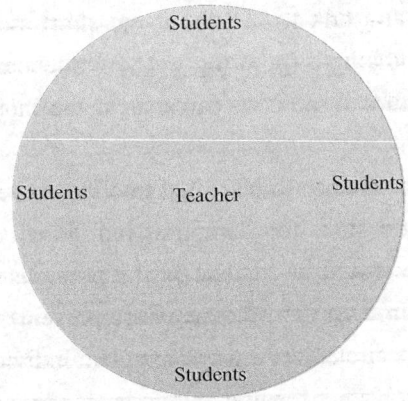

Figure 4.2 The Positions of the Teacher and Students in the Circle Exercise

Excerpt 4.9

Homework for preparation:
- Class discussion of Hemingway's short story *The Short Happy Life of Francis Macomber* (1936).
- Focus on understanding what is happening between the three main characters Francis Macomber, his wife Margot/Margaret, and their safari guide Robert Wilson.

Be well-prepared!

Teacher P explained to students that the idea came from the Danish word "Rundkredspædagogik"[①] which was a kind of joking way to make fun of the authority of schools and teachers in 1970s. Her idea of circle exercise came from the special pedagogy in the 1970s.

> TP: [...] that (rundkredspædagogik) reminds me of this exercise. But anyway, the idea is that hopefully, everyone will have time to come

---

① It is a Danish word that means "Circle Pedagogy" in English.

into the circle and talk to me about the short story. And we will go to follow the tools here (pointing to the whiteboard). So more or less follow the structure to see if we can analyse the short story together.

Everyone had the chance to be called into the circle and talked with the teacher about the short story for 2 minutes individually. When one student finished, another one would be invited by the previous student to continue. Finally, 19 students in total (25 students were present) were invited to talk with the teacher in the circle, like a way of student individual presentation for two minutes based on his/her reading and understanding of the short story. In Teacher P's words, she used this exercise in order to make students energetic and positive because talking with the teacher face to face made students feel a little bit nervous; they did not know who would be the next one in the circle so they needed to listen to what previous students said. It seemed that about 80% or so of students joined in the two-minute-long discussion with the teacher one by one, but in essence, the whole process was manipulated by the teacher.

Teacher P's manipulation can be seen in both her teaching tools and the way of talking with her students. Firstly, Teacher P followed a structured procedure of guidance. Before the class, she made homework for students to prepare in advance, so students received a guide that told them what they should focus on. During the class, she organised the talk with students in a structured way, following a structure of analysing — "How to Analyse a Short Story" — that was listed on the whiteboard when they were talking. Excerpt 4.10 includes the analysing structure of a short story (*The Short Happy Life of Francis Macomber*).

Excerpt 4.10

How to Analyse a Short Story
- Plot/Structure
- Characters

- Setting
- Narrator/Point of View
- Images and Symbols
- Style and Language
- Theme
- Title

Thus, before the class, as shown in Excerpt 4.9, Teacher P guided students to firstly read the whole text on their own, having an initial understanding of the story. Meanwhile, she told students what they should focus on in the story. Through preparation, students entered their initial envisionment (Stance 1 Getting started with the material). During the class, Teacher P's guide of analysing a short story and discussion with students helped students to develop their understandings of the story in detail (Stance 2 Developing understanding of the material). Secondly, the process and procedures were fully manipulated by the teacher, which was shown in Excerpt 4.11.

Excerpt 4.11

TP: [...] So everyone should be here for 2minutes.

<Ss: Oh>

TP: Is that long or short?

Ss: Long!!

TP: Long? ↑ No, no, no!!↓ As the first person who come here, I choose you (pointing to a boy near her). Then if you roll in here, and we just talk for 2 minutes, and you say when the time is up (pointing to another boy who kept the time). OK. ↓ Can you introduce the short story that you have read [...].

It was evident that on the one hand Teacher P claimed that the idea of this exercise came from a change of crisis in pedagogy in the 1970s in Denmark, which was a challenge for the authority in schools at that time. But on the other hand, she framed the interaction with students with full manipulation of procedures, time duration, content, structure, and tools followed, showing her manipulation of teaching in the classroom. Therefore, there was a tension in between.

During the conversation with students, Teacher P adjusted her way of speaking with different students. Excerpt 4.12 illustrated how the teacher talked with students with different levels in the *circle exercise*.

Excerpt 4.12

① TP: So that could (0.5), Could you also argue that is an accident? ↑ (gesture)

② J: Em ... (6)

③ TP: Could be an accident? ↓

④ J: Yes. (Changed her sitting posture)

⑤ TP: Yeah. We don't know actually.

⑥ J: I am not sure. (shake her head, in a very soft voice)

⑦ TP: So, it is a kind of open. (Looked down, reading the text) And at the end, Robert Wilson, they have this dialogue:

"I'm through now," he said. "I was a little angry. I'd begun to like your husband."

"Oh, please stop it," she said. "Please stop it."

"That's better," Wilson said. "Please is much better. Now I'll stop." (0.5)

That is the ending. What do you think this indicates about the relationship between his wife and the guy, (0.5) the way they talk?

⑧ J: Maybe she (0,5) wants to control him? ↑ (murmured)

⑨ TP: (nodded her head) She wants to control him. ↓

⑩ J: Yeah.

⑪ TP: Does she succeed? Who is in control at the end?

⑫ J: Em (0.5) him.↑

⑬ P: Yeah. (Nodded her head)

⑭ J: Because (Looked down) (...)

⑮ TP: Yeah, yeah, yeah.↓ He is in control because in the way he can say "were you killed your husband?".

(...)

⑯ TP: Why do you think she (the wife) compares them?

⑰ A: Probably she likes Wilson, but so, you can really, probably compare them (gesture), and say who most and (2), that is Wilson.

⑱ TP: <Yeah, yeah> How do you characterize Robert Wilson after being flirted?

⑲ A: Em (2) I don't kn: ow. ↑ I really (scratched head) think that he likes seems the same way as the other does. He doesn't really think it is a ruin of fame to sleep with the wife. He says it is Francis's own fault because he can keep her, or something like that.

⑳ TP: Yeah. What kind of, er (2) perspective does he have on the relationship between the two sexes, when he thinks that way on marriage and so on?

㉑ A: (shrugged, being amazed) E: r ↑ That is a good question! I don't think he wants to get married himself.

㉒ TP: No. (↑)

㉓ A: Er, maybe it is more like original sex with someone else, next one (gesture). They also talk something about the called ... And still drink some wine? ↑(pointing)

㉔ TP: Whisky. Yeah. (nodding)

㉕ A: Whisky. It is something they often do. And then (...) (gesture). Yeah.

Some active respondents cooperated with the teacher in some way,

157

actively engaging in the text reading and dialogue with the teacher, like Student A's performance in Excerpt 4.12. Student A spoke longer turns than the teacher did. Her behavior showed her controlling the direction of their talk sometimes, from talking about the personalities of characters in the fiction to the relationship of two main characters, from superficial layer to the deeper meaning behind. She even reminded the teacher of a reference in the text (turn ㉓), in order to support what she was saying. Correspondingly, the teacher was less controlling of Student A's talk. However, the shy student like Student J was forced to talk along with the teacher's thinking in the conversation. In this process, Teacher P had a longer speech than Student J. Further, finally, Teacher P gave the answer herself and also elaborated herself (turn ③, ⑤, ⑮). In this sense, *circle exercise* restricted the performance of weak students. Students' engagement in the interaction with the teacher in the *circle exercise* was effective for some students who were good readers and also active.

Teacher P noticed her different ways of treating different students. In her view, because of the language that was English rather than Danish, it was difficult for students to express some words appropriately, especially for shy students. She explained:

> If I know someone is shy, maybe it is OK they just say one word, and I probably treat them differently, because I know who I could push more, and who I cannot push. But maybe I should push everyone, the same. But it is also unfair not to push a student because you know she is shy. But it is also about building trust strongly.

Teacher P did not push shy students much to contribute something in the class; instead, she responded herself on their behalf, as with Student J, because she thought pushing shy students to say something seemed to be not easy. In this sense, Teacher P was deliberately positioning Student J with a notion of "shy" in her mind in advance, which influenced her way of speaking with the student. It consequently might have affected the student's chance for engaging interactions with the teacher.

Briefly, the *circle exercise* of framing interactions looks different from a traditional whole-class discussion, but it was essentially framed in the pattern of IRE between Teacher P and one student. Others were merely listening when the teacher was talking with one, so they were not given the opportunity to participate in discussions that the teacher and one student in the circle were talking about. Student A (Excerpt 4.12) who was commonly positioned by Teacher P as an active student in any class discussion described her feeling about the *circle exercise*: "Maybe in the circle where a new person talked with the teacher in two minutes (for each student). It was hard to keep concentrated when you did not talk." Thus, only the interaction between the teacher and one student occurred at that moment. There were no discussions among students who were listening, let alone contradictions raised in the discussions. Briefly, this exercise of the teacher-student interaction was a basic pattern of IRE between the teacher and one student, without the participation of other students in the discussion. In this sense, it was not helpful for sustained and substantive discussions that allowed multiple voices from others.

- ***Summing Up: Teacher P as an Initiator and a Controller in the Interaction with Students***

During the interaction with students, Teacher P positioned herself firstly as an initiator who often racked her brains to design unique activities as a way of making variations in her class. Although students might feel interested when engaged in a new activity, the results showed that their participation and engagement were partly controlled by the teacher, just like being in the *circle exercise*. Students with different levels were asked by the teacher or peers to be in the circle, and so they were forced (for some quiet students with poor academic performance) to respond in IRE pattern. So, in general, one student who was in the circle was forcedly positioned as a responder, instead of being willing to do so.

4.3.2 The Interaction between the Student and the Student: A Special Form *Double-Circle Exercise*

In Teacher S's classrooms, there were different kinds of group work for students with different levels (second-year and third-year students). By comparison, Teacher P did not offer students much independent group work during the observation; instead, she liked to use short pair discussions as one teaching method when she tried to vary the class activities. As mentioned earlier, Teacher P designed some unique activities in the class and *double-circle exercise* was one of them, as a form of pair discussion that was often used in her class.

The *double-circle exercise* was used in the process of working with two WW1(First World War) poems written by Siegfried Sassoon, in order to engage all students in talking during the exercise. When learning these two poems, students went through them starting with reading a poem aloud and then discussing the poem in pairs in a form of double-circle exercise, with a list of guiding questions on the whiteboard. Figure 4.3 is about the guidance of reading poems.

These questions on the form and content were related to students' basic knowledge about poems. In fact, at the beginning of the lesson, Teacher P asked students to review the poem terminology they learnt in the last lesson and asked them if they had any terms that needed to be explained further. Some students put forward some words they did not understand clearly, and then the teacher asked other students to try to explain. After that, the teacher supplemented or elaborated if needed. This kind of explanation of poem terminology, so to speak, was working as Stance 1 (Getting started with the material) — to tap students' related knowledge. When students discussed in pairs in *double-circle exercise* around the questions on the Powerpoint, they were stepping into the material, developing an understanding of the details, and connecting relevant details to build a more cohesive envisionment (Stance 2 Developing an understanding of the material) (Langer, 2011b).

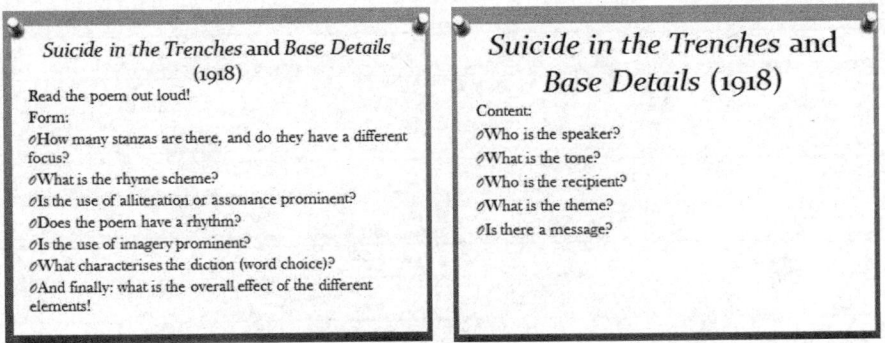

Figure 4.3   Questions for Discussing Poems of Siegfried Sassoon

The next step was the whole-class discussion on the topic that students had discussed in *double-circle exercise*. Teacher P and her students read through two poems together following the questions on the Powerpoint, hearing about what students had talked about and what they got from pair discussions. The observation notes showed that ten students responded and gave contributions afterwards. Two of the students shared their feelings about the poems and others merely answered the questions listed on the Powerpoint. So, although Teacher P seemed to start this topic with some stance tools, the students and the teacher focused more on the form and content of poems than students' personal readings and envisionment-building.

In fact, the *double-circle exercise* was designed to make everyone talk in English in the discussion. This exercise proceeded as follows: students stood in two circles; one was in the middle; the other circle was around the middle circle as the following Figure 4.4 shows. Thus, everyone in the outer circle faced someone in the inner circle so that every student had a partner right in front of him/her. The idea was that one student talked to someone in front of

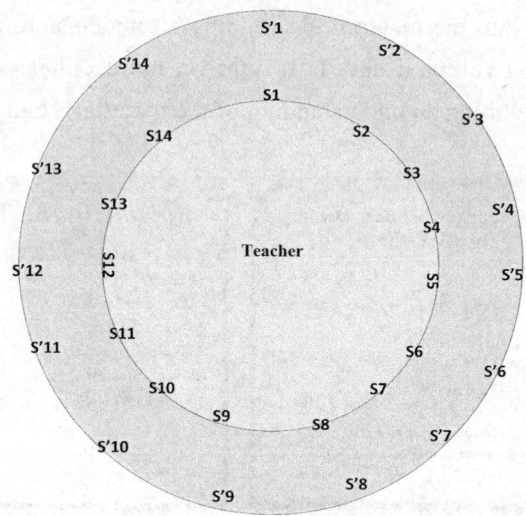

Figure 4.4 The Positions of the Teacher and Students in *Double-Circle Exercise*

him/her and then had the people in the outer circle move to the right for the next question. So, each student had a new partner to discuss a new question, and everyone had the chance to talk. Teacher P stood on a desk that located in the circle, so in the process she watched every student and organised the procedures by repeating questions on the whiteboard one by one. There were twelve questions for each poem, with around one-minute pair discussion for each question. In total, it took 30 minutes to finish discussing in the *double-circle exercise*. Excerpt 4.13 shows how the exercise went on.

Excerpt 4.13

TP: (...) the first thing I want you to do is to read the poem aloud. Just the first one. So, I don't want a person to read for you next.

(One minute later)

TP: So that was, shu! (Let the students be quiet) a short acquaintance, now you are all ready to move on to the next partner for the first question which has to do with form. What did I say before?

S: Outer circle to the right!

TP: Yes, outer circle to the right.

(Another one minute later)

TP: (showed a gesture of stop) Next question, new partner! "What is the rhythm scheme?"

(...)

Excerpt 4.13 demonstrates that Teacher P controlled what the students discussed, how they discussed, and how much time they discussed. Compared with Teacher S's framing approach, Teacher P controlled more in the process of student-student discussion. Obviously, Teacher P's class was more structured and goal-orientated than Teacher S's classes. In this exercise, the identities of the teacher and students that are authorized by the institution were clearly shown. If the exercise was seen as a game, Teacher P deliberately expressed her identity/the position of a master of the game, and accordingly, students were forced to be positioned as players of the game. However, the students preferred the *double-circle exercise*, in that they felt safer than when talking in the class discussion. One student described her feeling in this exercise:

> It is not so dangerous like stand in the class. So, it is safe. Because there is only one person you talk with rather than the whole class. Sometimes when you have to speak, you know, not your first language, it can be very difficult if you don't know the words and you might be scared (...)

This statement indicates that students cared about their performance in front of the whole class and the teacher who evaluated their daily performance at the end of each academic year (see Danish educational system). In this sense, *double-circle exercise* was helpful to encourage students to talk in English. But it was not necessarily helpful for encouraging students to engage in substantive discussions. It seemed that every student had time to speak English and talk with different peers. But within one minute, the interaction was limited within the conversation between two speakers at a time, just like the *circle exercise*, which excluded engagement of other students in the same conversation, preventing other views from these two speakers. Therefore, this exercise was another counter-example of the framing of interactions with the idea of *heteroglossia* (Bakhtin, 1981).

- ***Summing Up: Teacher P as a Manipulator and Students as Players***

Teacher P did not frame the discussion among students through group work; instead, she would like to frame the student-student discussion through pair work, such as *double-circle exercise*. During the interaction between the student and the student, Teacher P dominated the steps, process, content, and the time of discussing, whereas students were forced to be positioned as players of the game that was ruled by the teacher. Although students felt safer when they were in the *double-circle exercise*, the discussions in pairs were short and single, instead of long and multiple.

4.3.3 The Interaction with the Text: How to Instruct Students in Reading

As many teachers do, Teacher P liked to use worksheets to instruct students on how to read and analyse texts step by step. As she planned about the topic "Heroes", Teacher P arranged two lessons in learning WW1 poems. The class learnt different poems in these two lessons, and correspondingly Teacher P used different methods. In the first lesson, the class read WW1 two poems written by Siegfried Sassoon. The lesson was framed using the *double-circle exercise* which has been analysed. After reading WW1 poems in the first lesson, Teacher P brought two more difficult sonnets to the classroom for discussing and analysing. In this lesson, Teacher P made variations in her teaching method too, using different activities from the first lesson. She used a worksheet (Excerpt 4.14) with which students worked firstly in pairs for around 5 to 10 minutes about one question, and then the whole class talked about this question. Then student pairs worked in this way a bit more, and then the whole class talked about a bit more together again. So, the discussion was going back-and-forth between pair discussion and whole-class discussion.

In order to make it easier for students to read and understand, Teacher P separated the poem into different parts. She said:

> I tried to split it up into different parts, but if I see that no one is reacting, and then I know OK, it is too difficult for them. It is too difficult to do something in this situation, but maybe when I teach this poem to another class at another time, I know I have to do even more to help them with the poem.

This way in Teacher P's view helped her to know if students understood one part of the poem or not so that she could adjust her way in the following steps. Working with sonnets, she thought was difficult for students, so she prepared a worksheet (Excerpt 4.14) for students to work within the class.

Excerpt 4.14
Worksheet for two sonnets, Rupert Brooke's *The Soldier* (1914) and Siegfried Sassoon's *Glory of Women* (1918)

BASIC UNDERSTANDING/PREPARATION FOR ANALYSIS

1. **Rephrase** the two poems in your own words sentence by sentence to ensure your understanding of the whole poem. Don't skip difficult passages — on the contrary focus more on them, and ask if you need

help! Remember that words may have several meanings and the right understanding of a word can ensure your understanding of that part of the poem.

2. What are the characteristic features of a **sonnet**?

ANALYSIS
FORM:
3. Identify the **sonnet features** of the two poems.

4. Analyse **other features** relating to form such as figurative language, alliteration, etc.

CONTENT:
5. Use the guide to identify the **speaker, recipient, subject matter, choice of words, theme, and message** in both poems.

CONCLUSION
6. Why are the two poems so different, and **how do they use the sonnet differently**?

With the worksheet shown in Excerpt 4.14, Teacher P asked students in pairs to rephrase two poems in their own words sentence by sentence in order to ensure they understood the meaning of the poems. During the discussion, she walked around and helped them if needed. The sequence of the points in the worksheet indicates that Teacher P guided students to read the sonnet from the whole to the details — first rephrase the poems to have a holistic and initial understanding of what the sonnet was talking about, and then to analyse specific words and features in the form, and afterward the content, themes, and messages; finally, they stepped out of the poems and rethought them in a comparative way in order to make students see the differences between them, which might be helpful for students to understand more deeply.

This process, from a whole to details and back to the whole, was Teacher P's one way of teaching poems. Viewed from Langer's definition (2011b), it can be seen that Teacher P firstly used Stance 1 (Getting started with the material) — rephrase to have a holistic understanding, and then Stance 2 (Developing understanding of the material) — analyse specific poems, and finally Stance 3 (Leaving from the material) — rethought two sonnets in a comparative way. Again, the back-and-forth in Teacher P's class was established during the process: from reading the poem as a whole to analysing the details in the poem, and then stepping out to the whole poem again.

Compared to the first lesson with WW1 poems, Teacher P guided students more in the second lesson, especially because she thought of the two sonnets as difficult for students to read even though the topic was interesting. Thus, it was evident that Teacher P focused more on analysing the poems than attracting students' interests in the second lesson of WW1 poems, and hence she framed the interaction with students in a more guiding way in order to develop student deeper understanding of the sonnets.

During whole-class discussion, many students actively responded to questions and gave contributions about the form and content of the sonnets. But the conversation at the end of the lesson between teacher and students illustrated that some students did not really engage in rethinking the poems personally.

Excerpt 4.15

TP: Final question: I forgot to say that the sonnet is a very old poetic form. It goes back to the 1300s. It started in Italy. It was the most popular form for a lot of poetry also in England and Shakespeare's time. So, the sonnet is associated with this really noble and elevated poetic style. Why did Brooke and Sassoon choose the sonnet? Sonnet has this history of being the most refined poetic form. Does this make sense?

(Quiet for 10 seconds)

TP: One person has an idea and the rest? Maybe have something, but not quite sure? S1, what's your thinking? (Asking another boy who did not raise his hand)

S1: Em, I don't know.

TP: So, the sonnet is really like a refined form of poetry, so why do you think Brooke chose it?

S1: Because he thinks soldiers, something, were fine, good?

TP: Yeah, yes. I mean does it fit the atmosphere of the poem?

S1: Yes↑

TP: What is the atmosphere?

S1: Er, em. The atmosphere is (...) I don't know exactly how to (...)

TP: It is difficult to find the word. Em, is it, like, solemn quietly, or like every day?

S1: Yes, sole <T: solemn> Solemn.

TP: So, the sonnet has its way appropriately, and the sonnet also has the solemn feeling. So, this makes sense.

Here, Teacher P had a longer speech than S1 and also elaborated the answer herself. It is evident to see that S1 did not have his own idea about the sonnet; he just seemed to guess the answer that the teacher wanted, whereas Teacher P instructed S1 to agree with her idea finally.

Summing Up: Teacher P as a Teacher with a Structured Plan and Clear Goal

When teaching students how to read poems, Teacher P was always deliberately performing identity of a teacher who had a structured teaching plan, clear goal, and various ways of methods with different poems. She instructed students to read and understand poems step by step, poem by poem and also worked with students together. Thus, in contrast to Teacher S, Teacher P seems not to focus as much on fostering student independence in reading; instead, she set up the content of what students read and discussed, and as well as steps and procedures of how they discussed. Correspondingly, students were deliberately positioned to follow what the teacher instructed them to do.

4.4 Post-Observation: Comments and Reviews

In the interviews of the teacher (second time), Teacher P looked back at the actual teaching practices occurring in the class during observations, comparing with what she intended to do in the first interview and students' comments on the teaching.

4.4.1 The Teacher's Comments

After the observations, Teacher P commented on students' contributions, especially in working with poems of WW1.

Excerpt 4.16
(I: What do you think about students' contributions?)
TP: It is going as I expected, it is a topic that seems to interest them (...) I think the topic wouldn't work without their input (...) it is difficult for them to read the poetry. It is not something they are really trained to do in the Danish school system, I think. We like to read short stories, articles and speeches, but poetry is difficult to teach (...) because you also want to talk about what the poem is about, there are so many academic things you want to do with the poems. If you want to keep their interest, it is impossible to do both. So, I think when I do with the poems, I focus more on analysing the poems than to make interesting for them. But I need them to contribute because I know what the poem is about, so I need to know if they understand what the poem is about, so if they don't contribute, I don't know if they learnt anything, so it is my way to see what their understandings are (...)

The above statement reflects that Teacher P was not much satisfied with students' performance when they were learning poems in that she thought of students' contributions as a window through which to know their understandings and then to improve her teaching. Hence, according to students' contributions, she somehow adjusted her approaches. In order to motivate students, she was careful about choosing topics, texts, and methods of teaching, as with her aims stated in the first interview. Working with poems was an example of teaching difficult texts. In fact, she worked really differently with two sets of poems — one set was easier and the other was comprised of sonnets, which were harder to understand. As analysed earlier, she guided students in reading two sets of poems with different extents because she thought students needed more guidance and assistance to understand more difficult poems. Her comments verified her deliberate positioning of self and students when working with the difficult set of poems: she was a guide who offered guidance and assistance for students' learning according to students' needs, as she said in the first interview. But meanwhile, what she did in the class indicates that she played the role of the guide with more control over the process, and the students thus had less time to work independently.

Her purpose of controlling as she said was to lead the class discussion and to ensure students gained understandings. She noticed the problem of whole-class discussion; however, she had to have whole-class discussion especially when they were learning difficult texts and when students were passive. She explained that:

> I can see how many students put up their hands, and I noticed there may be one third, and it is more or less the same people (...) with the difficult poem, I left the class feeling that maybe the poems had been too difficult and too many students had to be passive. So, I wasn't sure they really got everything

out of it that I want them to (...) I want them to be active, but sometimes I have to lead the class (...) We need to have the class discussion because I need to hear what is right what is wrong, I need to hear answers, and we need to go through together when it is difficult (...) when it was difficult, they became passive, but I also have to like take over (...)

Teacher P on the one hand tried to attract students to be active with different exercises, but on the other hand, she cut down the chance for students to be active if she thought the texts were difficult for students to read and understand. In this sense, Teacher P's control over the process of learning partly depended on the complexity of the texts.

4.4.2 Students' Comments

The interview with selected students in Teacher P's class demonstrated that students seemed to communicate with the teacher when they needed help to finish tasks mostly in the class, but after class, they seldom had communication with the teacher. In the students' view, a teacher's questions and students' answers about texts, as well as students' questions and a teacher's help about tasks, were two common formats of the interaction with a teacher in Teacher P's class. They described the interaction with the teacher in the class as comfortable or good because they thought no matter in which format, Teacher P's interpretations made them understand something in the texts, and also learn something they did not know. Indeed, ten students in the class responded in the CIQ that they felt their expectations of the class had been achieved to a large extent because they had learnt something about the topic of "Heroes, Superheroes, Heroines and Anti-heroes". Students' comments demonstrate Teacher P's selection of the topic did interest students, which was in line with her aims. These comments also reflect the difference of student opinions on the most interesting thing in the class. The responses of CIQ showed that some students (3 students) liked the topic, some (10 students) liked a certain activity, some (4 students) liked a certain literary text, some (5 students) liked to make presentations, and the remainder (3 students) had other different interests. But usually, they commonly liked to join in different new activities. All five students in the interview said they enjoyed various activities especially when Teacher P designed a new one. They thought of the variety in activity as a way to get out of dullness in the class. For instance, seven students responded in the CIQ that they felt the *circle exercise* most interesting mainly because it was a new activity and an alternative approach to the ordinary type of teaching literature.

However, compared with Teacher S's students, students in Teacher P's class seemed to have fewer interests in reading and analysing texts, especially analysing poems. Three students interviewed including the active, average, and passive responded that they did not like much because they thought reading and analysing texts were boring and difficult. Indeed, another five students wrote in their responses to CIQ that their expectations in English class were practicing and improving both oral and written English. In this sense, in order to meet students' different needs, Teacher P created variations of activities on the one hand to make the analysis with texts interesting, on the other hand to practice students' English as much as possible.

4.4.3 Reviews of What Had Been Done

In the interview with Teacher P after observation, she explained some of her actions that she did not notice but were interesting for me as a researcher.

First, Teacher P always strictly followed her teaching plan. In the first interview before observation, Teacher P said that students had little chance to add something in her plan, and also her teaching plan of Heroes indicated her structured and goal-oriented planning. This planning style was verified by observations in class. Before each lesson, Teacher P assigned homework to students via Lectio, and then at the beginning of each class, she clearly wrote the structure and specific content of that day's lesson on the left side of the whiteboard to remind herself and students to follow step by step, without exception. It was common to see that she always checked her notes now and then during the lesson, in order to see if she overlooked something according to the structure and content. She elaborated that following a strict plan was helpful for her to ensure variation in the class:

> Sometimes you see I have a very strict plan, fifteen minutes for this, and ten minutes for that. I like that because it is important for me to have variation in the class ideally. It doesn't always succeed. Things take longer and so on. So, I like variation and then I need to know the structure to have the variation. I think I make choice all the time through the lessons.

Evidently, Teacher P cared greatly about making variations in the class. Hence, she needed a structure to follow and to see which activity had been used which one had not. In essence, this style of planning and following the plan was in line with the method she framed the class — in a structured and goal-oriented way.

Second, Teacher P's teaching is often organised in a comparative way. When teaching poems of First World War, Teacher P spent two lessons (90 minutes each) analysing four poems, with two poems in each lesson. For two lessons as a whole, Teacher P chose two sets of poems with different levels — in the first lesson, they worked with simple two poems and in the second lesson, they learnt to analyse difficult sonnets — it was the first comparison. Also, for each lesson, Teacher P put two poems together in one lesson, analysing them in a comparative way too. In Teacher P's view, having two things next to each other could help students see the differences and made them understand the individual poem from the difference. In the lesson, students had two poems, it was easier to understand that this poem had a rhythm if the other poem did not have a rhythm, or it was easier to understand that this poem was very simple if the other was very complex. This was the second comparison.

She explained that she did comparison because it was always easier for students to understand something when it was put in a contrasting context. Take two sonnets in the second lesson as an instance. For students, they might not really know what a sonnet was, but they could understand one was very patriotic when they saw another sonnet that was very ironic. The contrast of things next to each other made the difference clear. Meanwhile, she chose different levels of poems and started with the simple one in order to let students gain background and basic knowledge of poems written during WW1 from simple poems. Then working with difficult ones could be a way of challenging students. So, it was a process from simpleness to difficulty, in this way students were supposed to learn deeper and deeper.

Third, Teacher P often asked "why" questions. As another method to help students read and understand, Teacher P asked them to think about why she asked this question, why she asked them to do things in that way. For instance, she asked the students why she asked them to rephrase the poems first (T: *"When I asked you to rephrase the poems, why did I do that?"*); she also asked the students why she chose to read two sonnets together (T: *"Why did I choose for us to read two sonnets together, do you think?"*). In this way, she reminded the students to make it clear what the goals were and what they could learn from them. Teacher P thought that if students understood why they were doing an activity, and then they took it seriously and were more interested in it because they knew their purposes and plan, in short, they were motivated. Sometimes "why" questions were asked when students gave different responses from the teacher. Teacher P used them to check if students could find particular information as support for their understandings. So, it was also a way of close reading like many literary teachers do.

But it is worth mentioning that while Teacher P asked "why" questions or taught in a comparative way as strategies to motivate students, these strategies again illustrated her goal-oriented and structured style of instruction. By reminding students to notice her purpose through "why" questions, Teacher P was trying to guiding students to follow her thinking and plan step by step.

4.5 Conclusion

Teacher P was a young English teacher who always considered students' English level and opportunities for them to practice English when she made teaching plans and designed activities. She utilized multi-modal sources of materials for students, which was embodied in her plan of "Heroes" topic (Excerpt 4.2). This actually aligned with the school and the societal cultures that advocate the usage of ICT and electronic media. Meanwhile, she cared about the students' interests, student talk, and students being active in the class, which were also the aims of the school. While it seemed that students had many chances to speak in various activities, and students' active responses in CIQ also demonstrated that they were attracted by the variations of teaching methods, the observations illustrated that sometimes some exercises did not really engage students in substantive discussions or heteroglot interactions, as with *circle exercise* and *double-circle exercise*. On the one hand, she cared about student participation and tried to motivate them, but on the other hand, she controlled their engagement now and then. Thus, the tension that Teacher P confronted was created between the purposes of the school and the teacher and the actual teaching practices of the teacher.

The observations in Teacher P's class also illustrate that the classroom was a structured and ordered learning environment where the teacher often led the class and followed her structure and plan step by step. Thus, she often framed the interaction with students in the form of whole-class discussion, or the interaction among students in the form of pair discussion, rather than fully independent group work. The specific positions of the teacher and students, and the stance tools that the teaching was related to in the three types of classroom interactions are summarized as follows:

Table 4.3 Positioning and Envisioning in Teacher P's Class

Type of interaction	The Teacher's positioning	Students' positioning	Stance tools
Teacher-Student (Circle exercise)	*Deliberately self-positioning:* 1. A initiator of new activity 2. A controller of student engagement	*The Teacher's deliberately positioning of students:* 1. Participators of the activity 2. Forced responders in the circle	Stance 1, 2
Student-Student (Double-circle exercise)	*Deliberately self-positioning:* A manipulator of the game	*The Teacher's deliberately positioning of students:* Players of the game	Stance 1, 2
Student-Text	*Moral positioning:* A teacher with a structured plan and clear goal	*Moral positioning:* Students following the teacher's structure and worksheet	Stance 1, 2, 3

Obviously, Teacher P's control over the activities and student engagement in the activities impacted her positioning of herself and students. In Teacher P's class, moral positioning was more evident compared with Teacher S's class. She often used intentional positioning, which was similar to Teacher S. But in contrast to Teacher S who put her purpose into practice through positioning, Teacher P sometimes conducted teaching differently from the principles of the school (setting up a democratic climate with the emphasis on active student participation) and her purpose of designing some exercises (e.g., *circle exercise*) by means of expressing her self-identities as controller and manipulator in the activities. Students thus had little chance to take up other positions other than the positions that were deliberately or forced given by the teacher. Performative positioning was therefore rare in Teacher P's class. In short, compared with Teacher S's classes, Teacher P neither shifted her position nor offered many opportunities for students' multiple positions. During the lesson, Teacher P often led the class according to her teaching plan and structure. Although Teacher P's pedagogy of literature was also related to some stance tools, students' responses demonstrated that not all of them had personal understandings of the texts. As a matter of fact, some exercises were designed to push students to discuss and understand the literary texts deeply, but finally, the results showed that students might merely engage in speaking in English without engaging in discussions and argumentations (e.g., *double-circle exercise* and *circle exercise*).

Chapter 5
The Case of Teacher X

Chapter 5 and Chapter 6 present the findings of the Chinese cases study. This chapter shares the same structure of Chapter 3, 4, but the findings are presented by comparison with Danish cases.

5.1 Contextual Cultures

5.1.1 Profile of the School

Both Chinese schools in this book are located in a big city of China. Z High School, founded in 1947, has been one of the key high schools in the province since 1996. At present, it has both lower secondary school and upper secondary school, with 36 high-school classes and about 2000 high-school students. From 1959, it was in the charge of a well-known university from which the high school developed its own school motto-seeking for knowledge, truth, steadiness, creativeness, kindness. Because of its history, Z High School inherited the school cultures of the university, aiming at fostering students' personalities and training their spirits of seeking truth. Thus, the school's development strategy — using its school cultures and the curriculum to build a modern high school of lively academic culture — was established.

According to relations of four levels of contextual culture (Cheong, 2000), the macro-level societal culture in China influences the school cultures, such as the principles, mottoes, and curriculum of the school, the relationship between the teacher and students, and management of the class. Thus, on the one hand, the Z High School represents the disciplined, ordered, and uniformed school cultures rooted in Chinese ideology and traditional cultures. In the Z High School students are required to wear school uniforms and do morning exercises each day. And on the other hand, under the influence of the *National Curriculum Reform of Basic Education*, Z High School tries to seek something new to reform the traditional curriculum. As one strategy, this school utilizes Chinese cultures to establish interactional connections. So far, it has connected with some high schools from America, England, Germany, Japan, Australia, and Denmark. Another strategy is to set up a course selection system across the compulsory and selective courses so as to reach the goal that every student has the opportunity to develop his or her own personality by attending self-selected courses. But this system hasn't opened for senior students who have to prepare for the *College Entrance Examination* at the end of the third year.

The policy of the *National Fundamental Education Reform* plays an important role in forming the new trend of school cultures, such as international connections and an electives system in the Z High School. In essence, these new changes to school cultures indicate a new reform of students' position in teaching and learning — from teacher-centred to student-centred mode of teaching. Thus, classroom interaction has received more attention recently, including Chinese literature classes. With this perception, the analysis and discussion in this chapter consider whether new changes stemming from the societal cultures and school cultures affected the three types of interactions in Teacher X's class or not.

5.1.2 Profile of Teacher X's Class

Teacher X's first-year Chinese class, which was one of the elite classes in Z High School, had 55 students, almost twice as many as Teachers S or P. These

Chinese students wore school uniforms and were seated in rows, which made the class look ordered and structured. Table 5.1 is an overview of Teacher X's class.

Table 5.1 highlights two conspicuous numbers: one is the student numbers in the class and the other is time of each lesson. The number of students in Danish classes (Table 3.1, Table 4.1) was much less than Teacher X's class, whereas the lesson time of the Danish classes was double Chinese classes. This distinct difference raises the question: *"How did the Chinese teacher frame the large class and meanwhile maintain the classroom interaction during 40 minutes?"* The data analysis in Teacher X's class was conducted with consideration of the effect of student number and lesson time — that constitutes the classroom cultures — on classroom interactions.

Table 5.1   Profile of Teacher X's Class

Grade of class	Number of Students	Seating	Lesson length	Lessons per week	Number of lessons observed	Curriculum
1st-year	55	vertical rows	40 minutes	4	9	■ A long prose *The Temple of Earth Park and I*; ■ A short story *The Last Leaf;* An essay *Whistling of Birds;* ■ Student homework with short stories *Stranger Bear Word to the Spartans We ...* and *While The Auto Waits*

5.1.2.1   Seating Arrangement

Teacher X's Chinese classrooms were densely arranged in the traditional way. In Teacher X's classroom, there were four vertical rows with seven desks for each row. Around one student desk, two students sat together in pairs as shown in Figure 5.1.

The Chinese classroom looked smaller, but more ordered than Danish classrooms (Figure 3.1, Figure 4.1) because in Teacher X's class, it was rare

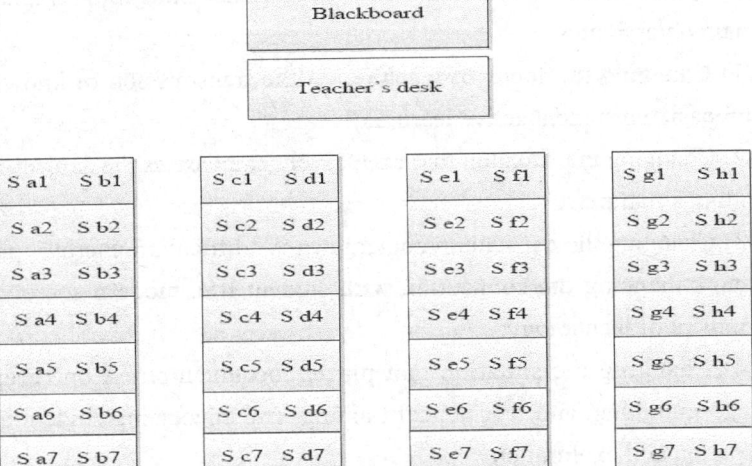

Figure 5.1　Seating Arrangement of Teacher X's Class

to change the desks and chairs, and thus seats were dense and fixed. In this way, more students could be accommodated in the smaller classroom, and also it made the class orderly.

Some Chinese teachers like Teacher X utilized the vertical-row arrangement to frame whole-class discussion. This way of framing was compared to the *metaphor of a train*, which means the teacher chose one row of students from eight vertical rows (a to h) and asked them to respond to the same question one by one, so each student in the row was like a car of a train.

5.1.2.2　Syllabus and Specific Learning Contents

In China, under the influence of the new curriculum reform, a new perception of teaching has been gradually coming into the focus of educators. Students are regarded as the agents of learning and the general goal of school education is to improve students' development, so teachers should support students' development through improving teaching and changing self-position, from being a representative of authority to being a facilitator of learning. The *National Curriculum Reform of Basic Education* emphasises four main objectivities:

(1) Changing the focus of teaching on the transmission of knowledge and emphasizing student active learning;

(2) Changing the situation that excessively emphasises the subject-based curriculum structure;

(3) Changing the curriculum content that is "difficult, numerous, partial, old" and enhancing the connection with student life, modern society, and development of technology;

(4) Changing the situation that places too much stress on receptive learning, cramming, and mechanical training, and advocating student active participation and exploration.[①]

The specific objectives of the curriculum reform indicate that a good teacher in China needs to consider how to engage students in active learning, how to arouse student interests, how to transform the subject-related curriculum in order to establish the connection between practice and real life, and how to create a platform for students to explore knowledge and improve competences. Therefore, in a classroom where the new curricular reform is being conducted, students' level of enthusiasm, their state of attention, the extent of participation, the state of mind, and the quality of interaction are the main criteria for the evaluation of a teacher's teaching. Correspondingly, local governments have adjusted the curriculum of *Chinese Language and Literature* as the main subject in upper secondary schools in terms of goals, contents, means, and evaluations. The biggest change is adding elective content into textbooks so that they contain both compulsory and elective texts. The elective texts are comprised of poems and prose, novels and

---

① The specific objectivities of the curriculum reform were proposed and emphasised in the website of Ministry of Education, China: 教育部关于印发《基础教育课程改革纲要（试行）》的通知 http://www.moe.gov.cn/srcsite/A26/jcj_kcjcgh/200106/t20010608_167343.html, 2001-06-08/2017-05-05.

dramas, news and biographies, application of language and characters, and works about cultures. The compulsory texts include five modules in order to achieve two goals: one is to improve the abilities of reading and analysis, and the other is to facilitate students' expression and communication. Through learning, students are expected to develop multiple abilities in several areas: accumulation and integration of various content and knowledge, imagination, and aesthetic reading, deep thinking and understanding the values and spirits through dialogue with literary texts, application, and putting the knowledge into practice, discovery, and innovation through observing, exploring the literature of China and foreign countries in different stances (*New Curriculum of Chinese Language and Literature in General Upper Secondary Schools*)[1]. In brief, the curriculum reform advocates student-centred teaching and stresses the student active participation in class and the development of student learning competencies as well.

However, Teacher X thought it was hard to achieve the ideal goal of the new curriculum. This was because the amount of content was too large to finish during two years[2]. In a half-semester, about two months, the teacher was required to finish teaching all the mandatory texts in one textbook including 16 compulsory texts and 16 selected texts. Teacher X was afraid that a large amount of content might lead to a problem that students were lost in the ocean of texts and might not grasp the importance of what they were learning. Teacher X was a little bit anxious, but she could not choose and decide what to learn. In contrast to Danish teachers, Chinese teachers have to follow textbooks and thus the learning content for the students is fixed and

---

[1] New Curriculum of Chinese Language and Literature in General Upper Secondary Schools(《普通高中语文课程标准》) put forward several aspects of the disciplinary objectives.
See: http://www.moe.gov.cn/srcsite/A26/s8001/202006/t20200603_462199.html.

[2] In China, it is usual to keep the whole third-year of high school exercising and practicing in order to prepare for the National College Entrance Examination, so nearly all the Chinese high school teachers try to finish teaching the entire curriculum in the first two years of high school.

unchangeable. What the teacher can choose are the elective texts. Chinese teachers usually try to predict and select texts that probably will be included in the final examination. In the first year of high school, students are usually busy learning compulsory texts in textbooks, as Teacher X's class was doing. Table 5.2 shows the curriculum with specific teaching methods of Teacher X's class.

Table 5.2 Curriculum Units and Activities in Teacher X's Class

Classroom observed	Curriculum units observed per course	Characteristic teaching methods
1st-year Chinese class (9 lessons)	Each lesson started with a student presentation	Student presentations before each lesson started
	A long prose *The Temple of Earth Park and I* (written by a Chinese contemporary writer, Tiesheng Shi)	Lecture and IRE (1st lesson); Whole-class discussion of a particular paragraph in the prose was framed like a train as a metaphor (2nd lesson); Reading aloud the prose (3rd lesson); Whole-class discussion to share student understandings (4th lesson)
	The Last Leaf (written by an American short story writer O. Henry)	Lecture and whole-class discussion
	Student homework including the reading of *Stranger Bear Word to the Spartans We ...* (a short story by the German author Heinrich Böll) and *While The Auto Waits* (a short story by O. Henry)	Whole-class discussion of the character in the story of *Stranger Bear Word to the Spartans We ...* was framed like a train as a metaphor (1st lesson); The teacher's comments on the homework about the story *While The Auto Waits* (2nd lesson)
	An essay *Whistling of Birds* by David Herbert Lawrence	Lecture and whole-class discussion

Teacher X and her students focused on reading literary texts that were across different countries and genres. But the teaching methods that Teacher X used to teach each text were almost the same. She spent more time on the lecture, but less time on the student-student discussion, let alone student group work. Instead, Teacher X preferred to frame whole-class discussion by the *metaphor of train*.

In addition, student presentation was another distinct activity in Teacher X's class. As a strategy to respond to the new curricular reform, each student in Teacher X's class was requested to do a student presentation at the beginning of each lesson. In Danish classes, the assignment of student presentation was often implemented in groups, whereas in Teacher X's Chinese class, the work of preparing and giving presentations was student individual work. By this means, each student took the opportunity to deal with their interesting topics on literary texts or literary events to gain an overview, to come to an understanding of that topic, and to form his or her own opinions.

With an overview of the curriculum and teaching methods, it seems that Teacher X was trying to do something new to align with the trend of reform. Indeed, what she said demonstrated that she cared about her students and the situation of Chinese literature education.

5.2 Pre-Observation: Teacher X's Perceptions of Literature Teaching

In the first interview with Teacher X, she talked about her thoughts on the current situation of literature education in China including the purpose and features of her teaching, indicating how she characterized her roles and responsibilities as a literary teacher.

5.2.1 Reflexive Positioning

Teacher X had around twenty years' experience of teaching the subject of Chinese language and literature. With the development of her teaching skills, Teacher X gradually noticed the role of the teacher in the class and the importance of student participation in the class.

Excerpt 5.1

TX: when I was a new teacher, I felt sad if somebody did not listen to my lecture. But gradually I was learning to adjust my emotions and thought from the perspective of students. I could not request all the pupils to follow my steps. As a teacher, I should actively interact with students, even if there were only one or two students were listening to me.

In my mind, an ideal teaching situation is that: on the one hand, students have the chance to choose what they are interested in, and on the other hand there are sufficient communications between the teacher and students. But it is a pity that this situation is rare in current Chinese classrooms especially in the elite high school (...) Thus, in the class, the teacher is usually the only speaker who speaks a lot, whereas students have few speeches. If the teacher makes more room for student speeches, s/he probably feels anxious that the teaching plan and compulsory learning content might not be finished on time (...) Hence, I think the reality often runs contrary to the ideality.

The long period of teaching experience enriched Teacher X's feelings of being a literature teacher in China — it lets her know more about students, the problem of current teaching in Chinese literature class, and the effects of the educational system on teaching approaches. She wanted to be an ideal teacher that she described and chose to be a literature teacher because she loved reading literature in her life. Every time she was interviewed, she was reading a literary book in her office. She expected to share her understanding with students after reading a book, but it was a pity that not many students would share their readings because there were some obstacles in reality that made them read less and less. The above statement reflects her awareness of the importance of student engagement in the interaction with the teacher, and that she positioned herself as a teacher who cared about the interaction with students and the current situation of literature teaching in today's high schools in China.

5.2.2 Purpose of Teaching

Teacher X's awareness of the situation in Chinese literature teaching and her reflexive positioning were also embodied in her stated purpose of teaching literature. She expected students to get benefits from reading and learning literature during three high-school years. Nevertheless, she was afraid that fewer and fewer students were interested in reading literature in their daily life. Excerpt 5.2 includes her explanation of the purpose of teaching literature.

Excerpt 5.2

TX: I hope after three-year learning in high school, for each student there will be a literary text, a writer, or a work of art that can impress his or her, so his or her inner world will be nourished by the spirits from literature (...) During my teaching life, it is rare to find that students really step into the texts and engage in reading personally. In fact, for most students, their time for reading literature has been occupied by other subjects like math, physics, and chemistry, so they are not willing to spend much time reading literature. Therefore, sometimes I feel depressed. If I care more, I feel more depressed (...) I think learning literature needs a loose environment rather than a tense environment (...) several years ago, there were still some students who wrote poems themselves and showed them to me, but now there are less and less. I guess the lesson time is not enough, so I hope, to help them and let them be interested in something in reading literature in the class. That is what I can do at present.

Here Teacher X repeated her anxiety about student attitudes toward literature and the current situation of student learning literature in China. Thinking about the nature of the literature, Teacher X knew how to read literature, in what kind of environment, and in which way. She recalled that in her early years, when the learning environment of students was not as restricted as today, there were many students who liked to read and even write literary texts. But the situation has changed a lot in recent years. Considering the obstacles that the educational background brought, she had to adjust her expectation and teaching approach in order to accommodate the contextual cultures in which she worked. Thus, at present she aimed to do her best in the class to help to trigger students' interest in literature through guiding and teaching, which was her general purpose.

5.2.3 Perceptions of How to Engage Students

As the Danish teachers, Teacher X also tried to attract students' interest. But the approaches were distinct. In Teacher X's class, students had to learn compulsory texts even though they might not be interesting for all students. In that case, Teacher X needed to think about which part she might talk more, and which part she might not, as following Excerpt 5.3 indicates.

Excerpt 5.3

TX: I can only say that sometimes students are in a good condition so that I can conduct my teaching activities well and they also cooperate well. But sometimes if they are not in a good condition, I have to change my plan or the structure. For example, I will teach a compulsory text, but they think it isn't interesting, and then I need to change the content and the way of talking, such as selecting an easier point or topic about that text. In other words, I try to teach them according to their needs and levels. I will not talk about something they are not interested in.

Teacher X's action of adjustment is understandable — to meet students' current level. But obviously, her adjustment was restricted. As a matter of fact, her statement indicates that Chinese teachers have little room to decide on the student learning content in the class, and students had no chance to choose what they wanted to learn. Under these circumstances, Teacher X interpreted her own ways to engage students in the class.

5.2.3.1 Plan a Goal-oriented and Efficient Lesson

When talking about her teaching plan, Teacher X always repeated a fact that her class was a big class but each lesson was only forty minutes.

Excerpt 5.4

TX: I don't give much time for student discussion because there are fifty-five students. It is impossible to let each student respond in only forty minutes, especially when I have to consider the requests for the College Entrance Examination. Usually, the most common format of interaction is teacher initiation and student response (...) sometimes I have to take the students who haven't read the texts before into account. If so, the class is easy to be a place where the teacher is giving a monologue. But according to my teaching experience, I know it doesn't make sense for students if they are talked much, rather than having personal understandings and explorations. But always I have to follow the goal and the time schedule (...) Besides, there are a lot of exercises and standardized tests for students. If no exercise, student thinking cannot be trained and supported, but too many exercises and standardized tests will stifle students' interests and enthusiasm because sometimes their active responses might not be confirmed according to the standard answers.

In the interview, she claimed that both the teacher and students had clear goals of learning in high schools. Students are mostly motivated by the College Entrance Examination. Her statement reflects three facts. **First,** the examination was the main purpose of learning for most students, so they would like to spend large amounts of time on other difficult subjects that might bring higher scores if they work hard, whereas literature is taught in mother tongue and easier to learn superficially, thus the subject *Chinese Language and Literature* was neglected by many students. **Second,** standardized tests made students lose interest in exploring personal understanding, in that sometimes a student's unique answer would probably be declined according to the answer key. Teacher X was afraid if things went on like this, students critical thinking would be weakened, and also their voices would be reduced. **Third,** Teacher X felt that the large curriculum pushed her to catch up with the schedule of each lesson and also of the whole semester, so in the only forty-minute lesson, the more time for teachers' lectures, the less time for student talk in the classroom, let alone group work.

With clear goals, Teacher X tried to make her classes efficient. Usually, in ordinary lessons, Teacher X only taught mandatory texts, even so, during each semester (two to three months), the class had to finish one textbook including four units, sixteen texts. Usually, she spent three to five lessons to read, analyse, discuss the text, and comment on student homework. In other extensive classes after ordinary classes, students learnt some selected texts. Even so, for the teacher, it was also a challenge to finish the large curricular plan on time. Teacher X said she had to lead the progress and structure of a lesson in order to make the lesson efficient, so sometimes she could not take students' talk into account. Her statement in fact indicated the effect of the reform as an aspect of the societal cultures in her teaching.

5.2.3.2 Be Aware of Fostering Student Reading Habit

Teacher X concerning with students' interest in reading was also embodied in her awareness of fostering their good reading habits. One is fostering the student habit of making notes. She explained that she thought writing and reading connected closely with each other, and making notes was a good way to accumulate materials for writing essays in the exam. Thus, she always reminded students to make notes, no matter if they read in the class or read in their leisure time. Even when other students gave presentations, students who were listening were also making notes of what they had learnt from the presentation. By this means, Teacher X pointed at the benefits of reading literature in the examinations, motivating students to read.

The other strategy of fostering student reading habits was that Teacher X was expected to guide students to read literature in their leisure time. As a way of guiding, at the end of each semester, she would give students a list of books that were ready for them to read on the holidays. From the list, students selected some interesting books to read, and meanwhile they were requested by Teacher X to write a review of one book after reading. At the beginning of the next semester, their reviews would be evaluated by the teacher. Some good essays would also be read and shared in the class.

Summing up, Teacher X positioned herself as a literature teacher who loved reading and was concerned with the situation of literature teaching in Chinese high schools. Thus, as a literary teacher, Teacher X expected to attract students' interest in reading that was beneficial for student spirits. However, her perceptions of engaging students demonstrate that she was also a traditional Chinese teacher who had to set up a clear goal and have a structured plan in order to finish the curriculum on time. Thus, on the one hand, she had to conduct teaching within the societal and school cultures, but on the other hand, she tried to motivate students by pointing at some interesting and beneficial aspects in literature.

5.3　During-Observation: Three Types of Classroom Interactions

Like many traditional Chinese classes, Teacher X's class had fixed seats, textbooks, exam-orientation, and disciplined students. It was common to see the teacher's monologic lecture and the interaction between the teacher and students, whereas it was rare to see group discussion during the class. But under the influence of the curricular reforms and new trends, a combined style of tradition and new changes in her class was also embodied in the classroom interactions.

5.3.1 The Interaction between the Teacher and Students: Whole-Class Discussion through the "Train" Metaphor

Except for the pattern of IRE, there were two other ways of framing interactions between the teacher and students found — one is the *circle exercise* in Teacher P's Danish classroom, and the other is the *train metaphor* in Teacher X's Chinese classroom.

The metaphor of the train describes a phenomenon where students in a row respond to the same question from the first student to the last as Figure 5.2 shows below. The row was like a train with each student as each carriage. When the students responded to the teacher's question, the next student could build on what the previous student had said or gave a new response. Each student in a "train" was forced to a position of the potential responder who had to contribute to the same question. This metaphor was often used in Teacher X's classroom. When one student responded, Teacher X walked from the head of the "train" (Sa1 or Sb1) to the end (Sa7 or Sb7), speaking with the student closely.

Excerpt 5.5 is an example of class discussion that was framed using the train metaphor. The transcript was selected from a lesson where the class was talking about a particular paragraph in long prose *The Temple of Earth Park and I* written by a Chinese writer Tiesheng Shi. This paragraph particularly described the scenery in the park. Teacher X started with an open question: "*What do you think is the most interesting, impressing, or touching in this paragraph?*" One row of students was invited to share their reading experience

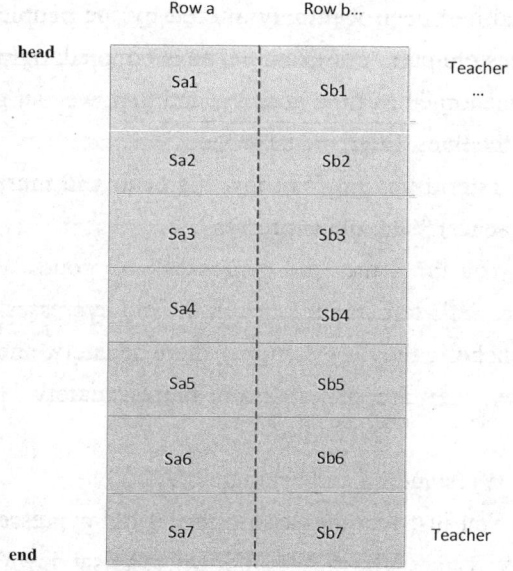

Figure 5.2 Train as a Metaphor

in the form of the train metaphor. The following contains the conversation between Teacher X and the third and fifth student in the selected row (Row a).

Excerpt 5.5

① TX: Well, I will ask a row of students to respond, one by one, like a train. You please (pointed to a student).

② Sa3: I think the park he described exited as nature, as truth, although everything is changing, it still stays there. I think the author also has something similar to the park. He is crippled, the park also becomes old and broken as time goes by, but they both have the same insights of life, which will not change over time, they are both pure, unworldly, and calm.

③ TX: Good. Please sit down. She makes the meaning more explicit. She means that not only the park but also the memory in the author's mind had been wantonly altered by the people who did not understand this old park. For example, he is crippled, right? Thus, life is simple and unadorned as time goes by, and then we can feel the law of life between the lines. Well, the next one!

④ Sa5: (stood up) En (5) (bow his head and murmur, and then look at the teacher) "Old, old cypresses".

⑤ TX: You think the "old cypresses" are good. Well, why they are good? OK, let's talk about a detail, the old cypresses "when you're feeling melancholy, they are standing there sedately, and when you're feeling happy, they are still standing there sedately ..." right? Why good?

⑥ Sa5: (7) (standing and being quiet)

⑦ TX: You just feel the description of old cypresses is good, but can't say why. Right? OK, please sit down. (Sa5 sat down).

We have met this sentence in the homework; you can think it further again: why the old cypresses are good? (...) what do you think is expressed? (3) What of life? What of life? (repeated)

⑧ S (Someone): Variability.

⑨ TX: Variability of life? ↑ (doubtfully) They stand firmly, although other things are changing, they still stand there firmly. We can think of, what kind of feeling? (3) What kind of feeling? (Repeated again)

⑩ TX: (6) Do you feel a little upset? Right? ↑ So, we should refine our thinking when reading it ...

In this conversation, Teacher X was playing the role of a magisterial teacher and correspondingly the students in the row were positioned as forced responders, according to their social roles. This is moral positioning (Harré & van Langenhove, 1999; Davies & Harré, 1990) through which Teacher X and students' institutional identities dominated. But different students in a row also had different identities achieved by their overtly different performance, which was related to the performative positioning of students (ibid). Some students felt uncomfortable when they stood up and did not know what to say. They just stood there and murmured in a low voice, such as S5. But this method did invite some students who might be shy to say something and yet in fact could do make contributions, such as S3 who had a long speech turn and her response was confirmed by the teacher. S3's understanding received a high evaluation from the teacher who elaborated a bit and built on S3's response. Conversely, Teacher X wasn't satisfied with S5's short answer. As a result, S5 was positioned on the periphery and into a passive receiving mode. He was forced to think about what the teacher expected. But obviously, he couldn't see what the teacher had seen. Instead of guiding, Teacher X closed the possibility of continuous interaction with S5 at that time when she asked a follow-up question that pointed to particular information in the text (turn ⑤ : *"let's talk about a detail"*).

As Langer (2011a, 2011b) stated, giving meaning can not develop envisionment-building. In this excerpt, Teacher X asked a question on the details of the text, intending to build a cohesive envisionment through developing student understanding (Stance 2 Developing an understanding of the material) of the text. But she did not use enabling strategies to help them explore other possible interpretations. Teacher X's starting with an open question indicated that at the beginning she positioned students as potential readers who could have some personal readings and feelings, but as the conversation continued, she became hurried to show her magisterial interpretation to students on behalf of the text, forcing them to tell something that was close to her thinking. At that time, the students' possibility of taking on a position of an independent reader was declined by the teacher. It can be seen that the classroom was designed to be dialogically organised, but finally, student engagement in the interaction was closed when the teacher pushed them to follow her magisterial

interpretation.
- **Summing Up: Teacher X as a Magisterial Teacher Who Confronted with a Dilemma**[①]

The above excerpt was one of the examples of the teacher-student interaction that was framed using the *train metaphor* in Teacher X's class. At other times she often interacted with students by this means. In the discussion framed in the form of train metaphor, Teacher X morally positioned herself as a magisterial teacher who controlled the procedure and pace, decided which row of students would respond and which question was to be answered, and gave magisterial interpretations on behalf of the texts. In this case, Teacher X started the discussion with an open question to invite students to share reading experience. This indicated that she noticed student personal reading and literature experience that was also emphasised by envisioning theory (Langer, 2011a, 2011b). It followed that on the one hand Teacher X hoped to reach her ideal teaching situation where there was active interaction between the teacher and students, but on the other hand she was confronted with a dilemma (Dilemma 1) when she found a student response was deviant or superficial.

5.3.2 The Interaction between the Student and the Student: Two Activities

There seemed to be few interactions among students such as group work and group discussions, but only some pair discussions in Teacher X's class. But under the circumstance of new curricular reform, teachers in China were requested to change the traditional teaching mode, from teacher-centred mode to the student-centred mode. Thus, there were two kinds of student-student interaction reflecting Teacher's efforts to echo this reform. One is student individual presentation, and the other is student self-check homework.

---

① There were three dilemmas identified in Teacher X's class.

5.3.2.1 Student Individual Presentation as a Way of Extending Class Interaction to the Outside

Student Individual Presentation has been widely used, as a typical interaction between the student and the student in Chinese classrooms. In Teacher X's class, each lesson always started with a student individual presentation which lasted for 10–15 minutes, nearly 1/3 of each lesson time (40 minutes). Every student in the class was requested to give a presentation with PowerPoint. It was an individual student's work that was prepared on their own before class, different from the typical form of student presentation in Danish cases of this book — both oral and written forms of student presentation were the product of group work during the class time.

The other difference is the topic of student presentation. In Teacher S's classes, the topic was set by the teacher, which was about a person or a literary text or period (third-year class), whereas the choice of presentation topic in Teacher X's class was diverse. The topics of presentation were freely chosen by students. At first, the topics of presentations were only about poems. Students were requested to talk about a poet and his/her poems. Gradually, after two months, Teacher X enlarged the range of student choice considering that some students hoped to read and talk about other genres. Hence, later the topics of presentation could cover various genres, such as fiction, essays, dramas, films, and even cartoons. Teacher X opened the choice of topics because she wanted to let students learn more about other genres from peers' presentations. She considered the student presentation as a way to establish interplay among students. Teacher X explained the purpose of framing student presentation:

> Students have more time in their first year than other to years, so I decided to try student presentation at the beginning of the class (...) The purpose is to create a chance for students

to express and show themselves, but also make a platform for student-student interaction and interplay. The effect of a teacher's talk on one's learning is less than the effect of another peer's talk. One student may feel impressed when he is listening to another peer's presentation. I think it is a beneficial interplay.

In brief, the intent of Teacher X was to make room for student talk in the class and also for them to learn from each other. So far, student performance had shown that the form of student individual presentation indeed pushed each student in the class to work with some literary texts on their own during their leisure time, encouraged them to study a topic they were interested in by searching for a wealth of relevant materials individually, and also pushed them to speak in front of the class. Thus, for student speakers, they were given the opportunity to engage in interaction with peers through the presentation. They were offered by the teacher a position of a speaker who is able to present something and express him or herself in public.

Meanwhile, in order to facilitate interaction among students, Teacher X asked the student audience to jot down notes that they found useful, touching, and interesting. As mentioned earlier, taking notes in Teacher X's class was seen as an approach to learning from others and accumulating materials for writing. If student audiences really engaged in taking notes, assimilated new information, and thought about it in their minds, the exchanging and learning did occur between the speaker and audiences. Thus, student listeners were intentionally offered positions as an audience and as learners who were expected to give feedback and communicate with the speaker in the external interaction, and as well as write down the notes and learn from the presentation in the internal interaction. In this sense, the teacher was facilitating the interplay between the student and the student. However, it was rare to see oral feedback among students after each presentation during observation. After class, three girls who sat in the front rows shared their thoughts — there were several peers who gave feedback to their presentations, but later there were fewer and fewer because they thought the quality of the presentation was going down.

Indeed, the fact is that students with different levels approached this activity differently. Some active students took this task seriously, so they prepared it well and then their presentations involved much information or other useful knowledge. But there were also some passive students who just finished a simple PowerPoint but prepared poor presentations. For instance, students listened to/watched a silent "written" presentation about Japanimation, which contained only a colorful PowerPoint but the student did not speak any words. During the presenting time, the student only played the PowerPoint slide by slide, without any interpretation. His written PowerPoint was a collection of information about Japanimation, the history, the representative work, and famous writers. Teacher X felt a little bit disappointed about this student's presentation, although she knew this student was quite weak in reading literature. In fact, this student did not interact with the teacher often, and even neither showed the slides to the teacher nor asked for advice before giving the presentation. It follows that some weak students had difficulty in working with a topic individually in a broader and deeper view.

Thus, in order to keep students interested in presenting and ensure the effectiveness of the presentation, Teacher X provided guidance in the process, which indicates her two main positions. ***First,*** Teacher X deliberately positioned herself as an examiner, who pre-read each student's written PowerPoint before their presentations in order to ensure the topics and contents were appropriate and relevant to literature reading. After the first reading, Teacher X gave her initial feedback to the student, reminding that the presentation should focus on the literary aspects, use of language, and the connotation of materials that were used in the presentation. It seemed that the teacher's first examination to some extent restricted students' choice of topics, forms and frameworks, and the content of the presentation.

But usually, Teacher X did not deny students' choice of topics in order to maintain their interests but guided them to see the literary aspects in the materials. For example, a student intended to talk about a Chinese TV show about a diet program, called "A Bite of China"[①]. It was a diet program but also contained other aspects of Chinese language and literature, such as stories, characters, the language of the narrator, the structure of the narrative. After the first examination, Teacher X did not ask him to change this topic; instead, she asked him to analyse the literary aspects, such as the language and structure of the text, as well as the cultures and values contained inside. Thus, the student presentation in Teacher X's class was manipulated by the teacher. Teacher X's manipulation was also embodied in her requests of writing notes. Student notes taken from peers' presentations were to be handed in each month, and then Teacher X examined whether students really listened to what their peers presented or not. **Second,** Teacher X deliberately positioned herself as a commentator when she was listening to student presentations. When a student presented, the teacher listened seriously as others did and after that gave her second feedback including her understanding and ideas of the topics. Many students said it was very helpful when Teacher X explained after each presentation, especially when they felt confused or did not understand something in the presentation, because they thought the teacher's comments and interpretations on the basis of the presentation made them clearer about the themes and meanings.

In short, student presentation in Teacher X's class can be seen as a means to extend class interaction to the outside of the class, where students need to prepare for the presentation and communicate with the teacher for advice out of the class. In this sense, student presentation in Teacher X's class functioned as a strategy to maintain the interaction and meanwhile to compensate for the insufficient lesson time. In this sense, student individual

---

① In China this TV program is titled as "舌尖上的中国".

presentation at the beginning of each class was the result of both societal cultures (new curriculum reform that stresses student talk) and classroom cultures (short lesson length).

5.3.2.2 Self-Check of Homework as a Way to Balance the "Correct" Answer and Critical Thinking

In Teacher X's class, students were given an answer key and required to check the homework themselves using red colour pens to highlight the mistakes and differences after checking with the standard answer key. After that, students' homework was submitted to the teacher, who would check which questions students probably had difficulties with. If possible, Teacher X arranged one lesson as shown in Excerpt 5.6, to discuss with students some questions on the homework. In this process, there were two types of interactions. One was an inner interaction, between one and oneself in one's mind. The other was the interaction with the teacher.

First was the internal interaction between one and oneself when checking the answers. This was ideal, which required students to have initiative and self-control, not to cheat the teacher by copying the standard answers. However, the reality was, as the interviewed students said: "Sometimes, standard answer key works like a double-edged sword." The statement below was extracted from an interview with a diligent student.

> Some persons did copy the answers because they were hurried to finish the homework on time. Some persons like me, sometimes when the question is difficult to understand, have a look at the answer and then rewrite the answer with their own words. But the answer did help us to know the "correct" answer in advance, so we don't need to waste time thinking in a different direction. But I will be much happy if I find my answer is nearly the same as the answer key.

It showed that self-checking of homework had its pros and cons. The active students might finish and check seriously, but the passive students might copy the answers without assimilation and understanding. Therefore, on the one hand, it might foster student ability of independent learning, and on the other hand, it could also create a large distance between active students and passive students.

Second was the external interaction with the teacher when she discussed the difficulties in homework. This interaction was sometimes substantive because, in the process of self-checking and discussion with the teacher, students were learning to be critical. They did not accept the answer key all the time; sometimes several students expressed their disagreements with the standard answers, based on their understandings and knowledge. If their understandings were not better than the standard answer but they did not understand why the teacher would find the evidence in the text or give her reasons to support the standard answer. But sometimes, the teacher was standing on the side of students' ideas, considering the standard answer as wrong; then the teacher asked students to share their ideas and argumentations. Usually, students in their first year had difficulty in expression and language use, thus not all the students who disagreed with the standard answers could clearly explain the reasons, but they might find the hints and evidence in the texts. The following excerpt illustrates how students questioned the standard answer key.

Excerpt 5.6

(*Stranger Bear Word to the Spartans We* ... by Heinrich Böll)

TX: About that character, the wounded soldier, I found there were many different answers from students' homework. Here I want to emphasise that you don't need to be the same as the standard answers given at the end of the exercise book. Even if your answer is totally unrelated to the standard answer, then you need to think further: why did you have the different and even opposite answer? This short story, I think, it is easy to understand when you read it, right?

S1: The standard answers are a bit strange!

Ss: Yes! (Many students murmured)

TX: Well. Indeed, I also feel confused about one question. Let's go back to Question 12 in the exercise book. I told you that you should read the whole story before you answer this question: "From the text, how to characterize the German wounded soldier? (...) The standard answer given in the exercise book is 'He is a muddleheaded person, a poor man (...)' What's your opinion? (...)"

The answer is to criticize the soldier, but according to your reading experience, do you think if the author is criticizing the soldier?

Ss: No!

T: Well, next, please share your ideas about the character of a soldier and find references in the text to support what you said, regardless of the standard answers. Please note to find the evidence from the text (...)

S2: He is fanatical about the war.

TX: How did you know that?

S2: On page 43, read the descriptions of the sound of artillery: *"To me there is something aristocratic about artillery, even when it's firing. It sounds so dignified, just like the war in picture books ..."* He did not realize the cruelty of the war, and next, it said: "Then I thought of how many names there would be on the war memorial when they reconsecrated it ...", I think for him war is an honor.

TX: OK, please sit down. I think S2 found the right paragraph that well describes the soldier's inner world. You could read this paragraph carefully again (...)

In Excerpt 5.6, Teacher X and students questioned the answer of one question in homework. From the perspective of envisioning theory, Teacher X was encouraging students to have some critical thinking on standard answers (Stance 4 Think critically about the material), which was valuable under the circumstance of a standardized-test educational system. However, in fact, the teacher was trying to make a balance between being close to the "correct" answer and retaining critical thinking. She said:

> In the examination, there is only one correct answer, one magisterial understanding, so students have to think about which one is the closest to the correct answer (...) So sometimes, I could not consider too much about students' thinking. To some extent, it will dampen their enthusiasm, but if I always agree with their personal understandings, their understandings sometimes might diverge too much. As a result, they might get a lower score, which is also a hit for them.

This statement indicated the second dilemma[①] (Dilemma 2) that Teacher X confronted. On the one hand, Teacher X expected students to remain critical of the standard answers, but on the other hand, she had to request that students learn to think more closely to standard answers because students had to complete an examination, which only had a single "correct" answer. In fact, S2's understanding was close to the teacher's; thus, it was supported by the teacher in that she also disagreed with the standard answers. Hence, so to speak, Teacher X was guiding students' understanding to be closer to hers, because for the teacher either her understanding or the standard answer were representative of the magisterial interpretation of the text. Although Teacher X thought that student readings should be diverse, she also accepted the fact that the "correct" answer was the only acceptable one

---

[①] The first dilemma was found in the teacher-student interaction in a way of *train as a metaphor*.

in the test. Therefore, she thought students should learn to distinguish which understanding was closer to the magisterial interpretation.

- **Summing Up: Teacher X as a Facilitator Who Offered Students Other Possible Positions**

Teacher X intentionally shifted her positions during the process of student presentation and self-checking of homework, but in general, she played the role of a facilitator who guided students to read and study on their own and deliberately created opportunities for students to occupy other positions such as being a speaker, a commenter, an independent learner, and a critical reader. The purpose of student presentation and self-checking of homework was to facilitate student-student interactions and encourage them to engage in reading and thinking about literature personally and diversely. But the results showed that the student-student interaction (external and internal) did not necessarily occur in the presentation, nor did one-oneself inner interaction necessarily work when students were doing and checking homework.

5.3.3 The Interaction between Students and the Text: Working with *The Temple of Earth Park and I*

In Teacher X's classroom, students' interaction with the text was led by the teacher step by step. In the process Teacher X applied several teaching methods at different phases. Usually, Teacher X started reading a long text with a lecture on the background and an overview and followed by the close reading of the details in the text, and finally usually ended with whole-class discussion of student readings.

Teacher X's class spent five lessons reading and analysing this long prose *The Temple of Earth Park and I* which involves seven sections in total. They not only read the first two sections that were selected and included in the textbook but also read the other five sections found from other materials. The first and second lessons were teacher lectures including an introduction of the background, interpretations of some meaningful words, characters, and images of two sections in the textbook. In the third lesson, Teacher X asked students to concentrate on a particular paragraph, which described the special scenery of the park. Whole-class discussion was framed using the train metaphor. The fourth lesson was filled with an activity of reading aloud the next five sections which were not found in the textbook. In the last lesson, students were invited to share their reading experience of the whole prose, and the discussion was also framed using the train metaphor. Thus, it followed that students participated in four different activities.

5.3.3.1 The Introductive Lessons (1st and 2nd lessons)

When the teacher gave lectures in the first two lessons that functioned as an introduction, students were forced to be positioned as passive receivers who were on the periphery. According to the teacher's plan, the goal of this first lesson was to "grasp the whole meaning, and make thoughts explicit". To be simple, it was to make students have an initial envisionment of the character, content, and theme in the text. After knowing about the content of the first two sections, the teacher and students talked a while about the characteristics of "I" (the first narrator) and the "Temple of Earth Park".

Excerpt 5.7

TX: Now, let's think and discuss:
— What is "I" like?
— What is the "Temple" like?
— What is "Mother" like?

Discuss with your partner next to you, and then I will ask some students to respond.

Note! Mark when you read and think!

(...)

TX: OK, let's discuss the first question, what is "I" like?

S1: It says: "when the park was finally ready for me (...)" So he is a man at loose ends. It also says: "(...)." So, I can feel that he is, unrest, and lost.

TX: Yes, a man who feels lost, S1 finds one point of "I", and also gives evidence from the text. Let's continue.

S2: "It was another world, one where I could escape this world." I could see something negative in this sentence. It seems that life means nothing for him.

TX: So, you think "I" am a negative man. Anything else? S3?

S3: I find "I" am a dedicated person.

TX: A dedicated person?

S3: Yes. He kept on thinking of "death" for several years. It says: "this kind of thinking went on (...)" He is persistent in the thinking of life and death, I think he is a man who focuses on his mind and soul, and he takes so many years to think about how to live, rather than to think about how bad the situation is for him.

Three teacher's questions in Excerpt 5.7 were all closed questions that pointed to the particular information in the text. So, three students found the specific information related to questions, and also summarized and interpreted it in their own words. From their responses, it can be seen that students used a close reading that was confirmed by the teacher. But their three responses about the character of "I" were diverse, on the basis of their personal readings. After each response, Teacher X did not give a negative evaluation, instead, she elaborated a bit based on the student response.

5.3.3.2 Train as a Metaphor in the 3rd Lesson

The third lesson focused on a particular paragraph that described the scenery in the park. The teacher guided the students to understand the meaning of the images. The discussion was framed as a train metaphor. For student readers, it was important that the teacher guided them to actively engage in reading and living through the literary experience. Thus, in order to engage students in thinking and sharing their understandings, the discussion started with an open question, but when confronted with a simple or superficial response from weak students, the teacher closed the possibility for these students' engagement in the continuous discussion, instead of enabling them to keep on reading and talking. In this sense, the possibility of student engagement in discussions depended on how students performed and whether students' interpretations were close to the teacher's understanding or not.

5.3.3.3 Reading-Aloud Activity in the 4th Lesson

The fourth lesson was a reading-aloud activity, where 10 volunteer students read aloud the next five sections one by one. Simultaneously, the other students were requested to think which one was the most impressive for them when listening, and also to write down notes that were useful for them. These five sections were found by the teacher as extensive materials for students' reading. The goal of this lesson was to draw a full map of the long prose in the students' minds.

From the perspective of envisioning theory, reading-aloud activity in Teacher X's classroom can be regarded as a strategy to develop their envisionment of the text, and on the whole, various teaching methods in Teacher X's class can be seen as different stances from which students could read the text from different perspectives. According to Langer's definition (Langer, 2011b), if the first and second lessons could be acknowledged as being out and stepping into an envisionment (Stance 1 Getting started with the material), the third one was being in and moving through an envisionment (Stance 2 Developing an understanding of the material) where students immersed themselves in narrowing the focus on the characters and developing understandings of some details. In the fourth lesson, they developed the understanding of the whole prose through reading the next five sections (Stance

2), to get a whole picture of the prose within and out of the selection, helping to have a holistic impression of the prose. As Teacher X explained that:

> What the book selected may be only a point; indeed, it is probably just the tip of an iceberg (...) You could imagine how the author designs and writes the next five parts when you have deeply read the selected two parts in the textbook. When we finish reading the total seven parts of the prose, then we could rethink what the author exactly wants to express with the title "The Temple of Earth Park and I".

At the beginning, the teacher was trying to engage students to explore the possibilities of the next five parts in the prose around the topic of *The Temple of Earth Park and I* through envisaging, anticipating, imagining before reading. With an initial envisionment, when the students read aloud the remaining five parts of the prose, they had the opportunity to rethink and revise what they had learnt and envisioned in their minds based on their understandings of the selected parts in the textbook (Stance 3 Leaving from the material).

5.3.3.4 Whole-Class Discussion in the 5th Lesson

After rethinking and revising in the mind, the fifth lesson was framed based on their reading experience of the whole prose. In this sense, the fifth lesson was using Stance 2 (Developing understanding of the material) and Stance 3 (Leaving from the material), developing the understanding of the material and rethinking what they had read in the textbook as a whole. In the fifth lesson, Teacher X asked students firstly to discuss in pairs and then to voluntarily share their readings and understandings in the class. It was a discussion time for the students to express their personal thinking and reading experience both on the whole prose or the details of the prose. She said to the class:

In this long prose, as a whole, which part is the most impressive for you? You could talk about the author's thinking, textual meaning, themes and characters of the prose, the writing styles, and even a sentence you like as well. From one idea of somebody, you may get inspiration and think further (...).

Similar to the discussion in the third lesson (Excerpt 5.5), Teacher X used similar open questions to start a discussion, but in the fifth lesson she framed the discussion in a different way. The discussion in the fifth lesson was not restricted by the train metaphor but depended largely on the student volunteers' active performance. The following Excerpt 5.8 is the transcript of conversations between the teacher and the third and fourth students who voluntarily raised their hands to give contributions.

Excerpt 5.8

(TX: In this long prose, as a whole, which part is the most impressive for you?)

① S3: The first several parts mainly describe that he was born at the wrong time. The author was crippled in his twenties, and then he fell down because of the terrible below. He then wrote about the runner who worked very hard but no one knew his success. At the end, when the runner was found by a coach, it was too late for him-he was too old to run faster. So, he wrote about his mother: His mother asked the author to see the flowers in the park many times, but he wouldn't like to go to the park. However, in the end, when he went to the park, his mother was spitting out blood from her mouth. So, I feel sad. Tiesheng Shi who could write this prose and still continue to live in his hard time is very strong.

② TX: OK, please sit down. What is this kind of feeling called? "Being down on one's luck and suffering many mishaps in one's life."

Is what he said about the author's mother learnt from primary school? ↑ So, he added this, right?

③ <S: murmured> S3: From the relevant materials at the back of this book!

④ TX: OK. Some students have read the relevant materials in the book and used it as a supplement (...) Any other thoughts and feelings? That is, after hearing this student's thoughts, you may know about his feeling, but is that the same as your thought? Otherwise, what do you think?

⑤ S4: I still want to say something about the runner. No matter how hard he works, he still has bad luck. It illustrates that in one's life, he not only needs efforts but also opportunities (...) then, the author was inspired by the runner. That is, I still have opportunities if I try my best. I think; indeed, it is also a life of experience.

It is evident in this excerpt that students had longer speech turns than the teacher (turn ①, ⑤) and Teacher X often invited students' thinking and talking (e.g., *"What do you think? Any other thoughts?"*). Also, students inspired each other during the discussion. S4 was inspired by the discussion between the teacher and S3 about the runner but he talked about something different from what S3 said (turn ⑤). Like them, there were four other responders who actively engaged later in the discussion, and their responses pushed the interaction between the teacher and students forward and also enriched readings from different student perspectives. In Excerpt 5.7 there were several closed questions with prescribed answers, but in Excerpt 5.8 Teacher X changed her ways of asking. This difference demonstrates the transfer of the teacher's positioning. This shift seemed to open the possibility of positions that students could occupy, such as active responder and reader that were ascribed by students' performance (performative positioning). Indeed, from turn ② and turn ③, it can be seen that S3 was powerful at that time when he revised Teacher X's comments;

Teacher X did not expect that S3 would read other relevant materials except for the textbook, to learn more about the author's mother. In other words, S3 modified the position the teacher offered: Teacher X positioned S3 as a receiver who usually learnt knowledge from the teacher or textbooks, but it turned out that she was wrong — S3 resisted this position and modified it by positioning himself as a reader who was engaging in a reconnaissance activity as a way of exploring horizons of possibilities (Langer, 2011b) and searching for other resources.

Through exchanging, students could learn about other perspectives and then reflect on previous understanding. Ultimately, during the last two lessons (fourth and fifth), more students were engaged in reading activities: reading aloud, discussing in pairs, and sharing ideas with the whole class. With a comparison of the two discussions respectively in the third and fifth lesson, something contrasting has been listed in Table 5.3.

Table 5.3   The Difference in Student Responses

Item	The 3rd lesson	The 5th lesson
Number of student responders	7	6
Voluntary or forced	forced	Voluntary
The teacher's follow-up questions	Closed questions: most questions either point to particular information in the text, or close to teacher's reading	Inviting questions (e.g., "Any other different thoughts?" Or "What do you think? What's your opinion?")
Interactive positioning	Students were passive receivers who are on the periphery; The teacher was the controller who represented the magisterial interpretation	Students were participants in reading and discussion; The teacher was the controller who made some room for student personal readings
Student response and reading	Short response and even a simple word, restricted in the text only	Long response; could connect to relevant materials to support his response. As for the same character, they also could have different responses based on their own readings

In the fifth lesson, students engaged themselves actively in the discussion, and students' responses inspired each other, while in the third lesson, the class discussion that was restricted by the train metaphor was not really sustained and substantial. The salient difference on the one hand shows that participating in a reading activity was helpful, on the other hand, it illustrated the third dilemma[①] (Dilemma 3) that Teacher X had — she noticed the necessity and importance of student engagement in discussions and tried to facilitate this, but still, she restricted students' exploration because of her controlling approaches. Compared with the Danish classroom Teacher X controlled more, including the reading materials, the activity, the topic, and the form of discussion. These constraints may to some extent limit student open-ended exploration of other possibilities of texts or exploring horizons of possibilities (Langer, 2011a, 2011b), because it was supposed that students might not consider searching for other relevant sources like an autobiography, historical background documents, and other work of the same author.

- ***Summing Up: Teacher X Shifted Positions to Engage Students in Various Activities***

This example demonstrates a method of framing the Chinese literature classroom where Teacher X tried to intentionally offer positions other than positioning students as passive receivers and tried to use some strategies to build a rich envisionment of the text, such as employing a reading-aloud activity and providing students with the remainder of the text to interest them. But in general, Teacher X still mastered the process of positioning and engaging students.

5.4 Post-Observation: Comments and Reviews

After observation, the teacher and students reviewed their teaching

---

[①] The first dilemma was found in the discussing form of *train as a metaphor*, and the second dilemma was found in the *self-check homework* activity.

and learning during this period. Their comments and reviews not only demonstrated the purpose of some actions and activities but also reflected the teacher's tension between reality and ideality under the influence of contextual cultures.

5.4.1 The Teacher's Comments

In general, Teacher X was satisfied with her students' performance in the class, but her comments showed that in fact, she had higher expectations for students.

Excerpt 5.9

I: What do you think about students' contributions?

TX: I was satisfied with the interaction with students during this period. But I feel it is hard to pull them in the process of reading because they don't ask questions themselves. But I had students who suddenly posed a question that I had not prepared before but inspired my thinking. At present, I haven't been confronted with a similar situation. Nobody will ask critical questions about what I am talking about. This is the general situation currently in my classes (...) Also, many students were weak at expressing, because they had less chance to speak.

In the second interview, Teacher X again expressed her expectation for students, hoping they would be active and critical when reading and thinking about literature. During her teaching life, she found two general phenomena of Chinese students in high schools. *First,* students would not like to initiate questions to the teacher. They had been used to being asked passively. *Second*, students did not know how to express their understandings. Sometimes they could find the hints in the text, but they might not express their understandings about the meaning behind them properly. They could not use accurate and refined words to interpret.

As she said in the first interview, Teacher X's above comments also indicate that she often considered student motivation and took the current situation of teaching and learning literature into account when she adjusted her way of teaching. She thought as a high-school teacher she needed to rethink and review her teaching now and then. For her, she was thinking about how to find an interesting topic that was related to the learning text to attract students' interest in the class. Also, she believed that good teaching should be based on students' needs rather than the teacher's needs, because she thought too many exercises requested by the school or the teacher was not necessarily helpful for improving students' reading comprehension. Thus, considering two general phenomena of current students, Teacher X maintained her expectations, hoping students would actively ask questions.

In fact, observations in Teacher X's class illustrated her trial to engage students in literary experiences, personal reading, and exploration of other possibilities of understanding. But observations showed that she failed sometimes because her institutional identity of magisterial teacher dominated, especially when students' responses were deviant and simple, and also because there were some obstacles stemming from contextual cultures (e.g., lesson length, large class, educational system).

5.4.2 Students' Comments

Students had opposite opinions from the teacher on the teacher-student interaction. All interviewed students agreed that they had little interaction with the teacher in class, let alone group discussion, and the most frequent form of interaction was whole-class discussion with the train as a metaphor. The following excerpt was an extract from one interviewed student comment.

Excerpt 5.10

S: In the class, I don't contribute much. I just listen most of the time, unless I am asked. Teacher X seldom interacts with us in a form of initiation and response; instead, she likes to use the form of train metaphor. In this way, sometimes I feel I am forced to say something, but sometimes I really don't have any ideas or sometimes previous students had said what I want to say. So, I hope the teacher would ask us some questions, rather than asking a question and a row of students respond one by one (...) maybe I could not catch the pace of the teacher.

This was the common comment of five interviewed students across different levels. They did not like to actively respond to questions but had to answer in the train metaphor. Thus, what the students said verified student passive positioning in this form of discussion. Students felt they could not catch the pace of the teacher or they often had a different understanding from the teacher or the standard answer. So, they concluded that this course was not as easy as the one learnt in secondary school. From the perspective of envisioning theory (Langer, 2011a, 2011b), the diversity of textual understanding was the result of engaging in reading and thinking literature individually. However, the difference from standard answers to some extent dampened students' enthusiasm for engagement and made them anxious about their scores in the exams. This anxiety manifested once more when student engagement was restricted by the system and the effects of contextual cultures.

As a matter of fact, in Teacher X's class student engagement in the interaction was extended to the outside of the school. 37 students (around 68%) responded in CIQ that the most impressive interaction with the teacher was the interaction before they presented individual presentations at the beginning of the class. One student agreed that Teacher X's advice on the structure, the content, and the language of the presentation did help her. Indeed, all the students interviewed loved the activity of student individual presentation because through listening they could learn other knowledge relevant to what they were learning, and meanwhile they had the chance to interact with the teacher in advance, and also teacher's comments after the presentation were very interesting and informative. But they agreed that increasingly some students did not prepare well for the presentation. Sometimes the presenting student added too many videos or their language was poor, or the topic was irrelevant to literature. Thus, students advocated setting some rules for the presentations.

Regarding the student presentation, Teacher X had a different opinion from the students. She would not deny students' long presentation:

> I will encourage students if they would like to present more. Meanwhile, I will remind them to notice the refining of words. It is not a good way to add too many videos in the PowerPoint (...) I plan to keep this activity to the next year, but the form will be changed a little bit (...) I like student presentation because it is a way of saving class time. Students are forced to present, so it requests them to spend some spare time on reading. I find it is working.

It can be seen from this statement that Teacher X hoped to make room for student talk as long as they wanted to express themselves. In this way, she wanted to push some passive and quiet students to speak in the class, and so she paid more attention to the advantages of the activity. But the difference between students' and teachers' comments on the teacher-student interaction and student presentation actually illustrated that Teacher X needed to know more about her students' needs and the effectiveness of interactions in the class.

5.4.3 Reviews on What Had Been Done

During observations, Teacher X was found to try putting her ideas on teaching literature into practice. Activities like a train as a metaphor, student individual presentation, and self-check of homework in Teacher X's class illustrated Teacher X's efforts to motivate, interest, and guide students in reading and thinking. In Teacher X's class, another way to attract students' interest was talking about something connected to their real life. She explained the purpose as follows:

> (...) this is something that is relevant to their growth and maybe in the future they will meet the same situation. So, I like to talk as long as it can be related to literature. I find students are interested in this. Literature itself is something that can nourish one's spirits and so it must be relevant to people's real life. After all, young students who are growing must be interested in guessing what kind of person they will become in the future, how society will be, and how to support their spirits. I think this point is very important for students.

Obviously, in Teacher X's mind, the literature was from reality and also helpful for students in their real life, thus she guided students in the way of bridging the gap between the class and life. That was her general purpose of teaching literature as she said in the first interview. But sometimes when she taught specific texts, she had to consider the realistic goal of students. The following statement reflects a tension between the reality and the ideality in her mind:

> What I could do was to guide them to be closer to my understanding, but in essence guide them to be close to the standard answer, because my understanding was usually close to it (...) If I want them to understand the standard answer, I must have evidence to support me. After all, they have to be marked in the educational system (...) I always tell them,

don't feel depressed if the teacher denies your answer, and you should adjust your emotion and think about why there a difference (...) Sometimes, one expressed a strange idea; I will not deny it directly. But sometimes, I also have to tell them what is wrong. So, I know how to balance. I need to know better of them because they have diverse backgrounds.

It can be seen from her statement that Teacher X knew this tension. As she said in the first interview, what she did was to try to guide students to be interested in reading and thinking rather than fully shifting to the student-centred mode of teaching immediately. This shift takes time, for both teachers and students.

5.5 Conclusion

Teacher X on the one hand made some pedagogical changes under the influence of an aspect of societal culture (*National Curriculum Reform of Basic Education*) and school culture (school principle), but on the other hand taught within the constraints of the classroom culture, such as the big class, the short lessons, the seating arrangement, the large number of texts, which is closely related to other aspects of societal culture such as the educational system, standardized-test, and the new curriculum of Chinese Language and Literature. Specifically, Teacher X often confronted three dilemmas during teaching: The *first* dilemma was confronted in the discussion using the train metaphor. On the one hand, Teacher X invited student reading starting with an open question, but on the other hand, she denied student reading that seemed to be deviant or superficial. The *second* dilemma related to Teacher X's expectations for students to sometimes question standard answers, while in general, she requested them to learn to think close to the standard answers. The *third* dilemma referred to a situation when the teacher tried to facilitate student engagement in discussions by changing some approaches, but still she controlled students' exploration through controlling the materials, the topic, the activity, and the form of discussion. The above three dilemmas commonly show a tension between Teacher X's concern for student development of reading and thinking competence and the real obstacles in the current learning environment. This tension in the teacher's mind also impacted her way of positioning. Sometimes she intentionally shifted her position in order to engage students in the classroom interaction, but in general she manipulated the classroom interactions which expressed her moral positioning. The specific positions of the teacher and students and the relevant stance tools in three types of classroom interaction are summarized in Table 5.4.

Table 5.4 Positioning and Envisioning in Teacher X's Class

Type of interaction	The Teacher's positioning	Students' positioning	Stances used
Teacher-Student (Train as a metaphor)	*Moral positioning:* A magisterial teacher who confronted with a dilemma	*Moral positioning and forcedly positioning of students:* Forced responders	Stance 2
Student-Student (Student presentation, self-check of homework)	*Deliberately self-positioning:* 1. A manipulator who also examined before and commented after 2. A facilitator of student thinking to be close to the standard answer	*The teacher's deliberately positioning of students:* 1. Speakers and audiences who learnt from each other 2. Active readers who were supposed to internally interact with self	Stance 4
Student-Text	*Deliberately self-positioning:* A guider of reading through adding different activities	*The teacher's deliberately positioning of students:* Different positions in different activities	Stance 1, 2, 3

Apparently, there were mainly moral positioning and intentional positioning in Teacher X's class, without performative positioning. This demonstrated Teacher X decided the positions that students could adopt in the interactions despite her shifting the positions sometimes. This shifting of positions indicated the teacher's efforts to engage students in the classroom interaction, however in fact students still had fewer possibilities to interact with peers, compared with Danish students. Even though it seemed that students' talk was increasing in Teacher X's class, the type of interaction was still unitary, and the interaction among students was rare. Thus, the possibility of positions that students could occupy was confined to the interaction between the teacher and students.

In conclusion, the above findings partly verify that Chinese classrooms had something new and different from traditional ways of teaching. But the findings also indicate that these new pedagogical changes that are facilitated by the new curriculum reform (societal culture) are at an early stage and are also partly impeded by some aspects of contextual cultures (e.g., the educational system, the classroom cultures), which brings restrictions for student development.

Chapter 6
The Case of Teacher Z

This chapter presents the findings of another Chinese case, Teacher Z, and the descriptions and analyses are done using a comparative view from which characteristic activities and different ways of interacting in Teacher Z's class are highlighted and discussed. When analysing this case, several excerpts are frozen-frame as with the previous three cases. But in contrast, fewer excerpts are adopted in this chapter because of the learning content of the class and the teaching style of Teacher Z.

6.1 Contextual Cultures

6.1.1 Profile of the School

This Chinese case school is E High School, which is a rising secondary school that was founded in 2008 and features foreign language teaching and aims for the long-term development of every student. This school, involving the lower secondary school and upper secondary school, has 33 teaching classes with over 1,150 students in total. As with the Z High School, Chinese societal cultures are also embodied in the school cultures of E High School. In the wake of the nation-wide fundamental educational reform (*National Curriculum Reform of Basic Education*), this school also offers both compulsory and elective courses. Meanwhile, E High School is a foreign language school, so its school culture is also partly influenced by some aspects of western culture. On the one hand, the school is a general Chinese secondary school that firmly supports Chinese traditional values and sets an aim of "fulfill moral education through teaching activities". On the other hand, the school aims to create a democratic, respectful, open, and active campus atmosphere through launching diverse campus activities. Considering the integration of two cultures, the E High School describes itself as a school that pays a considerable amount of attention to the fostering of students' interests, various abilities, and study habits. Thus, it claims to encourage students to develop active learning, the competence of independent learning, and collaborative study.

6.1.2 Profile of Teacher Z's Class

Not as large as Teacher X's class, Teacher Z's class was an ordinary second-year class with 35 students. The following Table 7.1 shows an overview of Teacher Z's class.

Table 6.1 Profile of Teacher Z's Class

Grade of class	Number of Students	Seating	Lesson length	Lessons per week	Number of lessons observed	Curriculum
2nd-year	35	Vertical rows	40 minutes	5	7	One volume of *The Records of the Grand Historian* by Sima Qian: *The Biography of Confucius*; One chapter in *Confucian Analects (Lun Yu)*: Do Something in Moderation; A topic on "How to Write a Good Essay on the College Entrance Examination"

The seating and the lesson length were the same as Teacher X's class. Because of the lower student number, there were only four to five students in each vertical row, which made Teacher Z's classroom looked less dense.

223

6.1.2.1 Comparing the Seating Arrangement in Danish and Chinese Classes

Comparing Chinese classes with Danish classes, the distinct seating arrangement indicates the differences between the classroom cultures. By and large, the seating arrangement of Danish classrooms, including Teacher S's and Teacher P's, were flexible, which means that the seats in the classroom could be changed and rearranged to prepare for some activities. For example, seats were rearranged in several groups (Teacher S's classes), in a circle (Teacher P's class), or in rows (both teachers' classes). On the contrary, the seating arrangement of the Chinese classrooms was stable and unified. This was not only because of the large number of students in the Chinese classes but also because of the ordered and disciplined school cultures.

Further, the flexibility of Danish classrooms was also embodied in the utilization of computers and electronic media. During the lesson time, especially when working with groups, Danish students were allowed to bring and use computers and electronic media to help them to reach various materials, whereas in the Chinese classes of this book, usually students were less allowed to use electronic media. As a matter of fact, Chinese teachers either offered other relevant materials for the students, as Teacher X did with *The Temple of Earth Park and I,* or extended the class time to the outside of the class where students needed to find materials on their own, for example, student presentations in both Chinese classes. These strategies were used to maintain the interaction with students and among students without occupying much lesson time.

6.1.2.2 Syllabus and Specific Learning Content

Teacher X and Teacher Z used the same series of textbooks that were published by the same publisher, although they taught different grades of students. Specifically, Teacher X was teaching the compulsory texts of the first-year textbook of the series, whereas Teacher Z, who had finished compulsory texts, was teaching elective texts from the second-year textbook.

Table 6.2 Curriculum Units and Activities in Teacher Z's Class

Classroom observed	Curriculum units observed per course	Characteristic teaching methods
2nd-year (7 lessons)	Each lesson started with a student presentation	Student presentations about student translation and interpretation of *Confucian Analects* in contemporary Chinese language before each lesson
	During class break	Putting up students' better written essays for others to read (exchanging written assignments)
	One volume of *The Records of the Grand Historian* by Sima Qian: *The Biography of Confucius* (from 1st to 3rd lesson)	Chose several students to read aloud the paragraph *The Biography of Confucius* one by one (1st lesson); The teacher's lecture (translation and interpretation) on in contemporary Chinese language (1st to 3rd *The Biography of Confucius* lesson)
	One chapter in *Confucian Analects:* Do Something in Moderation (4th lesson)	Chose several students to write paragraphs in *Do Something in Moderation* from memory; The teacher's lecture on the word of *moderation*; The teacher's lecture (translation and interpretation) on the words and content
	Confucian Analects (Lun Yu) (5th lesson)	Student presentations about a paragraph in *Confucian Analects*, sharing student personal understanding and comments based on comments of two other famous critics
	How to Write a Good Essay on the College Entrance Examination (6th lesson and 7th lesson)	The teacher's lecture; (1 lesson) A student who got a high score in an essay talked about his/her idea and way of writing (1 lesson)

In contrast to Teacher X's class, which focused on reading the modern and contemporary literary texts, Teacher Z's class spent all the time reading some chapters of a traditional Chinese classic work of art, *Confucian Analects*, and the biography of Confucius during the seven observed lessons.

For Teacher X's class, the compulsory texts were more important considering that these texts were part of the assessment. In fact, the observations in Teacher X's class showed that sometimes she was a little hurried to push students to be closer to her understanding. On the contrary, Teacher Z seemed to slow down her teaching pace, dealing with a traditional classic work that was difficult for students to read and understand. But meanwhile, the content of the last lesson during the observations demonstrated that she also took students' scores into account as did Teacher X, spending two lessons on the topic of how to write an essay in the College Entrance Examination.

As for the teaching activities, there were also commonalities and differences between the two Chinese teachers. In Teacher Z's class, student presentation was also applied at the beginning of each class, but the topic was only about *Confucian Analects*. Similar to Teacher X, there was no group work in Teacher Z's class too. But Teacher Z spent more time on the lectures (five lessons) and less time on whole-class discussion compared with Teacher X's class. In other words, other than student presentation at the beginning, other classroom interactions in Teacher Z's class occupied a small proportion of lesson time. It follows that another new way of framing interactions after class was designed by Teacher Z to compensate for the inefficiency of the lesson time, which involved putting up students' written essays or assignments for other students to read, compare, and discuss. This was named *exchanging written assignments*. Therefore, it can be seen from Table 6.2 that Teacher Z also made some new changes in her class to align with the trend of reform, while at the same time, she maintained some traditional methods.

6.2 Pre-Observation: Teacher Z's Perceptions of Literature Teaching

6.2.1 Reflexive Positioning

Teacher Z was an experienced literary teacher who has been teaching

Chinese language and literature for over twenty years. She thought that an ideal teacher not only taught students how to read and understand literature in the class but also taught them how to be human beings in society.

Excerpt 6.1

TZ: The class time is very short, so I think a good literary teacher in class should not only transmit knowledge to students but also show them the way in future, teach them how to be a human being. That is the way to connect what they learn in class with one's life after class (...) if a teacher wanted to be good at teaching literature, s/he needs to know about her/his students, be concerned about them, be observant, and conscientious person, and be aware of students' behaviors and their inner world.

The above statement indicates that Teacher Z was concerned with what students learnt from the literature and cared about students' inner world. She thought the essence of learning literature was to know about others' feelings and to acquire one's own perceptions and inspirations, thus she regarded literature as a subject of "Human Study". In her view, people's understanding of literature was something from one's perceptions and feelings, so the interpretation could not be seen as good or bad, but as appropriate or inappropriate. In her words, "appropriate interpretation" was something that "was acceptable for most of the people". Her perceptions of this subject reflect her focus on the essence of literature that nourishes people's spirits rather than on the acquisition of an understanding of literary texts. It indicates that Teacher Z reflexively positioned herself as a teacher who also had the responsibility of moral education through teaching literature, in line with the school aims — fulfilling moral education through teaching activities.

6.2.2 Purpose of Teaching

Teacher Z's focus on the essence of literature was also embodied in her purpose of teaching. She thought reading literature could help people to set up their views of life, thus the purpose of teaching for her was to help students "to set up a spiritual foundation for their future life" through reading. Meanwhile, she also aimed to foster students' literacy through engaging them in reading literature. The following statements explained her two purposes:

> The reading comprehension actually is related to literacy. Thus, teaching literature is to foster students' abilities of listening, speaking, reading, and writing, among which speaking is very important. But how literacy is taught? I think students need to be well cultured, and read texts by heart, so they may reach other people's internal world through words in texts (...) I think in class what a literary teacher can do is sparking students' interests in a text, a topic, or an idea, and then they may spend time on exploring it after class.

In line with what the school claims (encourage students to develop an attitude of active learning, the competence of independent study, and collaborative study), Teacher Z's purpose of teaching indicated that she also considered the development of students' abilities, but she also had to consider the reality of the class. The same as Teacher X's class, in Teacher Z's class the lesson time was not enough for students to have much talk. As an alternative approach, Teacher Z said in class she focused on how to spark students' interests, trying to inspire students somehow and guiding them to form good study habits. This was caused by the classroom cultures with the short lesson length and large student number.

6.2.3 Perceptions of How to Engage Students

Teacher Z's awareness of fostering students' learning habits influenced her perceptions of teaching and learning literature. She explained that according to the aims of the school, students in her class were also encouraged to have an active learning attitude. Thus, she did not care much about teaching methods but stressed the learning methods of students. In her view, if what the teacher said interested students, they would like to listen, learn, and assimilate actively. In the same class, students had different interests; some paid attention to this part of the content, and some might have interests in another part. As a teacher, she said she tried to talk about something interesting and informative, and students might understand this "something" from various perspectives, which made a variety of understandings in the classroom. Thus, in Teacher Z's view, students who actively engaged in reading might choose and learn what they needed and were interested in, using different methods that were appropriate to them. It followed that Teacher Z regarded understanding as a fluid and flexible thing, instead of a stable or mechanized thing. In this sense, as a literary teacher, Teacher Z had a reader-response inspired concept of the reader, which means that different students had diverse understandings based on their own perspectives.

Specifically, after talking about her purpose of teaching, Teacher Z also talked about her thoughts about how to encourage student active learning, which were embedded in the school cultures. As a strategy to train students active learning, Teacher Z noticed that the cultivation of students' interests depended on how she tried to foster their learning habits. As a whole, every year, the group of literature teachers in the school offered a reading list for students at the beginning of that year. As a leader of this literary teacher's group, Teacher Z suggested her students read in their leisure time as many books as they could and write a review of one book that they favored at the end of the semester. In this way, she offered the choice for students to select what they were interested in. Moreover, as she said, it pushed students to practice reading and writing every once in a while and helped them to develop their interest in reading and writing and to form a habit. What she did indeed indicated her concern with students' spirits since she thought of writing as a type of interaction, through which she knew about students' inner worlds.

Her purpose of fostering students' habits of reading and writing was also embodied in her selection of curriculum. Teacher Z selected *Confucian Analects (Lun Yu)*, which was one of the elective texts in the second-year textbook as essential learning content, and spent much time interpreting and discussing it. *Confucian Analects (Lun Yu)* as a widely-known traditional classic containing philosophy, politics, and history. Its core, the *Confucianism*, constitutes the mainstream of Chinese culture and ideology. Considering the significance and the ideological meaning, Teacher Z decided to teach *Confucian Analects* including the biography of Confucius through the old language and obscure meaning of *Lun Yu*, which increased the difficulty for student reading and understanding. As matter of fact, many teachers who had a clearer orientation toward the *College Entrance Examination* in the E High School did not select this topic, or spent much less time on reading and reciting some *"pearls of wisdom"* in it, because as an elective text *Confucian Analects* would probably not be included in the examination. In contrast, Teacher Z maintained this text as she thought that reading, interpreting, and discussing the meaning and principles of *Confucianism* could trigger students' interests in reading a Chinese classic, improve their literacy of ancient language, help them to understand Chinese culture more deeply, and influence their views of life and values. Again, this choice of Teacher Z indicated her focus on the essence of the literature and concern of students' spiritual world that she viewed as being nourished by reading literature.

Summing up, Teacher Z deliberately expressed herself (deliberately self-positioning) as a literary teacher who should consider students' interests, their perspectives, their learning attitude, and their spirits during teaching, similar to Teacher X who also noticed student interests. In contrast, Teacher

Z did not care much about ways of teaching, instead, she expected students to form their own learning methods. This perception of Teacher Z indicated her awareness of fostering student active learning attitudes and the habits of reading and writing, in line with the aims and policy of the school. But embedded in the educational culture, Teacher Z also had to follow the curriculum of the ministry at the same time.

6.3 During-Observation: Three Types of Classroom Interactions

Table 6.2 shows that in general Teacher Z used more lectures than discussions (either whole-class discussion or group discussion) to frame classroom interactions. Moreover, whole-class discussion was only framed in a one-to-many mode and intermixed in the teacher's lectures. She talked much when teaching *Confucian Analects*, though she also gave opportunities for student presentations in between. Thus, the classroom interaction in Teacher Z's class was not as varied as in the Danish classes discussed earlier.

6.3.1 Interaction between the Teacher and Students: *One-to-Many Mode*

In Teacher Z's class, there was the rare whole-class discussion between the teacher and individual students as was the case with Teacher X's Chinese class (e.g., the *train metaphor*). Teacher Z often applied a special mode of interaction with the whole class instead, which is termed *one-to-many mode* in this book. This mode refers to a pattern where more than one student answers a question when the teacher asks a question (Figure 6.1).

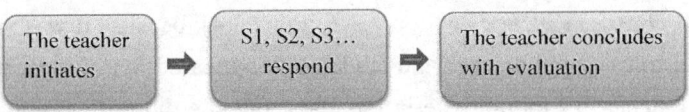

Figure 6.1 *One-to-Many Mode* of the Interaction between the Teacher and Students

Figure 6.1 shows the process of how the mode worked in the class. It can be seen that *one-to-many mode* describes a short and unidirectional pattern of IRE between one teacher and someone else in the classroom. For instance, Teacher Z asked a question to the whole class, if somebody or several students informally spoke out or murmured something when they were seated, this "something" was accepted by the teacher as a response from students. The interaction usually ended up with the teacher's evaluation if no other responses came from students. Hence, the interaction framed in this pattern was usually short without successive discussions between the teacher and students or among students.

During the period of observation, Teacher Z never invited an individual student to stand up and deliver an answer, because she thought the pattern of IRE was a single interaction between the teacher and one student, which was a time-consuming means of interaction. Instead, she often employed the *one-to-many mode* when she lectured on the biography of *Confucius*. There were seven lessons observed in Teacher Z's class. From the first lesson to the third lesson, Teacher Z interpreted the old language in the text and told the story in the contemporary Chinese language with a PowerPoint including details of Confucius's life. She told the story of Confucius for some time and then asked a question. After several students who were seated responded informally, she continued talking and after a while asked another question. In this way, the one-to-many mode was merged with her lectures. Obviously, in this process Teacher Z performed as the narrator of the story, and her identity as a lecturer who transmitted information to students dominated. Correspondingly, students were morally positioned as receivers of the information. This positioning was moral (Harré & van Langenhove, 1999; Davies & Harré, 1990, see Section 2.3.3, Table 2.4), because it was related to the social roles of the teacher and students. It appeared that this mode was a type of Teacher Z's monologue in the class, but she did not agree with that. She explained that if the teacher only talked with one student, others might be distracted from what they were studying, which was not beneficial for other students. Thus, she expected to provoke the thoughts of most students when she asked a question through this mode, creating a chance for those students who did not have the confidence to express their ideas in public but still wanted to contribute something to be able to answer the question. It can be seen that Teacher Z was concerned with the majority of students rather than the individual when teaching.

The occurrence of *one-to-many mode* of interaction was indeed affected by the classroom culture in Chinese classes. This *one-to-many mode* has been popular in many Chinese classrooms in the last few years, as a result of the increasing numbers of students in classes with short lesson lengths. Many Chinese teachers including Teacher Z prefer asking questions to the whole class together rather than individual students, as an alternative way of interacting with students. Further, the *one-to-many mode* of interaction also reflects Teacher Z's perception of the purpose of teaching literature. As mentioned earlier, Teacher Z thought of a literary teacher as a guide who sparked students' interests. She also thought a good literary teacher was a good speaker whose interesting talk could trigger students' interests and even thinking while they were seated and listening. If students actively engaged in thinking, gradually they could form the habit of reading and thinking. Thus, in her view, the kind of activities used in class was not so important, but whether students engaged in thinking by attending these activities was the key. From the perspective of envisioning theory, this idea of Teacher Z was consistent with Langer's *literary thinking* (Langer, 2011a), which emphasised the importance of thinking ability during the process of reading literature. But in Teacher Z's class students' thinking only occurred under a premise — that is, these students needed to be self-disciplined and really racked their brains to think when the teacher asked questions. Langer (2011a) advocated that literary teachers foster student literary thinking through some strategies, such as stance tools or "offering enabling strategies" to enable students to think and do. Nevertheless, as Teacher Z said in the first interview, she did not think about methods, instead, she only thought about the teaching content that could be interesting for students with an expectation that students were interested in and being active in studying and thinking. Her thoughts of students' active learning thus aligned with the aims of the school.

- ***Summing Up: Teacher Z was the Lecturer of the Biography of Confucius***

Teacher Z morally positioned herself as a lecturer and positioned students as the audience when discussing the biography of Confucius. During the lectures, Teacher Z indeed asked questions and students responded. This interaction between the teacher and students was framed in a mode of *one-to-many* in which more students seemed to join in the conversation with the teacher. But in reality, students' short and simple responses could not contribute to continuous discussions in class. While it was expected to produce the internal dialogic interaction in one's mind, the *one-to-many* mode was a type of traditional IRE/recitation formally.

6.3.2   The Interaction between Students and the Text

In Teacher Z's class, how the teacher and students read texts can be examined through analysing the teaching of two students' written assignments — one is a written task of *Confucian Analects,* and the other is the exam-oriented composition.

6.3.2.1   Written Assignment with Two Specialized Interpretations

The following example of working with Chapter XIII Tsze-Lû, Section XXIV in *Confucian Analects* demonstrates the incorporation of two sorts of interactions — one was the interaction between students and the text, the other was the interaction between the student and the student. Excerpt 6.2 shows the full version of the written task assigned by the teacher.

Excerpt 6.2

My Reviews

Chapter XIII Tsze-Lû

Section XXIV of *Confucian Analects*

Tsze-kung asked, saying, "What do you say of a man who is loved by all the people of his neighbourhood?" The Master replied, "We may not for that accord our approval of him." "And what do you say of him who is hated by all the people of his neighbourhood?" The Master said, "We may not for that conclude that he is bad. It is better than either of these cases that the good in the neighbourhood love him, and the bad hate him." (Translated by James Legge, 1893)

Written assignment: Read and think about two commentaries, and write down your commentary from your perspective.

[Two well-known commentaries]

Xi Zhu: All the people of his neighbourhood can judge good or bad, but they also like or dislike the people who belongs to the same group or not. So, one person who is loved by the good but not hated by the bad must have done something dishonest; one person who is hated by the bad and is not loved by the good must have something rebarbative.

Huaijin Nan: This dialogue from Confucius and his student tells a fact that "the masses are blind" in modern Chinese, so it is hard for one person to judge good or bad. Therefore, when held local elections, we have to notice that things that the masses deem wrong are not necessarily wrong; the things the masses deem right are not necessarily right. Thus, the difficulty of governing can be seen.

(Appendix 6.1 Chinese version)

This task requested students to read, interpret, and express understandings of the chapter in Chapter XIII Tsze-Lû, which is well-known and philosophically deep. In fact, there are many commentaries interpreted and reviewed in this chapter, and among them the task contained two famous examples, Xi Zhu and Huaijin Nan. From the requirement of the written task, it can be seen that Teacher Z not only expected students to interpret and understand the meaning of the chapter, but also asked them to compare the two specialized commentaries and think about them critically, and then to form their own understandings. In other words, translating the old Chinese language into contemporary language was the first step. Interpreting the meaning of the words was the second step. The most important step for students was writing down their ideas based on their interpretations and thoughts through a comparison of two famous commentaries. Various skills of students were practiced in the process of finishing this task, which was consistent with the aims of the school to foster students' various abilities of learning.

It was claimed in the first interview that Teacher Z did not care much about teaching methods. However, in reality, her way of teaching *Confucian Analects* could be related to stance tools in Langer's (2011b) sense. Teacher Z seemed to help students to build up a rich envisionment of Confucius and his philosophies through changing *stances* (Langer, 2011a) that were related to the text. Beginning with *The Biography of Confucius* during the first three lessons, Teacher Z gave lectures on the biography of Confucius and the specific chapters in *Confucian Analects*, connecting Confucius' life with his words and deeds that the class was reading *Confucian Analects*. Through this connection, students stepped into materials and built up a cohesive envisionment of Confucius and the meaning of some chapters, which can be seen as using Stance 1 (Getting started with the material) and Stance 2 (Developing understanding of the material). In accordance with the requirements of the written assignment, Teacher Z requested students to step out the whole book and focus on a certain chapter, and then to rethink commentaries from two reviewers as well, which can be related to Stance 3 (Leaving from the material).

Meanwhile, Teacher Z asked students to present their viewpoints and understandings from one perspective in papers that had been handed in after finishing. Thus, in other words, students had the chance to choose the angle of presentations. Indeed, there could be several perspectives/angles drawn from the meaning of the chapter, such as how to govern, how to judge the good and the bad, how to form strong values. In reality, eight students' written short papers that were collected from Teacher Z's class, demonstrated that some students were able to propose a viewpoint, elaborated the point, and discussed with evidence, not only interpreting the meaning. During writing, they used various perspectives based on their background knowledge, reading experience, and relevant materials they found to understand the meaning of the chapter. Also, some of them commented on the famous commentaries from Xi Zhu and Huaijin Nan who interpreted the meaning based on their life experience in their eras. Thus, these students were engaged in critical thinking through Stance 4 (Think critically about the material). The diverse perspectives that these eight students mentioned in their writings are summarized as below:

(1) The classification of human being in Confucius's view.

(2) How to judge the good and the bad?

(3) The saying "the masses are blind" is not necessarily right.

(4) What is a real gentleman like?

(5) The relationship between the judgment of good or bad and relativism, in other words, moderation, the golden mean of the Confucian school.

(6) Confucius words "the good in the neighbourhood love him, and the bad hate him" is not necessarily right.

(7) Hypocrite and the real villain.

(8) Confucius' words "Your good, careful people of the villages are the thieves of virtue".

Clearly, the above perspectives were different from each other. Comparing these perspectives with the two commentaries listed in the task, it is evident that these students did not follow the two commentators' views, but rather they queried some points in the two commentaries, discussing and arguing using some evidence found from other relevant materials. Also, they picked up something new from the meaning of the chapter through making connections to other relevant knowledge and materials they knew, such as resources from other chapters, or the thought of moderation, and the culture of the Confucian school. Excerpt 6.3 shows two students' written assignments. One criticized the commentary of Huaijin Nan[①], and the other proposed a new point of view.

Excerpt 6.3

R: it seems to be impossible to govern the country in an ideal condition. I don't think Huaijin Nan's words "the masses are blind" are right. It is said that the masses are blind because they cannot go together facing the same direction. I think each person in the community has his/her aim, so when all the persons orient toward their personal aims, this community will be in chaos.

F: "The good or the bad" are two opposite concepts, but they are coexisting too. Huaijin Nan thinks that it is hard to judge the good or the bad for the masses, which I think is the same for all people. What we judge is in accordance to our moral standards. It is relativism.

These two students really engaged in critical thinking by criticizing Huainjin Nan's point of view (*"the masses are blind"*). They discussed and questioned one specialized interpretation (Huaijin Nan) and further expressed their own views. Thus, through thinking, discussing, and arguing, these students had further interaction with the text, rather than just sitting

---

[①] Huaijin Nan is a contemporary famous scholar, writer, and educator. He wrote a book regarding the stories and interpretation of *The Analects of Confucius*.

and listening to Teacher Z's lecture of Confucius and the meaning of chapter Tsze-Lû. In this sense, Teacher Z intentionally performed like a coach who firstly lectured on the topic, talking about her interpretations and understandings that represented the common understandings in this field, and then trained students to think critically and express their ideas, allowing other perspectives and understandings. Thus, she engaged students in reading and thinking by deliberately offering them multi-positions-reader, thinker, and commentator. But it is worth mentioning that these eight students' writings were selected and evaluated by both the teacher and students' peers as top written papers because of their rational and appropriate interpretations and unique points. It is probable that not every student was able to discuss and argue as these eight students did. As Teacher Z said in the first interview, she tried to trigger students' interests, but meanwhile, students had their own methods of learning. In other words, on the one hand, Teacher Z offered the chance for students to engage in reading, critical thinking, and expressing ideas, but on the other hand, she thought student learning also depended on whether they had interests or actively joined in. In Teacher Z's view, teaching was a cooperative work with students who were the agents of the action of learning.

6.3.2.2 Exam-Oriented Composition

How Teacher Z guided students to read and think about materials was also embodied in her teaching of writing exam-oriented compositions in the exams. In a lesson during the observations, she firstly gave a lecture on writing skills, commented on students' writing, and then invited students to reread and rewrite their essays using the skills.

Excerpt 6.4
What is the assessment rubric of a good essay?
Students are expected to write their thoughts on current issues in

society.

How to write a good exam-oriented essay? Four points:
Keep writing on the theme → have original conception and composition → include interesting examples → highlight the theme

Five steps of writing
a. Citation: Summarize materials given in the exam
b. Analysis: analyse materials and highlight the key point
c. Viewpoint: propose viewpoints and express essential points
d. Connection: make connections and demonstration with evidence.
e. Conclusion: recite materials and deepen the argument.

These skills refer to the specific procedures and steps of writing in the exams where students were requested to write based on textual material given in the exams. This means that the genre, the structure, and the main theme are restricted by the task. Teacher Z realized that it was difficult for students to get higher scores in writing instantly. Thus, after reading the first version of students' writings, she decided to give a lecture on the topic of writing, telling the students about writing skills. Apparently, this way of teaching was led by the exam-oriented goal, which might possibly result in the stereotyped essays of students. However, it is worth noting that Teacher Z did not only discuss writing skills with her monologic lecture, instead, she invited one high-achieving student to present his experience and approaches to writing in class. Excerpt 6.5 includes part of the student's presentation.

Excerpt 6.5
S: I don't think I am a clever student. I did not expect that the teacher would give me a good score. I only think as long as you grasp the methods of writing, all of you will get a better score. First, I extract

the theme of the material given in the test. Then I asked myself "What is the team spirit?" Around this question, I make a connection to real life in society. Frankly speaking, I don't think my understandings and interpretations are deep enough. But I point out the themes and explain my thinking and opinion.

This student presentation indicated that despite being restricted by the material in the exams, it was possible for some students to write differently and originally with personal understanding and opinions. Other students were expected to learn something useful from their peer's presentations. As a matter of fact, after the class, three essays written for the second time were evaluated as better by the teacher. This lesson demonstrated the teacher's combination of exam-oriented lecture and student-student interaction, which was influenced by two sides of societal cultures (the educational system and new reform of curriculum).

- *Summing Up: Teacher Z as a Coach Who Trained Students' Critical Thinking and Essays Writing in the Exams*

The interaction between students and the text indicated Teacher Z's awareness of the school's aim, attracting student interests and fostering their various abilities including writing skills in the exams. In the process, Teacher Z played the role of a coach who intentionally trained students to critically think of specialized interpretations and grasp the skills of writing exam-oriented compositions, indicating the effect of the educational culture and the teacher's purpose of teaching. In the process of completing the written assignment, students were deliberately offered positions as readers, thinkers, and commentators, expected to express their own views based on their knowledge background, the comparison of two commentaries, and other materials they found. It was also individual work which means that student active learning and independent learning were also encouraged and practiced in the process of dealing with the task.

6.3.3 The Interaction between the Student and the Student: in Class and after Class

As a way to replace student group discussions, in Teacher Z's class student presentations in class and the *Corner of Exchanging* after class were two typical ways of student-student interaction. Student presentations were framed similarly to Teacher X's class, but the *Corner of Exchanging* was a unique activity in Teacher Z's class.

6.3.3.1 Student Individual Presentation in Class

By coincidence, both Chinese teachers employed the student individual presentation at the beginning of each lesson as a way to engage them in talking. The topic of student presentation in Teacher X's class was diverse as long as it was relevant to literature, whereas in Teacher Z's class the topic was definitive. When working with *Confucian Analects,* each of the students was requested to give a presentation based on his/her interpretation and understanding of some words in the *Analects* at the beginning of each lesson. While Teacher Z assigned the big topic, she did not provide students with detailed materials or reference books. As students did in Teacher X's class, student presentations in Teacher Z's class were also the individual work of each student. They had to choose which chapter in the *Analects* they were interested in and search for relevant materials and reference books to help and support them to understand the meaning and philosophy behind the words. In contrast, students in Teacher Z's class were not requested to show their presentations to the teacher before they gave them. But some student presentations showed that supported by the evidence they found from materials out of class, some of them were able to give rational and interesting presentations. In this way, students were learning how to prepare a presentation on their own, search for materials, build interpretations on materials, provide evidence, and support ideas. In this sense, one of the aims of the school — fostering student independent learning competence — was carried out through student individual presentation without the teacher's guidance in advance.

In general, Teacher Z intentionally occupied the position of a commentator or evaluator who often supplemented something from different angles after the students finished their presentations, but sometimes Teacher Z also deliberately positioned herself as a listener who communicated and assimilated something new from these presentations. Simultaneously, other student audience members were expected to be thinkers who listened to, thought over, and discussed with presenters in and out of class. In the situation when Teacher Z applied the *one-to-many mode* of interaction with students, students were expected to be active thinkers who could choose what they were interested in learning. Similarly, during the student presentation, students were also deliberately positioned as thinkers who actively engaged in thinking on peers' presentations and learnt from them. In reality, the discussion between the student and the student in class that was ignited by a student presentation did occur sometimes (Excerpt 6.6).

Excerpt 6.6

P: It is said that there are the good and the bad. But they are not absolutely good or bad. So, society denies the absolute good or bad, thus the majority of people can live in the society. This idea is in line with the idea of Confucius — that is, benevolence means to love others.

L: I agree with what you said. In fact, the definitions of the good and the bad are obscure. For instance, a lie is not good, but if it is a white lie, we say it is not bad. Thus, there is no strict boundary. We need to use the Confucian moderation when looking at one thing.

K: I have a question. (P: Fine.) I think what you said about the good and the bad is objective, but I think the judgment of the good or the bad is subjective for each person (...)

Student P was the presenter, and Student L was invited by the presenter to give feedback. Even though Student L agreed with Student P's views, she used other evidence to support (e.g., she gave an example of "a white lie"). Afterwards, Student K actively engaged in the discussion between them, expressing his different opinions from Student P. Thus, the discussion among three students was established through giving feedback, addressing questions, and expressing his own opinions. Their positions were ascribed by their actions, which were related to performative positioning (Harré & van Langenhove, 1999; Davies & Harré, 1990). Five students interviewed agreed that the student presentation brought benefits for both the speakers and the audience. But one student also pointed out that whether the learning really occurred largely depended on whether they were well prepared and seriously listened and thought.

6.3.3.2 The Corner of Exchanging after Class

The above discussions on the teacher-student interaction like the *one-to-many mode*, and on the student-student interaction like student presentations have shown that the classroom interaction in Teacher Z's class was not sustained in class. In Teacher X's class, student presentations were seen as a way of extending class interaction to the outside, while in Teacher Z's class, other than student presentation another activity named *Corner of Exchanging* after class was framed by the teacher with the same purpose. Literally, the *Corner of Exchanging* was a space, in a corner of the classroom, where students exchanged their written assignments after class or during the class break. This corner was set by Teacher Z at the left back corner of the classroom. Figure 6.2 shows students' written assignments about Chapter XIII Tsze-Lû (Excerpt 6.2), which were put up on the *Corner of Exchanging*.

This activity about student written assignments was named as "My reviews" as written on the green paper at the top left corner. The big white paper included all students' written assignments, without students' names.

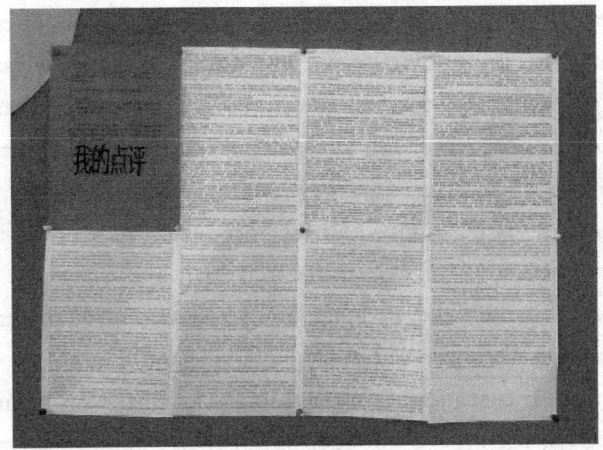

Figure 6.2 The *Corner of Exchanging* with the Written Task of "My Reviews"[①]

So, it was an anonymous exchange of homework. Specifically, the idea of the *Corner of Exchanging* was to let students exchange written assignments with peers, such as reading other's written assignments, thinking about others' ideas, writing styles, and opinions, and evaluating them as well. After that, according to students' evaluations, Teacher Z re-evaluated students' written papers again to see if her final evaluations were close to the students' evaluations. Then, the teacher selected the top papers and asked the writers to share their understandings by means of giving presentations. Thus, the *Corner of Exchanging* after class was connected to the student presentation in class.

Take working with one chapter in the *Confucian Analects* as an example. After students learnt *The Biography of Confucius* (1st to 3rd lessons) and one chapter in *Confucian Analects* (4th lesson), Chapter XIII Tsze-Lû, Section XXIV, they were assigned a task of written homework after class as shown in Excerpt 6.2 above, based on their interpretations

---

① The actual content of the students' homework is not shown in this book out of respect for copyright laws.

245

and understandings in different perspectives. Then the teacher numbered all the homework anonymously and put up all of them at the *Corner of Exchanging*, asking all the students to vote for 10 interpretations they thought most appropriate and the rationale for their opinions during lesson break. After voting, these 10 students were invited by the teacher to give presentations based on their interpretations during the fifth lesson. This type of presentation was requested to include a short discussion between the presenter and at least one student audience member who should comment on the presentation.

The presenting student was encouraged to give an opinion in his/her perspective, provide evidence, support his/her interpretation, and argue with others. Other student audience members had read different or new perspectives at the *Corner of Exchanging* before they listened to the presentations, so they had time to think, to compare all students' homework, and then to select.

In this process, all the students had the chance to interact with others and learn from others — no matter in an external oral way in the discussion after the presentation or in an inner way in their minds when they read and compared these written papers. Thus, in different phases, students adopted different positions — evaluators, presenters, or commentators, while Teacher Z was intentionally performing a guide who drove and meanwhile facilitated the whole process. As usual, Teacher Z was the only evaluator of student written assignments, but in this example, students joined in as co-evaluators. This shift supported students in learning something different and new from others through reading others' work and comparing it with their own, Teacher Z explained. In other words, this sort of assignment required each student to be involved, and usually, they needed to spend much time on reading, thinking, and comparing before evaluation. In this way, students were engaged in the task with multiple positions and corresponding responsibilities.

This example was the embodiment of Teacher Z's purpose of sparking students' interests, and the school's aim of facilitating student collaborative learning. Teacher Z insisted that an ideal teacher should trigger students' interests in what they were studying so that she designed the *Corner of Exchanging* to keep students interested in the topic after class. The main purpose for exchanging was to help students learn from each other, such as how to think about an issue from others' perspectives. Teacher Z thought, usually when students were studying something, their ideas were more easily influenced by peers than by the teacher. In this sense, in the *Corner of Exchanging*, students were working cooperatively by means of engaging in the joint task and cooperating through exchanging written assignments and inspiring each other.

- ***Summing Up: Teacher Z as a Facilitator Who Facilitated Multi-Positions of Students***

During the interaction between the student and the student, Teacher Z deliberately played the role of a facilitator who left some space for students to express their interpretations and understandings on some chapters of Confucius through presentations and written assignments, both inside of the class and outside of the class. Correspondingly, students were positioned variously — being presenters, audiences, commenters, and co-evaluators that were connected to their actions and responsibilities (performative positioning). In this way, different abilities of students were practiced through undertaking different responsibilities. Gradually, they were expected to improve their various learning competencies as the school aimed to help them to do so.

6.4 Post-Observation: Comments and Reviews

Teacher Z and her students reviewed and commented on the teaching practices after observation, highlighting the feature of Teacher Z's way of framing classroom interactions.

6.4.1 The Teacher's Comments

Teacher Z found that the presence of the researcher in the class did bring some effects on student engagement. The following excerpt presents how the teacher commented on students' contributions during observation.

Excerpt 6.7
I: What do you think about students' contributions?
TZ: I think the students were not active as much as before. Usually, there are many students responding when they are seated, but if somebody is present, they will be quieter. It might be because they are afraid to make mistakes (...) It might be also because now we are learning the *Confucian Analects*, but before that, we were studying proses, so I think the *Confucian Analects* may be more difficult for students to read and understand (...) In general, I can accept different readings of students if they get the point but the expression or the understanding is not deep enough. In my view, the understanding of literature is diverse (...) so I have to know about students' learning situation that varies from student to student. But I should set a goal that the majority of students can achieve.

Teacher Z's comment on student performance in class illustrated the mentality of students who care about their performance in public and are afraid of making mistakes in front of the whole class, just like some Danish students in the case of Teacher P's class. It also indicated that student engagement partly depended on how difficult the text was, and this is similar to Teacher P's class (students performed differently when working with two sets of WW1 poems-one was easier and the other was more difficult). In the second interview Teacher Z reiterated her thoughts about literary understanding that should vary from person to person. Therefore, compared with Teacher S who tried to guide students in deep understanding, Teacher Z did not demand a lot on student understanding but focused on their thinking in the process, which was one of the reasons for her using one-to-many mode as a form of teacher-student interaction. Indeed, the observations in Teacher Z's class verified that she did not care much how deep student readings were, but allowed diverse readings to be presented in the class (student presentation) or out of the class (exchanging written assignments). She did not talk with individual students in class, but was concerned about the overall learning achievements of the whole class by means of utilizing the interplay of students with different levels (e.g., she put up all students' written homework on the *Corner of Exchanging* and invited high-achieving students to share what they wrote and thought through student presentations).

6.4.2 Students' Comments

Five student interviewees agreed that Teacher Z's speech often dominated the class. However, students' responses indicated that they were fond of the teacher's lectures on something interesting. All five students interviewed expressed their enjoyment of listening to the teacher's talking that was relative to the history, politics, and culture of the text.

As a matter of fact, the result of CIQ also confirmed students' attitudes toward the teacher's lectures. There were 23 students (nearly 65%) who thought listening to the teacher's speech on the stories of Confucius and the background of *Confucian Analects* was the most interesting, in that they regarded listening as a way of knowing something divergent from the knowledge in the textbook. This, on the one hand, implies that the Chinese students preferred listening to talking in class, and on the other hand, verified the purpose of Teacher Z who thought of an ideal teacher as an attractive lecturer.

One student presented her impression of Teacher Z's teaching, indicating that students also noticed the feature of the teacher's framing:

On the one hand, Teacher Z taught us the skills of improving reading comprehension and writing a composition in the exams. And on the other hand, she told us much other useful information that will be of benefit for our future study and life. For example, we are learning the *Analects* that had nothing to do with the College Entrance Examinations; through reading, we can learn these predecessors' thoughts and views of point (...)

The above description reflects two orientations of Teacher Z-one is exam-orientation, the other is the orientation toward benefits of reading literature. It appears that sometimes there was a gap between these two goals, especially when students had to finish the curriculum in the limited lesson time. Another student interviewed thought Teacher Z's teaching tried to bridge the gap through a combination of teaching, balancing their exam-oriented thinking, and divergent thinking. Working with *Confucian Analects* was an example of Teacher Z's effort to bridge the gap. Indeed, Teacher Z accordingly applied a combination of teaching as the above student described — that is, a combination of the exam-oriented pedagogy (e.g., she asked students to recite some well-known chapters or sentences; taught skills of writing in exams) and the interactive pedagogy (e.g., student presentation, exchanging written assignments). In the students' view, the former way might rigidify their thinking, whereas the latter way could open their minds.

6.4.3 Reviews on What Had Been Done

The observations in Teacher Z's class verified that she did not pay much attention to the teaching method, as she said in the first interview. In contrast to the previous three teachers, Teacher Z did not make effort to attract students by changing teaching methods in the class. In one lesson, except the student presentation at the beginning of each class, she often talked and talked in a way of lecture with some *one-to-many* mode of interaction. Take the teaching of *Confucian Analects* as an example. In order to attract students' interests in learning, Teacher Z talked about *The Biography of Confucius,* interpreted the old language, introduced his life, and told historical stories of Confucius as a way to combine with interpreting meanings of chapters in *Confucian Analects.* The responses of her students showed that the majority of students liked this approach. Despite no active engagement in responding, some students, as the student interviewees said, engaged in thinking when the teacher talked about something that interested them or asked questions by means of the *one-to-many* mode. Furthermore, the student-student interaction during the student presentations and exchanging written assignments also demonstrated that students were indeed encouraged to think either in an oral way or a written way.

Regarding the student presentation, Teacher Z noticed students' abilities and their effect on the students' thinking. She said:

> In fact, what they present reflects their abilities of reading and understanding. I think it is reasonable. So, the student presentation is like an appetizer that opens a topic regarding one chapter of *Confucian Analects,* but my lecture that comes after their presentation works like the main meal that fills them with more knowledge built on what they have known. In this way, student thinking goes deeper and deeper.

The above statement again indicated Teacher Z's awareness of student thinking in the process of engaging in activities. She thought students' thinking was improved by the process — having initial thinking when they prepared the presentations and then learning deeper through comparing this with the teacher's interpretations presented in the lectures. As a matter of fact, two of the students who were interviewed agreed that the selection of relevant materials was challenging work, in that they had to read, compare, and integrate into their own ideas on the text. Also, they thought giving a presentation was offering the chance for peers to think through sharing others' ideas collected from the materials and build one's own ideas based on the materials.

Teacher Z also paid attention to student thinking in the process of exchanging written assignments. She confirmed the student-student interaction during the exchanging written assignments:

> I think they do (exchanging) because they need to vote, which is based on reading and comparison. They need to be pushed in this way. But they have criteria when voting because I think readers' understandings are divergent. By comparison, they will find which one is more rational. That is the feature of the subject, literature. There is no fixed answer in literature learning, which is the essence of literature education.

Teacher Z expected to engage students in reading and thinking through comparing with one other's homework. Some students responded that they really read peers' writings and thought over them, which was one way to enrich knowledge and learn from others. Further, it pushed students to take the assignment more seriously.

In brief, students' comments to some extent supported Teacher Z's expectations of students in engaging in these activities. But it is worth mentioning that students in Teacher Z's class had little chance to question what the teacher said or the answers to homework during the class. Students explained that sometimes even though they had different opinions from the teacher in class, they preferred talking with the teacher after class because the lesson length was short and they did not want to disturb the teacher's teaching procedures. This scruple of students showed the effect of the classroom culture of Chinese classes and also students' self-positions in the class — that is, they positioned themselves as powerless to challenge the teacher's authority in class.

6.5 Conclusion

The combination of exam-oriented pedagogy and interactive pedagogy was agreed by Teacher Z and her students as a means to integrate two orientations of literature education, aiming at keeping students interested. The teacher expected to attract students' interests in reading in class and then extended their interests from the inside of the class to the outside of the class. Thus, with the purpose of fostering students' active learning (the school aims), she on the one hand employed teacher's lectures that aimed to trigger student interests and thinking in class, and on the other hand, focused on student-student interaction that engages students in thinking and learning by utilizing students' lesson break time.

The combination of two pedagogies with two orientations affects the teacher's ways of positioning and instructing. Hence, with the shift of the type of interaction, the possibility of student positions that the teacher offered increased. The specific positions and the instructional tools used in the three types of classroom interaction are summarized as below:

Table 6.3 Positioning and Envisioning in Teacher Z's Class

Type of interaction	The Teacher's positioning	Students' positioning	Stances used
Teacher-Student (One-to-many mode)	*Moral positioning:* A lecturer	*Moral positioning:* Audiences who had the internal interaction in the mind	Stance 1, 2, 3, 4
Student-Text (Written assignments and exam-oriented compositions)	*Deliberately self-positioning:* A coach with two goals	*The teacher's deliberately positioning of students:* Readers, thinkers, and commentators	
Student-Student (Student presentation, exchanging written assignment)	*Deliberately self-positioning:* A facilitator of student-student interaction and critical thinking	*Performative positioning:* Multiple: presenters, audiences, commenters, and co-evaluators	

The above table demonstrates three types of positioning in Teacher Z's class, which is similar to Teacher S's classes. Using moral positioning, Teacher Z generally positioned herself as a lecturer who presented something interesting to motivate them to be active. Meanwhile, she deliberately positioned herself as a coach who trained students to form study habits by offering them the opportunity to actively engage in learning from others. Thus, during the engagement of student-student interactions (e.g., student presentation, exchanging written assignments), students' positions varied depended on their actions which were relevant to performative positioning.

Accordingly, Teacher Z's reading instructions aligned with her ways of positioning. As a whole, Teacher Z extended the interaction from the inside of the class (1st to 4th lesson: students learnt about *Confucian Analects* and Confucius' life through teacher's lectures intermixed with *one-to-many mode*) to the outside of the class (*exchanging written assignments*), and then returned to the inside of the class again (5th lesson: student presentation based on the results of exchanging written assignments). In this sense, when working with the whole unit of *Confucian Analects*, Teacher Z utilized both the inside of the class and the outside of the class, showing the combination of teacher-centred approaches (lecture, one-to-many mode) and student-centred approaches (student presentation and exchanging written assignments). It was also in line with the policy of the new curriculum reform (societal culture). In short, under the influence of the societal cultures and school cultures, Teacher Z's class featured two combined ways of teaching, creating the platform for utilizing after-class time and extending the student-student interaction beyond the class.

Chapter 7
Going Further with Comparing the Cases: Discussions and Conclusions

This chapter first synthesizes the empirical findings relative to two main research questions (RQ) of this study: (1) *How are the interactions between the teacher and students, the interaction between students and the interaction between students and texts framed in the Danish and Chinese literature classes?* (2) *What are the differences and commonalities between the framing approaches in Danish classes and Chinese classes?* The teacher-student and student-student interactions were investigated by means of analysing oral and written communications in class, whereas the student-text interaction was examined through analysing how the teacher instructed and facilitated students to read and think about literary texts. Based on the findings, the present chapter then discusses the research findings before discussing the pedagogical implications of the study. In closing, the chapter concludes by stating the contributions of this study.

7.1 Synthesis of Findings for RQ1: Summaries of the Findings

The main findings for RQ1 are presented in Chapters 3–6. This section summarizes these main findings in terms of the pattern of framing classroom interactions, and the notable features of positioning and reading instructions.

7.1.1 The Case of Teacher S

As analysed in Chapter 3, Teacher S framed different classes (2nd-year and 3rd-year) with different demands in accordance with student levels, aiming at gradually fostering the development of students' ability of independent learning from the first year to the third year in the Danish Gymnasium. With this intention, she used a wealth of group work and discussions (both whole-class discussion and group discussion) that were helpful for student-centred cooperative learning.

7.1.1.1 Pattern of Framing Classroom Interactions

Teacher S employed multiple methods for different objectives at different phases, such as lecture, teacher-led discussion/whole-class discussion, group work including student-led discussion, student presentation (oral and written), and student written assignment. But the focus of Teacher S was evident when she framed classroom interactions. She seldom applied the teacher's lectures. Even though she sometimes did, the lectures were short and also merged with whole-class discussions. In contrast, project-based group work, including group discussions and group presentations, was prolonged over several lessons. In the second-year class, Teacher S sometimes started with an instructional lecture when the class studied a new unit with new concepts (e.g., when they started to learn the horror fiction), sometimes group work occupied the whole process of studying (e.g., when they dealt with the miniature project of a British singer). In the third-year class, Teacher S directly began with group work that was maintained by the teacher during the whole semester (e.g., a project of different literary periods with different representative texts). In brief, the group work in Teacher S's classes was based on project work, which facilitated student independent and cooperative learning.

In summary, the pattern of the framing in Teacher S's classes can be depicted as shown in Figure 7.1.

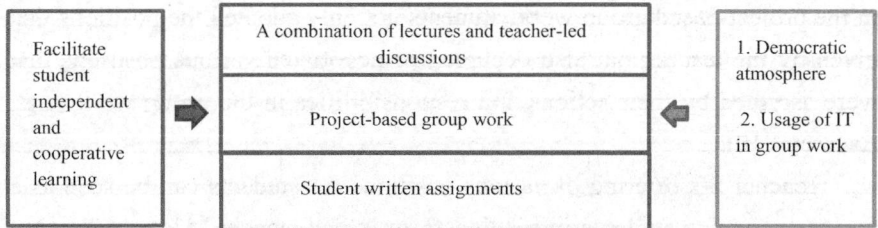

Figure 7.1 Pattern of Framing Classroom Interactions in Teacher S's Classes

This pattern involves three types of interactions, purposes of teaching, and the influence of contextual cultures. The three rectangles in the centre denote three parallel types of interactions: the teacher-student interaction, the student-student interaction, and the student-text interaction. The rectangle on the left refers to the central purpose of teaching. The purpose indicates the teacher's awareness of school policy and the influence of contextual cultures, which are included in the rectangle on the right.

In the case of Teacher S, her awareness of democracy affected her way of framing classroom interactions, opening other possibilities from student cooperative studies, such as group work and group discussions. Further, the usage of computers and electronic media in class supported students to work in groups independently and cooperatively. During interactions, Teacher S often shifted positions and reading instructions to guide students in deep reading.

7.1.1.2 The Feature of Positioning and Reading Instruction: Teaching Methods Relative to Stances

The analyses in Chapter 3 demonstrates that Teacher S always intentionally shifted self-positioning according to different tasks with different levels of students (Table 3.4). Meanwhile, through assigning different tasks and responsibilities, she offered various possible positions for students to occupy both in whole-class work and in group work. Especially in the project-based group work, students not only adopted the positions that given by the teacher but also occupied or negotiated various positions that were ascribed by their actions and responsibilities in the group work (e.g., Excerpt 3.10).

Teacher S's offering of various positions for students can be seen as a means to engage students in reading from varied stances. Also, in Teacher S's classes, different teaching methods that created various positions and responsibilities for students can also be related to the different stances (Langer, 2011b) from which students read and reflected on the texts. In lectures, when beginning to work with a literature topic or genre, Teacher S used questions to tap students' knowledge, guiding them into the text (Stance 1 Getting started with the material). In group work, students dealt with the chosen texts closely, making meaning of the text sentence by sentence with the teacher's guidance. At that time, they were in the texts and developing their understandings to move through the envisionment (Stance 2 Developing an understanding of the material). When giving presentations in the matrix groups (2nd-year class) or in the class as a way of student teaching (3rd-year class), students left the texts and stepped out of the presentations, rethinking what they had done and meeting new ideas (Stance 4 Think critically about the material), which they had not thought of, based on feedback from peers (e.g., Excerpt 3.12) and the teacher (e.g., Excerpt 3.16). The study findings have demonstrated that sometimes students did not engage in literature reading and thinking individually. Indeed, there was a tension between teachers'/schools' expectations and students' realities. But Teacher S's ways of positioning and teaching can be seen as a strategy of reading instruction, which is beneficial for students to build a cohesive and coherent envisionment of a topic, a genre, or a history of a certain period of literature.

7.1.2 The Case of Teacher P

As a quite young teacher, Teacher P usually made a goal-oriented and structured plan for each lesson, which is in contrast with Teacher S. Also, Teacher P preferred whole-class discussions and pair discussions to group discussions or group work that were more demanding in terms of students' independence. In Teacher P's class, making variations in her teaching is the main characteristic, which was used as a strategy to capture students' attention.

7.1.2.1 Pattern of Framing Classroom Interactions

Teacher P employed four interesting activities in the five lessons observed, namely *describing-terms exercise, drawing exercise, double-circle exercise,* and *circle exercise.* The previous three exercises were types of interaction between the student and the student, and *circle exercise* was an interaction between the teacher and students. These activities were designed not only to attract students' attention but also to engage students in practicing English as much as possible. In order to make the teaching varied, in one lesson each activity was combined with other methods or electronic media. For example, the first lesson of First World War (WW1) poetry was the introduction — the background, representative writers and poems, and terminologies of poems. Around the content, there were five activities involved in this lesson: brainstorm in pairs, whole-class discussion, playing videos, analysing propaganda posters, and a describing — terms exercise. In order to finish all the activities on time, Teacher P strictly manipulated the time of each activity, thus the lesson seemed to be a bit compact in ninety minutes. Through changing methods, Teacher P simultaneously shifted or switched the type of interaction to instruct students in reading between pair discussion and whole-class discussion. In the class of *Paradise Lost*, there were six switches in one lesson. By means of these "switches", students stepped into the poems, read them sentence by sentence, and interpreted them step by step with the guiding points from the teacher. But it is also worth noting that usually, the discussion in pairs was very short with only two to five minutes, whereas whole-class discussion was much longer. Further, in all cases, the duration of time, the form, the steps in the process, and the means of participation were planned and controlled by the teacher.

In summary, the pattern of framing classroom interactions in Teacher P's class is shown in the following Figure 7.2.

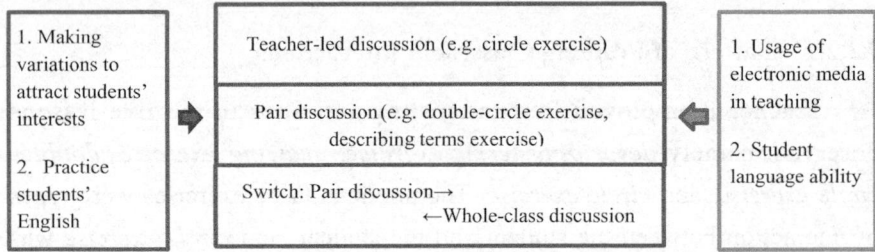

Figure 7.2 Pattern of Framing Classroom Interactions in Teacher P's Class

The third rectangle in the middle indicates that Teacher P usually shifted the type of interaction to instruct students to read and interact with texts (e.g., WW1 poems and *Paradise Lost*). As an English teacher of an English B-level class, Teacher P also took the purpose of practicing English and improving language ability into account when she designed various teaching methods. Besides, the usage of electronic media and IT also enriched the variety of teaching methods in the class.

7.1.2.2 The Feature of Positioning and Reading Instruction: Goal-Oriented and Structured Approach

In contrast to Teacher S, Teacher P did not intentionally shift positioning often. As mentioned earlier when describing the *double-circle exercise* (Excerpt 4.13), if an exercise in Teacher P's class was seen as a game, Teacher P always used deliberately self-positioning to express the role of a master of the game, and accordingly, students were deliberately positioned as players of the game, because it was the teacher who laid down the rules of the game, and students were forced to follow these rules during the participation (Table 4.3). This positioning affected how students learnt the text. Obviously, when studying a text, students were led by the teacher to understand and discuss the text step by step (e.g., in the *circle exercise* and *double-circle exercise*, student discussions were led by the teacher's questions), talking about the form, structure, theme, writing style, the background of the story, author's life, which might lead to a stereotyped interpretation based on the text and the author, rather than on the reader's personal experience. As a matter of fact, Teacher P and her students already classified the WW1 poem as war hero and *Paradise Lost* as the anti-hero, so their interpretations and understandings had to be relevant to these two themes. From the perspective of Langer (Langer, 2011a), Teacher P's questions were to some extent help students to develop understanding from more than one stance, as Excerpt 4.14 has illustrated, but for students with different ability levels, not all of them could engage in the literary thinking personally (Excerpt 4.12 Student J). While she always asked "why" questions or taught a topic with a comparative view because she wanted to motivate students by asking them to notice the purpose, this action again indicated Teacher P's goal-oriented and structured instructions.

7.1.3 The Case of Teacher X

Teacher X's class was one of the typical Chinese classes, which are jointly affected by the *Reform of Basic Education*, as well as the educational culture. Thus, Teacher X's teaching had the feature of combining traditional ways and new changes of teaching.

7.1.3.1 Pattern of Framing Classroom Interactions

In Teacher X's class, there were teacher's lectures, student presentations, and whole-class discussion (e.g., *train as a metaphor*), with rare group work. Her framing of classroom interactions represents a transition from teacher's dominated monologue to more dialogic interactions with student engagement. Being in the transition, it was almost inevitable that she would confront dilemmas that indicated tension between her traditional authoritative position and her consideration of the new trends based on student-centred teaching.

The tension was embodied specifically in whole-class discussion that was framed in the *train as a metaphor* (Excerpt 5.5, Figure 5.2). Of the nine lessons observed, five lessons included the teacher-led whole-class discussion framed by means of the train as a metaphor. The discussion was designed dialogically, but the result showed that not all the students had the chance to join in the dialogue with the teacher. Student engagement was also affected by their abilities and performance. The dialogue with the teacher was closed when the teacher pushed students to think in line with her thinking (Sa5 in Excerpt 5.5). But meanwhile influenced by the new reform, student presentation is becoming increasingly regarded as a preferable activity in many Chinese classrooms, indicating that the teacher is no longer the only speaker and students have the chance to be speakers in the class. Student presentation in Teacher X's class was individual work that involved external interactions between the teacher and students before the class, and internal interactions between the student and the student in the class. Thus, Teacher X framed her classes to extend the interaction inside the class to the outside of the class. Similarly, another kind of student-student interaction, self-checking of homework, also integrated the internal way of talking to oneself in one's mind and the external interaction with the teacher after self-checking (Excerpt 5.6). This approach was supposed to foster student independent learning and critical thinking. Figure 7.3 shows the pattern of framing classroom interactions in Teacher X's class.

When working with *The Temple of Earth Park and I,* Teacher X applied several teaching methods in different phases and positioned students differently, indicating her efforts to facilitate the interaction between students

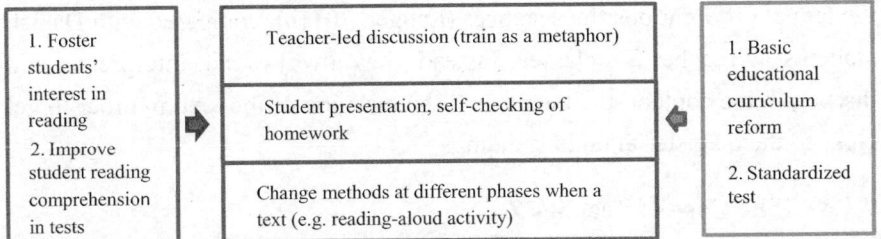

Figure 7.3 Pattern of Framing Classroom Interactions in Teacher X's Class

and the text, such as using reading-aloud activity and framing the whole-class discussion based on student volunteers rather than using train metaphor. Her efforts also demonstrated her awareness of the new curriculum reform in the literature classroom. While she expected to foster students' interests in reading literature, her teaching had to be shaped by the realities, such as the standardized tests and the large class with short lesson time.

7.1.3.2 The Feature of Positioning and Reading Instruction: Guiding Closely to the Magisterial Interpretations

Generally, Teacher X morally positioned students as learners who needed to think along the standard answers or the teacher's understandings when doing reading comprehension as homework or exams (Table 5.4). Through deliberately self-positioning and positioning of students, Teacher X attempted to create the opportunity for students to think independently and critically (e.g., whole-class discussion that started with open-ended questions and the self-checking of homework). However, finally, she closed the opportunity by presenting the magisterial interpretations or "correct" answers (e.g., Excerpt 5.6). In other words, she often guided students to think closely to her interpretations of the text. Besides, she did not offer the chance for students to explore the meaning independently through group work, or exchange ideas and reflect on the previous understandings through student-student discussions. In Teacher X's class, students had less chance to read the text at different positions/stances (Langer, 2011b), compared with Danish students in Teacher S's classes. Instead, they always read, interpreted, and discussed the content, the theme, and the meaning of the text, in order to get close to the magisterial understandings.

7.1.4 The Case of Teacher Z

Teacher Z's teaching methods used involved both traditional teacher-centred pedagogy and new student-centred pedagogy, indicating the influence of educational culture in China.

7.1.4.1 Pattern of Framing Classroom Interactions

When working with *Confucian Analects,* Teacher Z applied lectures, the *one-to-many* mode of IRE, student individual presentation, and student written assignment (exchanging written assignments). Apparently, the teacher's lectures were considered efficient for students to receive information from the teacher, indicating an orientation toward examination. For instance, after each lecture, she requested students to recite the well-known chapters and sentences in *Confucian Analects* and interpret selected chapters that were probably included in tests. But in Teacher Z's view, lectures could also produce interactions. She believed that interesting lectures could spark students' interests and then trigger their thinking and inner responses in students' minds through choosing what they needed and were interested in. In this sense, some active students might respond to the teacher's lectures in their minds and assimilate the words from the lecture to build up an *active understanding* (Bakhtin, 1981). Obviously, it was hard to infer if student response or assimilation did occur in their minds, thus whether the internal interaction occurred largely depended on how students responded to the teacher's lecture — being active or passive. The *one-to-many* mode of IRE in Teacher Z's class (Figure 6.1) also had two sides — the mode could be regarded as traditional IRE/recitation (external and oral) or a sort of internal interaction between students and the teacher. Student individual presentations and exchanging written assignments were products of working with some selected chapters in *Confucian Analects*. Joining these activities gave students the chance to make their voices heard through presenting viewpoints and understanding both in oral (student presentation) and written (exchanging written assignments) modes. In short, Teacher Z's pattern of framing the classroom can be summarized as a combination of teacher's monologue with an orientation toward examinations (e.g., the lecture on how to write essays in exams, one-to-many mode of IRE) and interactive ways of framing (e.g., student presentation, exchanging written assignments). The following figure depicts the specific pattern in Teacher Z's class.

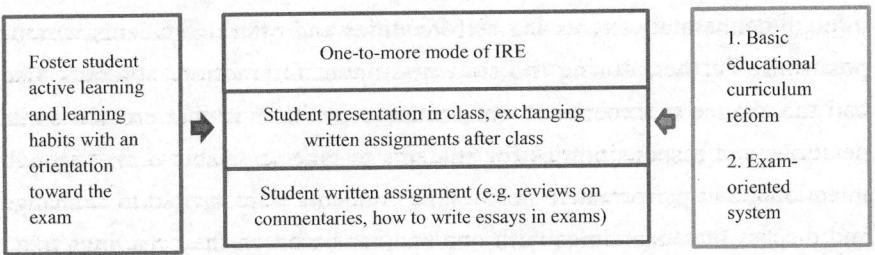

Figure 7.4   Pattern of Framing Classroom Interactions in Teacher Z's Class

When working with *Confucian Analects,* Teacher Z started with lectures and the one-to-many mode of IRE to set the background of the topic. But in between, student presentations in class and exchanging written assignments after class were employed to engage students in talking and discussing based on their readings. The student written assignments about students' reviews on two commentaries on Chapter XIII Tsze-Lû, Section XXIV could be seen as a strategy to engage students in the interaction with the text (Excerpt 6.3), because by joining in this activity, students were requested to think critically and have personal understandings. This assignment was designed to attract students' interests and encourage active learning, as well as foster their study habits, which were part of school cultures. But still, Teacher Z cared about students' writing skills in exams, which indicates the effect of educational culture.

7.1.4.2 The Feature of Positioning and Reading Instruction: Combining Two Pedagogies

The combination of two pedagogies in Teacher Z's class was also embodied in her positioning and reading instruction. **On the one hand**, Teacher Z played the social role of a lecturer. When she used lectures intermixed with one-to-many mode IRE, students were experiencing teacher-centred pedagogy in which knowledge was transmitted from the teacher. **On the other hand**, Teacher Z engaged students in continuous interactions through deliberately expressing self-identities and offering students various positions. Further, during the student-student interaction, students also had the chance to experience performative positioning that created some positions and responsibilities for students to take up (Table 6.3). Through intentional and performative positioning, students were invited to exchange and discuss understandings with one another based on their readings (e.g., student presentations, exchanging written assignments), which was related to the interaction-based pedagogy. Especially when dealing with the written assignment about Chapter XIII Tsze-Lû, Teacher Z was mostly using Stance 3 (Leaving from the material) and Stance 4 (Think critically about the material), pushing students to read and think of commentaries critically and then to form their own opinions.

In summary, the above interpretations of the framing patterns and the features of the positioning and reading instructions present one aspect of the distinctions among these cases, and also stress the influences of contextual cultures on the framing of classroom interactions. Other aspects of the distinctions will be explored in the following section which also discusses the commonalities shared by these classes.

7.2 Synthesis of Findings for RQ2: Differences and Commonalities

This section identifies differences and commonalities between case study findings of the four teachers as detailed in Chapters 3–6, responding to RQ2 of this study. Specifically, the differences between the cases are mainly embodied in the social participation structure (SPS) (Erickson, 1982), which indicates the divergent roles and relationships of participants in different classes. The commonalities are embodied in two interesting phenomena that are notable in both Danish classes and Chinese classes.

7.2.1 Difference in the Social Participation Structure (SPS)

Decades ago, there was some research in classroom discourse that drew attention to two aspects of the classroom. One was called the *Academic Task Structure* (ATS) and the other was termed the *Social Participation Structure* (SPS) that attracted sociolinguistic researchers' attention (e.g., Erickson, 1982). The *Social Participation Structure* (SPS) that was addressed by Erickson (1982) refers to a patterned set of restrictions on the configuration of interactional rights and obligations of participants of the interacting group; it "governs the sequencing and articulation of interaction" (Erickson 1982, p.154). The *Academic Task Structure* (ATS) refers to "a patterned set of constraints provided by the logical sequencing of instructional moves in the subject-matter content" (Erickson, 1982, p.154). Erickson asserted that the teaching in the classroom should involve these two structures together, considering that SPS was easy to neglect (Erickson, 1982).

Because the classroom interaction in this study involves both written communication and the interaction with the text, SPS is seen as not merely means a way of allocating different roles of partners in the interaction, but also is related to the ways of framing the three kinds of classroom interactions. In comparing the classrooms, there are two clear differences in SPS.

Firstly, the difference in positioning reflects the divergent SPS of each case. According to Erickson (1982), SPS in the classroom indicates the interactional partnership in learning and various communicative roles that participants take, for example, questioner (e.g., teachers) and roles in relation to answerer (e.g., students) roles (Erickson, 1982, p.167). Put simply, the roles and the relationship of partners are unfolded in SPS that are discourse-based. These roles can be regarded as positions that the speaker and audience occupy in an interactional conversation (Harré & van Langenhove, 1999). Specifically, the roles of teachers and students in SPS indicate how they position themselves and each other, and how much chance students have to engage in classroom interactions. The specific differences in SPS have been analysed in Table 7.1.

Table 7.1 The Feature of Allocation of Roles in SPS

Case	The feature of allocation of roles in SPS (Related to positions)
Teacher S	*Varied:* The teacher mastered main dimensions of ATS, but meanwhile offered multiple positions/roles for students to occupy/take. *Democratic:* Teaching activities were organised in a democratic way that respected the responses of students and emphasises the collaboration of each participant.
Teacher P	*Fixed:* Students were offered fewer possibilities to occupy other positions. *Structured:* The teacher controlled each step of ATS and SPS during class time.
Teacher X	
Teacher Z	*Combined:* The teacher controlled steps of ATS during the class time, but she extended SPS to out-of-class study and offered a platform for students' interaction after class.

In Teacher S's classes, students took up various situated identities or occupied multiple positions when they participated in different activities, which created pluralistic interactions in the classroom. In other words,

Teacher S used multiple ways of positioning. While Teacher S did some controlling of the ATS (e.g., the task, the topic of the group work), in the process, students still had possibilities not only to engage in each round of group work, but also to engage in the discussion of the whole project (e.g., students commented on the miniature project a British singer); students had opportunities not only to work individually, but also to work cooperatively (e.g., each group member was responsible for a part of the assignment, and then discussed together); students had the chance not only to learn from others but also to teach others (e.g., student teaching in the 3rd-year class). Therefore, so to speak, SPS in Teacher S's classes is varied. These teaching activities in Teacher S's class were organised in a democratic way that showed the teacher's respect for students' responses and emphasised the collaboration of each participant.

In Teacher P's and Teacher X's classes, students did not have many possibilities to occupy various positions, much less than in Teacher S's classes. The patterns of framing classroom interactions shed light on Teacher P and Teacher X's structured framing of the interactions with a clear goal. In other words, their positioning ways were limiting and goal-oriented. In Teacher X's class, student-student interaction was rarely other than student presentation at the beginning of the class. Thus, students had little chance to establish interactional partnerships with peers. While there was student-student interaction in Teacher P's class, such as the *double-circle* and *drawing* exercises, the teacher strictly orchestrated procedures of these activities, so students were forcedly offered a passive position where student-student interactions were restricted — they had to follow the teacher's plan on ATS. Thus, Teacher P's and Teacher X's classes demonstrate a fixed and structured SPS which leads to a stable and compact class environment.

Teacher Z applied combined pedagogies, which were embodied in SPS of her class. When she used teacher-centred methods, there was less space for students to engage in interactions with the teacher and peers in class; the teacher decided what she would talk about and the tasks for students — namely controlling the ATS. When she invited students to join in presentations, students were given the chance to interact with others in class internally and externally. Further, especially by using the platform (*Corner of Exchanging*) for exchanging written assignments, Teacher Z enlarged the space of student engagement in student-student interactions, extending from the inside of the class to the outside of the class. In this sense, SPS in Teacher Z's class was moderate, namely the combination of a fixed structure in class and a dynamic form out of class.

Secondly, the difference in the extent of student engagement suggests the extent of adaptiveness in SPS. When discussing two structures of the classroom, Erickson also addressed the concept of *classroom discourse as improvisation* (Erickson, 1982; Cazden, 2001), which views classroom discourse as the collective improvisation of meaning and instant social participating organization in the lesson, emphasizing the necessity to involve both of the academic and social aspects of lessons as learning environments (Erickson, 1982). *Improvisation* is the keyword of the concept, which demonstrates the classroom interaction is immediately social and radically cooperative from moment to moment. It was seen as a strategically adaptive action (Erickson, 1982), and from this perspective adjustments both in ATS and SPS usually should be made by teachers according to the learning capacity of students when they do not understand teachers' intentions or can not respond as teachers expect. With this concept, teachers are supposed to choose an appropriate teaching style to fit a particular student at a particular point in time in order to make student learning coherent within social interaction.

In this book, the concept of *improvisation* implies the possibility of student engagement in the discussion with the teacher. The findings from Teacher X's class demonstrate the tension between the teacher's expectations and the students' realities, which also indicates that the teacher might not know how to instantly improvise the interaction with students. It followed that she did not change her prepared words to follow up students' responses as Excerpt 5.5 shows (Student Sa5). Similarly, the tension could also be found in Teacher P's class. Excerpt 4.8 from Teacher P's class shows the tension when the student's response conflicted with the teacher's expectation. In that exchange, Teacher P did not deal well with the student's instant and unexpected response (e.g., Student G addressed an opposite example). If the teacher does not cope with the tension brought by a student's unexpected creativity, the discussion will certainly be closed without collaborative improvisation. In short, Teacher X and Teacher P did not do any adaptive action to meet students where they were because they followed what they had planned in a goal-oriented way. In comparison, Teacher S was better at adjusting her prepared words to follow up students' responses, even when the responses were not what she expected (e.g., Excerpt 3.4 in the discussion about first person narrators). Using combined approaches, Teacher Z sometimes rejected improvisation in the *one-to-many mode* of IRE or lectures, but sometimes she organised the teaching to accommodate to students' responses in the written assignments (e.g., she added student presentations after exchanging written assignments). Hence, different teachers used adaptive strategies or improvisation to different extents, reflecting the extent of student engagement in the interaction with the teacher.

7.2.2 Commonalities: Two Phenomena

This section presents two commonalities shared by both Danish and Chinese classes. One is termed *dancing with shackles*, which is a situation that students experience, and the other is the *double-bind problem* of the teachers.

7.2.2.1 Dancing with Shackles

The new focus that the *Basic Education Curriculum Reform* brought to teaching literature did to some extent change the way of framing classroom interactions, including some dialogic aspects in the Chinese classroom. Teachers in China have begun to be aware of student engagement in the classroom and are trying to engage students in some activities that create space for student talking such as the self-checking of homework and reading-aloud activity in Teacher X's class, exchanging written assignments at the *Corner of Exchanging* in Teacher Z's class, and student individual presentation in both teachers' classes. Joining these activities, the Chinese students had the chance to express their thoughts, learn from one another, and develop understandings. In short, student engagement was promoted by the new educational policy, which provides a macro-level cultural backdrop for some new changes. However, it is worth noting another aspect of the societal culture — the new changes indeed occurred in the educational culture. For instance, the findings from Teacher X's and Teacher Z's classes showed that the syllabus, the learning content, the activities, the organization of the classroom, and the structure of the lesson were largely determined by the teachers, schools, and institutions. Thus, Chinese teachers are requested by the new policy to consider creating possibilities to involve students in interactions with teachers, peers, and texts, but meanwhile, their teaching had to orient toward examinations, which creates restrictions for students' engagement and development. This situation is depicted in this book by the metaphor — *dancing with shackles* — that describes a situation where students have some opportunities to participate, but meanwhile, their actions are limited by some constraints. Put simply, the meaning of the metaphor is to encourage students to effectively use their limited possibilities to actively engage in learning activities, to learn and develop as much as possible, just as a dancer may still dance even though her or his hands or feet are bounded by the shackles.

The student individual presentation in both Teacher X's and Teacher Z's classes is a typical example of *dancing with shackles*. As described in

Chapters 5 and Chapter 6, some aspects of the presentation were controlled by the teacher. For instance, the theme should be relevant to what the students were studying; the focus should be on the literary texts; the presentation should be five to ten minutes; all the students had to join in; presenters were requested to use PowerPoint that had to be reviewed by the teacher before the presentation; the presentations were also expected to be helpful for student development of reading comprehension or writing essays in the standardized tests. These limitations served as rules of the activity — students were participants/players, and the teacher was the framer and referee. Even though students had to conform to these rules, they still had some space to perform other positions (e.g., speaker, audience) that created other responsibilities for students (e.g., presenting, giving feedback). Furthermore, in the process of engaging, students had choice in selecting different subtopics, content, and the style of presentations. Thus, in other words, students had the opportunity to dance differently, being restricted by some rules as shackles.

Based on the investigation in the Danish classes, *dancing with shackles* may be considered a common phenomenon shared by all of the cases in this book. Teacher S cared greatly about her ways of talking with students, showing her respect for their responses, which made the discussion between the teacher and students in the class usually continuous. In other words, she tried to set up a democratic atmosphere in which students could have much room to express their thinking, ideas, and views. This is a kind of *dancing*, like the free choice in the project about a British singer in Teacher S's second-year class: students chose the topic, the particular text and the picture, and the group. Meanwhile, their choice was limited by the teacher's intention and curricular plan: they had a choice, but not too much; the teacher adopted their choice of the topic because it was consistent with the curriculum and teacher's intention; they worked in groups but guided by the teacher's step-by-step written guidance that might result in stereotyped interpretations;

their written presentations were evaluated by the teacher. These restrictions, like shackles, were set by the teacher, the curriculum, and the school requirements. The restrictions in Teacher P's class seemed to be greater than Teacher S's classes. The findings of the case of Teacher P show that she preferred framing the classroom in a structured and goal-oriented way, which did set limitations for student participation. Thus, students had less choice in selecting the topics and the texts compared with Teacher S's classes. They were required to follow the teacher's goal and structure step by step. Even though Teacher P tried to vary activities to attract students' attention, the procedures, the forms, the time duration, and the task of the activities were decided by the teacher. The activity of *circle exercise* is a typical example. In this exercise, students had the chance to talk with the teacher, and moreover, some other active students (e.g., Student A in Excerpt 4.12) could even lead the discussion with the teacher, and in so doing, dancing well; but the performance of some weak students (e.g., Student J in Excerpt 4.12) was restricted and even lowered by the pattern of IRE and rules of the activity, which were the shackles for the students.

In summary, *dancing with shackles* was shared by both Danish classes and Chinese classes. The big difference between them depends on how much room the students have to dance, and how tight the shackles are.

7.2.2.2 Double Bind

Another interesting phenomenon shared by the cases of Teacher X and Teacher P is called *double bind* in the literature classroom. According to Mark Faust, *double bind* is inevitable for literature teachers who on the one hand seek to "validate students' personal responses to literature" from the perspective of reader-response theory, but on the other hand try to avoid students' "unbridled subjectivism" from the text as an object (Faust, 2000, p.19). Put simply, the *double bind* is produced when literary reading involves both subjective readers and objective texts. Faust (2000) claimed that because literary texts could not be read in the same way anywhere without consideration of the context and also because reading could not be purely subjective, teachers whose teaching practice is connected to principles of reader-response theory must confront the *double-bind* problem.

Indeed, the findings have shown that both Danish and Chinese teachers in this book on the one hand, invited students' understandings based on their personal readings, but on the other hand, rejected student personal readings in the end if these understandings deviated from teachers' interpretations. For instance, in Teacher X's class, especially when she framed the whole-class discussion in the metaphorical form of a train as Excerpt 5.5 shows, the inconsistency between the teacher's intention of initiating the discussion and what she actually did, in the end, was clear. In line with the earlier discussion about the differences among the teacher's usage of improvisation, students' personal readings were encouraged by the teacher's inviting question, but their engagement in the continuous discussion with the teacher based on their readings was declined by the teacher's closed questions and her interpretations. Instead, Teacher X hurried to ensure that the literature was presented more or less in its full capacity, no matter by the teacher herself or by students. Then the *double bind* occurred through the non-uniform combination of invitation and rejection of student responses (Hetmar, 2014).

This study uses the word *double-bind* to examine the problem from a broader perspective, arguing that the problem of *double bind* reflects the tension between the teacher's expectation and students' real performance. The findings also suggest that the *double-bind problem* can be related to the teacher's skill of framing classroom discourse as improvisation. On the basis of a comparative study of 30 schools in five countries, Robin Alexander (2001) found that there was a common tension for teachers in some classes in America, where teachers planned in considerable detail on the one hand, but also had to accommodate the unexpected element of improvisation within a predetermined lesson sequence on the other hand. In other words, this tension requires teachers' instructional skills to be a combination of flexible curriculum structures and on-the-spot creativity. Thus, the *double bind* occurs between the teacher's detailed plan and students' unexpected improvisation. Similarly, Excerpt 4.8 in Teacher P's class also indicates this sense of *double bind*, when Teacher P went back to her prepared lecture notes ("Satan is an anti-hero") and rejected the student's on-the-spot creativity.

Summing up, the differences and commonalities among the different cases indicate that the different teachers had different styles of teaching and framing ways, and also that the different contexts in which the cases are embedded contribute to the differences. Meanwhile, the common focus of these cases, literature teaching, produced the commonalities shared by them. The study's findings give rise to further discussions on the teaching methods, the meaning of dialogic teaching, and the factors in the student engagement in dialogues.

7.3 Theoretical and Empirical Discussions

This section deals with three main points that arise from the empirical data, which contribute to discussions on three dimensions: (1) Cross-model with modification, (2) empirical re-interpretations of dialogic teaching, and (3) factors in engaging students in dialogues.

7.3.1 Modified *Cross-Model* Based on Empirical Cases

The *Cross-model* (Bundsgaard, 2009) that has been discussed in Chapter 1, led to a theoretically based thinking of *dialogic* and *monologic*, and a discussion of classifying different teaching methods. The ***dialogic interaction*** in this book refers to a framing approach that creates possibilities for student engagement in multiple interactions and validates the engagement as substantial and sustained by means of changing positioning and reading instructional tools. During this study the typical teaching methods in each case were examined, the findings of which support a further discussion and modification of the *Cross-model*. This modified cross-model is shown in Figure 7.5[1].

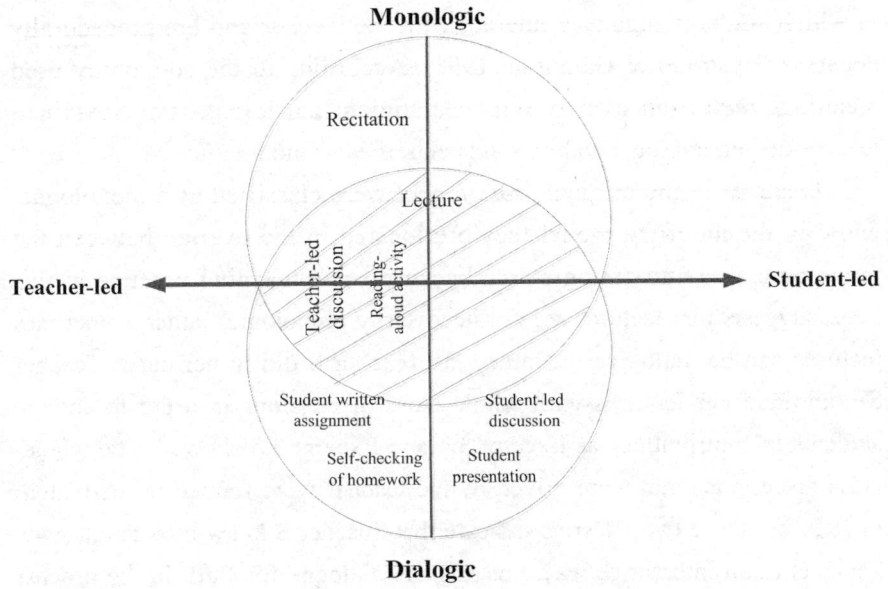

Figure 7.5 Modified *Cross-Model* of Teaching Method

The difference between the modified model and the original *Cross-model* centres mainly on the two circles that represent the sets of *Monologic* and *Dialogic* respectively. In the overlapping part the teaching methods have two sides — may be both dialogic and monologic. The left arrow indicates the tendency for teacher-led instruction, while the right arrow presents the tendency for student-led activities.

Recitation, during which "teacher talk dominated the lesson, the teacher asks known information questions, and students' role is limited to answering the teacher's questions" (Mehan, 1998) has been shown to strangle the

---

[1] The original model is shown in Figure 1.1.

teacher-student discussion and to induce student passivity (Alexander, 2008; Galton, 2007; Mehan, 1998; Nystrand, 1997). It was claimed to have a typical form "Initiation-Response-Evaluation (I-R-E)" (Mehan, 1979, 1998), in which students regularly interact with the teacher and are procedurally engaged (Nystrand & Gamoran, 1991). According to the commonly used meaning, *recitation* overtly impedes student participation in sustained discussion and talking, and hence it is classified as monologic.

Lectures in the original *cross-model* were classified as a monologue, while in the modified model they are located in the overlap between the monologic area and dialogic area because some teaching practice in this book suggests that lectures are not necessarily monologic; rather, sometimes lectures can be dialogically framed, as Teacher S did in her class. Teacher S combined her lectures with whole-class discussions in order to engage students in contributions as Excerpt 3.4 and Excerpt 3.5 showed. The whole-class discussions that were driven by the teacher were framed in the pattern of IRE, but these two excerpts indicate that Teacher S knew how to talk with students in an interactive way, pushing the dialogue forward. In the process of discussing, students' talk and opinions were often supported and invited by Teacher S's authentic questions, uptakes, and high-level evaluations, which marked them as dialogic IRE (Liu, 2016). Aligning with Rine's definition of *dialogic lecture* (Rine, 2009), Teacher S's lectures can be seen as dialogic lectures in which students were engaged or dialogued with through questions and answers during class time. In Rine's words, they were a "particular kind of interactive lecture(s)" (Rine, 2009, p.5). Besides, in Teacher S's third-year class, not only did the teacher give lectures but also the students gave lectures during the project with literary period and representative texts. Student presentations were organised as dialogic lectures including the small-group and teacher-student discussions around the presentation as Excerpt 3.15 shows. Thus, through student presentation, students were offered many possibilities to engage in talking and discussing with both the teacher and peers.

Student written assignment which contains the teacher-student and the student-student interactions is regarded as a dialogic teaching method in Teacher S and Teacher Z's classes, because in this process students had the chance, in a written way, to exchange their ideas with the teacher and other students. The student written assignment in Teacher S's second-year class is an example of this as Excerpt 3.6 shows. Through this written interaction, each student had the chance to interact with the teacher about his/her understanding of some texts. Correspondingly, the teacher interacted with students by means of giving responses and comments to push students to think further, and meanwhile, sometimes Teacher S was also open to students' new ideas based on their readings. Afterward, the findings have shown that teachers' comments were partly assimilated by students in their second-version writing, which created the *active understanding* in Bakhtin's (1981) sense. It followed that a dialogue between the teacher and students was set up during the back-and-forth exchanging of understandings and ideas. In Teacher Z's class, student written assignment offered a chance for students to exchange ideas and learn from each other (e.g., exchanging written assignments) through putting up all students' written assignments on the *Corner of exchanging*. This platform, therefore, created a space for the juxtaposition and contradiction of multiple interpretations, which was in line with Bakhtin's sense of *heteroglossia* (Bakhtin, 1981). Thus, the way of framing student writing, involving students in thinking, discussing, and exchanging is identified as dialogic in this study.

Student presentation, the same as student written assignment, is seen as a dialogic way of teaching in this book. This is because it involves students in reading, thinking, discussing, and expressing, which makes students' engagement authentic and substantial. In Teacher S's second-year class, student presentations as products of group work were given by each working-group member in new matrix groups (e.g., Excerpt 3.12). Therefore, group members contributed to the same presentation through discussing and cooperating when they were working with a British singer's songs, and in new matrix groups, they gave presentations on behalf of the working groups, receiving feedback from others. In Teacher Z's class, student presentations after exchanging homework about Chapter XIII Tsze-Lû, Section XXIV were the products of comparing all students' written assignments (Excerpt 6.6). Each presentation was required to involve feedback from one student audience member. As Excerpt 6.6 shows the student presentation followed by the student-student discussion in Teacher Z's class can be seen as an interactive activity for students to express and discuss their own views with others.

Teacher-led discussion in the modified model (Figure 7.5) can be monologic or dialogic, depending on how the teacher organises the discussion. Take the case of Teacher P as an example. She organised the discussion with students in the form of a *circle exercise* (Excerpt 4.12), which looked novel. But as discussed in Chapter 4, it was essentially framed in a pattern of IRE between Teacher P and one chosen student. Except for the student in the centre, others were not given chance to engage in continuous discussions with the teacher and the student in the centre. The extent of student engagement in discussions with the teacher sometimes depended on student performance. If the student was active, his/her discussion with the teacher was substantial (e.g., Student A in Excerpt 4.12 led the discussion). On the contrary, if the student was passive, his/her discussion with the teacher was short and superficial (e.g., Student J in Excerpt 4.12). Similarly, the discussion framed by means of the train metaphor (Excerpt 5.5, Figure 5.2) in Teacher X's class was also double-sided. The discussion was designed dialogically, but the findings showed that not all the students had the chance to join in the dialogue with the teacher in the end. The student engagement was also affected by their levels and performance. The dialogue with the teacher was closed when the teacher pushed weak students to think along with her thinking (Student Sa5 in Excerpt 5.5). Thus, it is too simplistic to say that the *circle exercise* and whole-discussion framed in the *train metaphor* are dialogic or monologic. In Teacher S's classes, the teacher paid attention to students' responses that were often supported and invited by Teacher S's authentic questions, uptakes, and high-level evaluations, which marks it as dialogic IRE (Liu, 2016). Excerpt 3.5 in Teacher S's class demonstrates the possibility of student discussion facilitated by the teacher who initiated the topic and pushed the students' (Students K, G, A) discussion forward. In this sense, the teacher-led discussion in Teacher S's classes can be clearly referred to as dialogic according to the definition in this study.

Student-led discussion in this book mainly refers to the group discussions as a part of group work in Teacher S's classes. In the process of group discussion, students had much time, from the beginning in choosing subtopics to the end in presenting products, to interact with the teacher and their peers (e.g., Excerpts 3.10, 3.12, 3.15). Thus, they are classified as dialogic teaching, the same as in the original *Cross-model* (Figure1.1). As an implied type of student-led discussion, exchanging written assignments in Teacher Z's class offered the chance for student-student interaction out of the class. Firstly, students individually finished the assignment by themselves, and they were expected to present to others, interact with one another, discuss outside of the class, and learn from others through *Corner of Exchanging* (Figure 6.2). In short, by joining in this activity, students had the chance to make their voices heard through presenting viewpoints and understanding in a written way.

Self-checking of homework was a kind of student-student interaction in Teacher X's class. As student individual presentation, the self-checking of homework also integrated the internal way of talking to oneself in one's mind and the external interaction with the teacher after self-checking (Excerpt 5.6). This was supposed to foster student independent learning and critical thinking. Thus, the self-checking of homework was also designed as a sort of dialogic interaction, although in reality student performance depended on whether they were active and self-disciplined or not.

Reading-aloud activity in Teacher X's class was seen as a kind of internal interaction in this book. Each voluntary student read a paragraph that told a story of a character in the prose. In the process of reading aloud, the teacher expected students to read with emotion and understand deeply by immersing themselves in the prose. So, in this process, students who listened to a peer's reading may have responses triggered by the readings, such as emotional responses like anger, passion, sorrow, distress, and occasionally laughter; it was regarded as the reason that older adolescents enjoy listening to and reading nonfiction in early research by Sanacore (1992). The student readers also had these emotional responses in reading and could transmit their emotional responses through different intonations when reading aloud. There could be an internal dialogic interaction between the voiced readers and silent audiences whose responses were triggered by the voiced readers, so to speak. Indeed, the importance of reading aloud in the development of student literacy has been studied for a long period (Amer, 1997; Sanacore, 1992). It is regarded as a tool to help students learn to read smoothly and build fluency skills, continuity, and confidence; also, it can help students comprehend what they are reading.

Summing up, the modified model is built based on the data of this book, but it indicates that there are more methods than those in the original model, and provides one possibility of revision. The reclassification of different teaching methods gives rise to the rethinking of the meaning of dialogue in this study.

7.3.2 Empirical Reinterpretations of Dialogic Teaching in the Literature Classroom

Dialogic instruction has been studied by many researchers so far (Applebee, Langer, Nystrand & Gamoran, 2003; Christoph & Nystrand,

2001; Nystrand, 1997; Nystrand & Gamoran, 1991, 1993) in secondary schools, however, apparently, there are rare studies that consider the student-text interaction and effects of the contextual cultures in the literature classroom. The present study seeks to bridge this gap, investigating three types of interactions with the objective of developing new understandings of dialogic teaching in the literature classroom rooted in contextual cultures. This development was built on both theoretical and empirical re-interpretations of dialogic teaching. Based on the findings of empirical research and the above discussion on teaching methods, this section re-interprets and identifies three characteristics of dialogic teaching in the literature classroom.

Firstly, the literary teacher frames the classroom as a reconstructed marketplace (Faust, 2000), considering the interaction between students and the text. The *double-bind problem* of many literary teachers has been discussed previously. Nevertheless, it is worth mentioning that not all teaching practices in the book produced the *double-bind problem*. In fact, some ways of the framing could be associated with the metaphorical construction — reconstructed marketplace addressed by Faust (2000) who argued that two dominant forms (metaphors of courtroom and marketplace) of framing the classroom discussion were not useful, because the metaphor of courtroom was associated with the formalistic approach to the text that was seen as objectivity, and the metaphor of marketplace that left too much room for subjectivity seemed to misinterpret of reader-response theory (Faust, 2000). As an alternative approach, he turned to transactional theory (Rosenblatt, 1978, 1995) which regards literary art as experience. In Faust's sense, the teacher who values literary experience and the interaction between reader and text frames the classroom discourse in the reconstructed marketplace metaphor. He thought in the classroom where the reconstructed marketplace metaphor played a role, teachers negotiated differences in students' understandings by taking the sociocultural context where reading events happened into account and taught students to view others' experiences as other possibilities of meaning-making in order to enrich their own perspective. In this sense, the *Corner of Exchanging* in Teacher Z's class can be an example of the reconstructed marketplace.

The *Corner of Exchanging* offered a platform where students' different interpretations of the same text (one chapter of *Confucian Analects*) were presented (Excerpt 6.2). Instead of transmitting the meaning of the old Chinese language to students and imposing the teacher's interpretation on them, the written assignment set by Teacher Z encouraged students to have their own interpretations and understandings based on their background knowledge and their reading experience inside and outside of class. All the students' written papers were posted on the wall at the *Corner of Exchanging* where all the students could read, compare them, reflect on them, discuss the difference, and make a choice. The *Corner of Exchanging* may be considered as a *Contact Zone* in Pratt's sense of the word (Pratt, 1991) where different understandings, derived from different social and cultural backgrounds, meet and conflict. Further, when dealing with the two specialized interpretations from two famous critics of Chapter XIII Tsze-Lû (Excerpt 6.2), comparing and critically thinking specialized interpretations can be considered as a way to teach students that there are no single or authoritative conclusions on how to read and understand a particular literary art. In this sense, the *Corner of Exchanging* as a *Contact Zone* not only created the possibility for students to learn from one another but also offered "an opportunity to achieve thoughtful responses testifying to their enhanced awareness of multiple possibilities for making meaning with literature" (Faust, 2000, p.29).

Secondly, the SPS of the dialogic literature classroom is flexible, thus students can choose and have an influence on the processes of teaching and learning. The Social Participation Structure (SPS) stresses the collaboration and roles of participants in the interaction (Erickson, 1982). From the view of SPS, learning is not only the transmission of information in order to finish an academic task, but also a social occasion where knowledge is constructed mutually and collaboratively considering the students' social participation. The previous discussion on the SPS of each case has shown three patterns. The SPS in Teacher S's classes, which is defined as varied and democratic, leaves some room for students to choose and decide something through negotiating with the teacher in the process of learning (e.g., the topic of songs and lyrics of a British singer was suggested by students; students were invited to comment on the project). Thus, there was a possibility for students to dialogue with the teacher on what they learnt and how they learnt. In comparison, in Teacher P's and Teacher X's classes the SPS that was fixed and structured, to some extent, impeded the possibility of collaboration and negotiation between the teacher and students. This difference between SPS demonstrates the dialogic classroom should have a flexible SPS, opening to students' contributions that might bring some changes in the ATS (Academic Task Structure, Erickson, 1982).

Thirdly, dialogic interaction can occur both in class and out of class. The cases of Teacher X and Teacher Z illustrate the possibility of extending the classroom interaction inside the class to the outside of the class, such as the student individual presentation in Teacher X's class and exchanging written assignments in Teacher Z's class. This approach was made under the influence of the *New Curriculum Reform* and the class realities. Obviously, in these two activities, Chinese students were pushed to the centre of the activity — expressing ideas, discussing with others, having an influence on something through engagement (e.g., students could choose the topic, the content, and the form of presentations; students had the right to evaluate a peer's written assignment). In this sense, the shift from teacher-centred mode to the student-centred mode, which the new curriculum reform advocates, was achieved in these two activities. But the cultural context of the Chinese classes, such as the 40-minute lesson time, the big classes, and a large amount of learning content, impact the teacher's teaching somehow. Thus, in order to echo the reform and meanwhile take the class reality into account, both Chinese teachers utilized students' leisure time to enrich interactions between the teacher and students, and the student and the student.

In summary, the above three new re-interpretations of dialogic teaching in the literature classroom are synthesized with a consideration of the effect of contextual cultures. The first point considers the joint context of four cases, the literature classroom, stressing the encouragement of multiple readings based on the reading theory. The second point on SPS indicates the democratic environment of the dialogic classrooms, showing the influence of the school culture and societal culture of Danish classes. The third one is summarized based on two Chinese cases, taking the macro-level societal culture and the micro-level classroom culture into account. In this sense, the contextual culture of each case can be an important factor impacting teaching in this study. The next section deals with the factors that impact student engagement in the dialogue in the literature classroom within different cultures.

7.3.3 Factors in Engaging Students in Dialogue in the Literature Classroom

Dialogic teaching has been a concept of growing importance in discussions of learning and teaching in recent years. However, carrying out dialogic teaching seems to be not always easy and a variety of reasons were offered (Burbules 1993), including the power of tradition and the crowded public classroom (Burbules 1993). Taking the realities of the classroom into account, this book suggests two main factors in engaging students in dialogue based on the empirical data-culture and language.

7.3.3.1 Cultural Factor

In addition to the differences in the patterns of framing and SPS, the findings also highlight the difference between Danish classes and Chinese classes embedded in the two cultures. This significant difference raises a question about the effect of cultural factors on education. There is a proposition that the culture in which the schools in a country are located, and which is shared by its teachers and pupils, is as powerful a determinant of the character of school and classroom life as are the unique institutional dynamics, local circumstances, and interpersonal chemistries that make one school or classroom different from another (Alexander, 2001). This proposition manifests the influence of contextual cultures on daily teaching. The results presented in Chapters 3 to 6 indicate that the teacher's purpose and methods of teaching were connected to the contextual cultures in each case. By and large, the societal cultures of the two countries, including the educational system, the policy, the ideology, and the syllabus impact the school cultures and classroom cultures including the school purpose, the school ethos, the classroom environment, and the perceptions of teachers and students of teaching. For instance, Danish teachers had some autonomy by which they could decide what materials to be read, how to read, what teaching methods to use, and what kind of activities to use; Chinese teachers usually follow a schema made by the ministry which also assigned textbooks, learning content, and requirements of the examination. This difference was a result of the educational culture of the two countries, which impacted on the interactions between the teacher and students.

The effect of culture is also embodied in the students' performance. Indeed, in a relevant study of the relationship between cultural dimensions and students' performance in the classroom, Sulkowski and Deakin (2009) discussed whether cultural conceptualizations could explain student behavior. They realized that the students from different cultures had purely different preferences for teaching styles. They claimed that students from a collectivist background preferred didactic teaching styles, and Chinese students, in particular, relied on the lecturer to transmit information but seemed uncomfortable with exercises that expected them to present their opinions openly. In contrast, students from individualist backgrounds preferred independent learning and they were found to be more comfortable in participating in the classroom discussions (Sulkowski & Deakin, 2009). This claim can be seen as an interpretation of the different purposes of teaching embedded in two societal cultures.

By and large, the difference between the educational culture affects the teaching focus — focusing on the individual or the collective — in the classroom. Danish teachers of this study tried to invite each individual in the classroom to engage in various activities or group work. Thus, they either preferred combining more than one method in one lesson to engage students (e.g., Teacher P used variety to attract students' attention) or encouraging students to work on their own (e.g., Teacher S liked students to study in groups). Chinese teachers seem to focus on the result of students' participation in learning. They often applied lectures or a pattern of IRE (e.g., one-to-many mode, train as a metaphor) to organise classroom discussion, which is effective for the large class and reflects their focus on the students as a collectivity. In addition, on the one hand, Chinese teachers tried to engage students in some new forms of activity (e.g., student presentation, self-checking of homework, exchanging written assignments) in order to respond to the requirements of curriculum reform, but on the other hand, they expected students to learn something useful and to prepare thoroughly for the examinations in future.

Therefore, contextual cultures do impose some constraints for student engagement in classroom interactions by partly influencing the teacher's teaching methods and student performance. Besides, student engagement in discussions can be also restricted by their ability to use language, which is presented as the other factor.

7.3.3.2 Language Ability

The cases in this study were comprised of English language classes in Denmark and Chinese language classes. Obviously, this difference resulted in the asymmetry of cases with two teaching languages. Indeed, Danish students' performance and participation partly depended on their English ability despite the fact that the students in the two Danish cases (Teacher S's classes being English A and Teacher P's class being English B level) could communicate, present, and discuss fluently in English. As a matter of fact, English B was mandatory for students in Danish Gymnasiums, whereas English A was the advanced course for students who incorporated English into the study package and aimed to improve English. The different motivations of students at different levels of English contributed to the impact of language ability on student engagement.

One student in Teacher P's class (English-B level) described her experience of joining in the *double-circle exercise* as "not so dangerous" but "safer" (see Section 4.3.2), in contrast to talking in front of the whole class. The student statement indicates that she did care about her language ability when she considered joining in some activities, especially when she had to speak in public or with the teacher because the teacher evaluated their daily performance at the end of each academic year. In contrast, students who were not good at speaking English felt comfortable and "safe" when they talked with peers, as the above student said. Similarly, some students in Teacher S's classes (English-A level) noticed the effect of language ability on their participation. Student G who was actively engaged in contributing to both whole-class and group discussions clearly pointed out the anxiety of some students who did not actively participate in talking, because "they are afraid of their English that is not adequate enough". His statement again explained how language ability impacted student engagement in talking.

Furthermore, language ability does not only mean the ability to use a foreign language but also means the ability to express in one's mother tongue. Findings show that students' ability of expression did impact their participation. For instance, in Teacher X's class, students with different expressive language competencies approached the student's individual presentation at the beginning of each class differently. This situation was discussed with an example of a weak student "silent" presentation (see Section 5.3.2.1). This example indicates that even though sometimes the students who struggled in expressing themselves were forced to participate in some activities (e.g., student presentation), their language ability was a resistance for them to substantially engage in.

7.4 Implications for Reading Pedagogy from the Perspective of Positioning

Chapter 1 discusses the use of *positioning* in some studies as a perspective to examine the student learning in literacy or literary discussion (Vetter, 2010; Wee, 2010). Similarly, this book also suggests a possibility to combine the perspective of positioning with literature reading. In particular, the findings of the cases study demonstrate that different positions offered by the teacher can function as various stances (Langer, 2011b) from which students read and reflected on the text and content.

The miniature project of a British singer in Teacher S's second-year class is analysed as an example of the connection between various stances and multiple positions in Chapter 3 and earlier in this chapter (the feature of positioning and reading instruction). From the perspective of envisioning theory (Langer, 2011a, 2011b), during the group work on the British singer, students read and discussed the songs from Stance 1 (Getting started with the material), Stance 2 (Developing understanding of the material), and Stance 3 (Leaving from the material). In the last lesson, students commented on the whole project, which was related to Stance 4 (Think critically about the material). Afterward, these comments were collected by the teacher who would take these comments and the experience of working with a miniature project into account in future study, indicating the usage of Stance 5 (Going beyond the material). The analysis of this case suggests that changing positioning when students read literary texts created various reading stances, which were seen as instructional tools by Langer (2011b). In Langer's view, shifting different stances in reading supports students to build a rich envisionment, which students can utilize and go beyond in future studies (Langer, 2011b). Hence, in the process of working with the miniature project, students' envisionment was built and enriched with the shifting of positions.

Teacher X's class also used stances when she taught the long prose *The Temple of Earth Park and I*. She tried to apply various teaching methods during the five lessons, offering the chance for students to occupy other positions as the discussion in Chapter 5. The first two introductory lessons could be considered as using Stance 1 (Getting started with the material) where students were positioned as receivers of information. The third lesson including a discussion on a particular paragraph in a train metaphor was framed by using Stance 2 (Developing understanding of the material) where a group of students were expected to be responders. The fourth lesson filled with reading-aloud activity was a using Stance 1 again, getting the whole map of the long text. Students were partly performing voiced reader and partly performing silent listener. The fifth lesson including the discussion on the whole prose was using Stance 2 and 3 (Leaving from the material), leaving from the given text in the textbook. At that time, students were expected to be readers and thinkers who rethought his or her initial reading of the chosen part in the textbook after reading the whole prose. The findings indicate the discussion in the 5th lesson seemed to be more sustained than the discussion framed using the train metaphor in the 3rd lesson. However, it is also worth noting that during the whole process, students were often guided with Stance 1(Getting started with the material) and Stance 2 (Developing understanding of the material), being in the text — reading, interpreting, discussing the details — but were seldom given the chance to step out, reflect on, and think critically about what they had already learnt from the teacher (using Stance 3 Leaving from the material and Stance 4 Think critically about the material), let alone going beyond utilizing what they learnt in the future study (using Stance 5 Going beyond the material).

The above two cases jointly illustrate that the teacher's positioning approach affects her reading pedagogy. Hence the perspective of positioning theory (Harré & van Langenhove, 1999) provides a way of thinking about how to improve reading instruction, which contains two specific *approaches*, one is facilitating students to be literate readers, the other is facilitating students' reading from the outside of the text.

First, facilitating students to be literate readers can be approached through engaging them in working with literature from the beginning to the end, or namely engaging them in student-led activities. This means students have the chance to seek materials relevant to texts, work with the materials, and present their understandings based on their independent work, just as the project-based group works in Teacher S's classes. In other words, students may not gain information transmitted by the teacher's lectures. Thus, instead of monologic lectures, the teacher can use Stance 1 (Getting started with the material) and ask questions to tap students' relevant information gained from searching, inviting students to engage in thinking and talking based on what they have obtained. This approach makes room for students to work with a literary text independently, as a literate reader should do.

Second, facilitating students' reading from outside of the text is a way to engage students in critical thinking through shifting positions. Fostering critical thinking is helpful for multiple readings of a text in the classroom. Apparently, using Stances 1, 2 students usually were immersed in the text, while using Stances 3, 4, 5 students step out. Therefore, shifting the stance in the text to the outside of the text is necessary for fostering student critical thinking. This approach facilitates students to reflect on with a broader view, supporting them not only to be a reader in the text but also to be a thinker from the out-of-text perspective.

7.5 In Closing: Contributions of the Study

The insights from the present study emphasise the importance and necessity of facilitating dialogic interactions in the literature classroom. The theoretical combination of positioning theory, envisioning theory, and teaching-method model suggest a combined perspective to other empirical research on classroom interaction and literary education.

In addition to the above pedagogical implications, the present study mainly contributes to three aspects of the educational field.

First, this study opens an alternative way to analyse classroom discourse in the literature classroom instead of four analytical indicators of dialogic teaching from Martin Nystrand — authentic questions, uptake, high evaluation, and substantive engagement (Nystrand et al., 1991, 1997, 2003). Specifically, this study examines interactions in the literature classroom based on a theoretical framework drawing from three main streams: positioning theory, literary reading theory, and Bundsgaard's *cross-model* of teaching method (Bundsgaard, 2009). Positioning theory is chosen because positioning has not received major attention, while studies about literature teaching have focused primarily on reading theory. The present study also focuses on the classroom discourse in the literature classroom because the roles of literary thinking and literature instruction have been largely ignored (Langer, 2011a, 2011b), whereas dialogic discussion has been viewed as a way to prompt students' participation and literary thinking in the process of discussing, arguing, and negotiating (Applebee et al., 2003; Christoph & Nystrand, 2001; Mercer, 1995; Nystrand, 1997). Again, this study emphasises the importance of dialogue in literature teaching and learning, expanding the understanding of dialogic teaching by analysing different patterns of framing classroom discourse.

Second, this study makes a unique contribution to teaching practice by comparing patterns of framing discourse in Danish and Chinese literature classes. A variety of teaching methods are analysed and discussed in different contexts, and Bundsgaard's Cross-model is discussed, revised, and supplemented. In so doing, the study engages literary teachers from selected Danish classes and Chinese classes in reflection on the classroom interactions and teaching methods used after observation (comments and reviews in the post-observation part). By comparison, the findings can provide some inspirations for educators and researchers in both countries.

Third, the present study also suggests a possible use of positioning theory as a lens for analysing interactions including oral and written modes in the literature classroom. *Position*, which was originally a psychological concept, has recently been increasingly used in the field of education. Much research has used positioning theory to examine the construction of teacher and student identities (cf. Barnes, 2004; Clarke, 2006; Leander, 2002; Murphy & Pinnegar, 2011; Vetter, 2010; Yoon, 2008). Some research demonstrates that teachers' saying and doing show the way that they position the students, and this positioning way will over time shape students' identities (Rex & Schiller, 2009; Vetter, 2010; Yoon, 2008); some illustrates that students' reactions that show how they position themselves and each other will also over time influence their learning (Anderson, 2009; Wee, 2010); others have used positioning theory or the concept of positioning to investigate interpersonal relationships in literacy events (Blackburn, 2005; Clarke, 2006; Enciso, 1997; Evans, 1996; Lewis, 2001). Nevertheless, positioning theory has not been widely used, despite its potential as a lens to observe the dynamics of relationships. Few studies focus on classroom interactions in the context of reading literature. In the current study, positioning is connected to literary teaching; examining positioning thus also becomes a window through which the ways in which the literature is read, discussed, and taught can be exposed in different settings. The purpose of applying positioning theory is not only to demonstrate the effects of positioning theory and its workings, but also to compare ways of framing literature classrooms by comparing ways of positioning, and to discuss the possibilities of student engagement by investigating the possible positions student can occupy, resist, and modify.

In conclusion, this book is only the first step for studying and discussing classroom interactions and literature teaching methods in different contexts, built on which the further exploration of the combination of positioning theory and literary theory is strongly needed. In doing so, I hope the present study will extend the application of positioning theory in educational research and contribute to the development of literature education. The comparative study in Danish and Chinese literary classes is expected to illuminate other educators and researchers in both countries to communicate, reflect on, and learn more.

Bibliography

Alexander, R. (2001). *Culture and Pedagogy: International Comparisons in Primary Education*. Malden, Mass.: Blackwell.

Alexander, R. (2008a). *Essays on Pedagogy*. New York, NY: Routledge.

Alexander, R. (2008b). *Dialogic Teaching*. Retrieved from the homepage of Robin Alexander http://www.robinalexander.org.uk/dialogic-teaching/.

Anderson, K. T. (2009). Applying Positioning Theory to the Analysis of Classroom Interactions: Mediating Micro-Identities, Macro-Kinds, and Ideologies of Knowing. *Linguistics and Education: An International Research Journal, 20*(4), 291–310.

Applebee, A., Langer, J., Nystrand, M., & Gamoran, A. (2003). Discussion-Based Approaches to Developing Understanding: Classroom Instruction and Student Performance in Middle and High School English. *American Educational Research Journal, 40*, 685–730.

Bakhtin, M. M. (1981). *The Dialogic Imagination: Four Essays by M.M. Bakhtin*. Austin, TX: University of Texas Press.

Bakhtin, M. M. (1984). *Problems of Dostoevsky's poetics*. London: University of Minnesota Press.

Bakhtin, M. M. (1986). *Speech Genres and Other Late Essays*. Austin: University of Texas Press.

Ball, A. F. & Freedman, S. W. (2004). Ideological Becoming: Bakhtinian Concepts to Guide the Study of Language, Literacy, and Learning. In Ball, A. F. & Freedman, S.W. (Eds.) *Bakhtinian Perspective on Language, Literacy, and Learning*. Cambridge: Cambridge University Press (pp.3–33).

Barnes, M. (2004). The Use of Positioning Theory in Studying Student Participation in Collaborative Learning Activities. Paper presented at the Symposium *Social Positioning Theory as an Analytical Tool* at the Annual Meeting of the Australian Association for Research in Education, Melbourne.

Baxter. P. & Jack, S. (2008). Qualitative Case Study Methodology: Study Design and Implementation for Novice Researchers, *The Qualitative Report*, 13 (4), 544–559.

Benwell, B., & Stokoe, E. (2006). *Discourse and Identity*. Edinburgh: Edinburgh

University Press.

Billings, L., & Fitzgerald, J. (2002). Dialogic Discussion and the Paideia Seminar. *American Educational Research Journal*, 39(4), 907–941.

Blackburn, M. V. (2005). Talking Together for Change: Examining Positioning between Teachers and Queer Youth. In Vadeboncoeur & Stevens (Eds.), *Re-Constructing "the Adolescent"* (pp.249–270). New York: Peter Lang.

Brookfield, S. D. (1995). Critical Incident Questionnaire.

Bundsgaard, J. (2009). Krydsmodel for Undervisningstilrettelæggelse. *Dansk Universitetspædagogisk Tidsskrift*, 7, 10–17.

Burbules, N. C. (1993). *Dialogue in Teaching: Theory and Practice*. New York, NY: Teachers College Press.

Cazden, C. B. (2001). *Classroom Discourse: The Language of Teaching and Learning*. Portsmouth, NH: Heinemann.

Cheong, (2000). Cultural Factors in Educational Effectiveness: A Framework for Comparative Research, *School Leadership and Management*, 20(2), 207–225.

Christoph, J. N., & Nystrand, M. (2001). Taking Risks, Negotiating Relationships: One Teacher's Transition toward a Dialogic Classroom. *Research in the Teaching of English*, 36(2), 249–286.

Clarke, L. W. (2006). Power through Voicing Others: Girls' Positioning of Boys in Literature Circle Discussions. *Journal of Literacy Research*, 38(1), 53–79.

Cohen, L., Manion, Lawrence, & Morrison, Keith. (2011). *Research Methods in Education* (7.ed. ed.). London: Routledge.

Collins, J. (1982). Discourse Style, Classroom Interaction and Differential Treatment. *Journal of Reading Behavior*, 14(4), 429–437.

Creswell, J. (2013). *Research Design: Qualitative, Quantitative, and Mixed Methods Approaches* (4. ed., international student ed.). Thousand Oaks, Calif: Sage Publications.

Dale, E. (1946). *Audiovisual methods in teaching*. New York: Dryden Press.

Davies, B., & Harre, R. (1990). Positioning: The Discursive Production of Selves. *Journal for the Theory of Social Behavior*, 20(1), 43–63.

Denzin, N., & Lincoln, Y. S. (2011). *The Sage Handbook of Qualitative Research* (4.th ed.). Thousand Oaks: Sage.

Diaz A. A. (2009). Interpretive Research Aiming at Theory Building: Adopting and

Adapting the Case Study Design. *Qualitative Report*, 14(1), 42-60.

Doecke, B., Grill, P., Van de Ven, P.-H. (2009). The Literature Classroom: Spaces for Dialogue. *Educational Studies in Language and Literature, 9*(1), 5-33.

Dressman, M. (2004). Dewey and Bakhtin in Dialogue: From Rosenblatt to a Pedagogy of Literature as Social, Aesthetic Practice. In Ball, A. F. & Freedman, S.W. (Eds.) *Bakhtinian Perspective on Language, Literacy, and Learning.* Cambridge: Cambridge University Press (pp.34-52).

Dysthe, O. (1993). *Writing and Talking to Learn. A Theory-based, Interpretive Study in Three Classrooms in Norway and the USA* (doctoral thesis). Tromsø: University of Tromsø.

Dysthe, O. (1999). *The Dialogical Perspective and Bakhtin (Conference Report).* Bergen, Norway: University of Bergen.

Enciso, P. E. (1997). Negotiating the Meaning of Difference: Talking Back to Multicultural Literature. In T. Rogers & A. O. Soter (Eds.), *Reading Across Cultures: Teaching Literature in a Diverse Society* (pp.13-41). New York, NY: Teachers College Press.

Erickson, F. (1982). Classroom Discourse as Improvisation: Relationships between Academic Task Structure and Social Participation Structure in Lessons. In L. C. Wilkinson (Ed.), *Communicating in the Classroom* (pp.153-181). New York: Academic Press.

Evans, K. S. (1996). Creating Spaces for Equity? The Role of Positioning in Peer-Led Literature Discussions. *Language Arts, 73,* 194-202.

Faust, M. (2000). Reconstructing Familiar Metaphors: John Dewey and Louise Rosenblatt on Literary Art as Experience, *Research in the Teaching of English,* 35 (1), 9-34.

Freedman, S. W., Delp, V., & Crawford, S. M. (2005). Teaching English in Untracked Classrooms. *Research in the Teaching of English, 40*(1), 62-126.

Freedman, S. W. & Delp, V. K. (2007). Conceptualizing a Whole- Class Learning Space: A Grand Dialogic Zone. *Research in the Teaching of English, 41*(3), 259-268.

Galton, M. J. (2007). *Learning and Teaching in the Primary Classroom.* London, UK: SAGE Publications Ltd.

Gee, J. P. (2001). Critical Literacy/Socially Perspective Literacy: A Study of Language in Action. In H. Fehring & P. Green (Eds.), *Critical Literacy. A Collection of Articles from the Australian Literacy Educators' Association* (pp.15-39). Delaware &

Norwood: International Reading Association.

Gee, J. (2011a). *An Introduction to Discourse Analysis: Theory and Method* (Third Edition), London: Routledge.

Gee, J. (2011b). *How to Do Discourse Analysis: A Toolkit.* New York: Routledge.

Goffman, E. (1981). *Forms of Talk.* Philadelphia: University of Pennsylvania Press.

Harré, R., & van Langenhove, L. v. (1999). *Positioning Theory: Moral Contexts of Intentional Action.* Oxford; Malden, Mass: Blackwell.

Harré, R., & Moghaddam, F. M. (Eds.) (2003). Introduction: The self and others in traditional psychology and in positioning theory. In R. Harré & F. Moghaddam (Eds.), *The Self and Others* (pp.1–11). Westport, CT: Praeger.

Hetmar, V. (2014). Different Perspectives on Dialogue in the Literature Classroom. Key note presented at the conference "*2014 International Conference on Understanding and Dialogue: Education of Literature and Language in the context of Globalization*", China.

Holquist, M. (1990). *Dialogism: Bakhtin and His World* (Repr. ed., New Accents). London: Routledge.

Howie, D., & Peters, M. (1996). Positioning Theory: Vygotsky, Wittgenstein and Social Constructionist Psychology. *Journal for the Theory of Social Behavior*, 26(1), 51–64.

Hsieh, H., & Shannon, S. (2005). Three Approaches to Qualitative Content Analysis. *Qualitative Health Research, 15*(9), 1277–1288.

Klein, H. K., & Myers, M. D. (1999). A Set of Principles for Conducting and Evaluating Interpretive Field Studies in Information Systems. *Management Information Systems Quarterly, 23*(1), 67–88.

Kozulin, A., Gindis, B., Ageyev, V.S., & Miller, S.M. (2003). *Vygotsky's Educational Theory in Cultural Context.* Cambridge: Cambridge University Press.

Lalley, J. P., & Miller, R. H. (2007). The Learning Pyramid: Does It Point Teachers in the Right Direction? *Education* 128(1), 64–79.

Langer, J. A. (2011a). *Envisioning Literature: Literary Understanding and Literature Instruction.* New York and London: Teachers College Press, Columbia University.

Langer, J. A. (2011b). *Envisioning Knowledge: Building Literacy in the Academic Disciplines.* New York and London: Teachers College Press, Columbia University.

Leander, K. M. (2002). Locating Latanya: The Situated Production of Identity Artifacts in

Classroom Interaction. *Research in the teaching of English, 37*, 198–250.

Legge, J. (1893). *Confucian Analects.*

Lewis, C. (2001). *Literary Practices as Social Acts: Power, Status, and Cultural Norms in the Classroom.* Mahwah, NJ: Lawrence Erlbaum Associates.

Liu, T. (2016). Dialogic Teaching and the Dialogic IRE Model: Discussing the Features and Forms of Dialogic Teaching Based on the Case Study of a Second-Year English Literature Class in a Danish High School. *Journal of Chinese Language Education.* 14(1), 45–66.

Lyle, S. (2008). Dialogic Teaching: Discussing Theoretical Contexts and Reviewing Evidence from Classroom Practice. *Language and Education, 22*(3), 222–240.

Mason, J. (2002). *Qualitative Researching* (2nd. ed.). London: SAGE.

Mehan, H. (1979). *Learning Lessons.* Cambridge, MA: Harvard University Press.

Mehan, H. (1998). The Study of Social Interaction in Educational Settings: Accomplishments and Unresolved Issues. *Human Development*, 41(4), 245–269.

Mercer, N. (1995). *The Guided Construction of Knowledge: Talk amongst Teachers and Learners.* Clevedon: Multilingual Matters.

Middendorf, M. (1992). Bakhtin and the Dialogic Writing Class. *Journal of Basic Writing,* Middendorf 11(1), 34–46.

Mroz, M., Smith, F., & Hardman, F. (2000). The Discourse of Literacy Hour. *Cambridge Journal of Education, 30*(3), 379–390.

Murphy, M., & Pinnegar, S. (2011). Teacher Educator Identity Emerging through Positioning Self and Others. *Studying Teacher Education,* 7(2), 155.

Nystrand, M., & Gamoran, A. (1991). Instructional Discourse, Student Engagement, and Literature Achievement. *Research in the Teaching of English,* 25(3), 261–90.

Nystrand, M., Gamoran, A., Kachur, R., & Prendergast, C. (1997). *Opening Dialogue: Understanding the Dynamics of Language and Learning in the English Classroom.* New York, NY: Teachers College Press.

Nystrand, M., Wu, L. L., Gamoran, A., Zeiser, S., & Long, D. A. (2003). Questions in Time: Investigating the Structure and Dynamics of Unfolding Classroom Discourse. *Discourse Processes*, 35(2), 135–198.

Nystrand, M. (2006). Research on the Role of Classroom Discourse as It Affects Reading Comprehension. *Research in the Teaching of English,* 40(4), 392–412.

Pratt, M. (1991). Arts of the Contact Zone. *Profession,* 33–40. Retrieved from http://www.

jstor.org/stable/25595469.

Probst, E. R. (1987). Transactional Theory in the Teaching of Literature.

Reeves, J. (2009). Teacher Investment in Learner Identity. *Teaching and Teacher Education: An International Journal of Research and Studies, 25*(1), 34–41.

Rex, L. A., & Schiller, L. (2009). *Using Discourse Analysis to Improve Classroom Interaction*: Routledge.

Reznitskaya, A. (2012). Dialogic Teaching: Rethinking Language Use during Literature Discussions. *The Reading Teacher, 65*(7), 446–456.

Rine, E. F. (2009). *Development in Dialogic Teaching Skills: A Micro-Analytic Case Study of a Pre-Service ITA*. Available from ProQuest Dissertations & Theses Global; ProQuest Education Journals.

Rex, L. A., & Green, J. L. (2008). Classroom Discourse and Interaction: Reading Across the Traditions. In B. Spolsky & F. M. Hult (Eds.), *The Handbook of Educational Linguistics*. (pp.571–584). London: Blackwell.

Rosenblatt, L. M. (1978). *The Reader, The Text, The Poem: The Transactional Theory of the Literary Work*, Carbondale, IL: Southern Illinois University Press.

Rosenblatt, L. M. (1985). Viewpoints: Transaction versus Interaction: A Terminological Rescue Operation. *Research in the Teaching of English,* 19(1), 96–107.

Rosenblatt, L. M. (1993). The Transactional Theory: Against Dualisms. *College English,* 55(4), 377–386.

Rosenblatt, L. M. (1995). *Literature as Exploration* (5th Ed.). New York: The Modern Language Association.

Sanacore, J. (1992). *Reading Aloud: A Neglected Strategy for Older Students.*

Schiffrin, D. (1994). *Approaches to Discourse* (Blackwell textbooks in linguistics). Cambridge, Mass: Blackwell.

Skidmore, D. (2006) Pedagogy and Dialogue. *Cambridge Journal of Education, 36*(4), 503–514.

Smidt, J. (1999). "All the World's a Stage": Discourse Roles and Student Positionings in the Great Dialogue. In Dysthe, O., (ed.), *The Dialogical Perspective and Bakhtin* (pp.89–99), Bergen. Norway: University of Bergen.

Sulkowski, N.B. & Deakin, M.K. (2009). Does Understanding Culture Help Enhance Students' Learning Experience? *International Journal of Contemporary Hospitality Management,* 21(2), 154–166.

Soter, A., Wilkinson, I. A., Murphy, P. K., Rudge, L., Reninger, K., & Edwards, M. (2008). What the Discourse Tells Us: Talk and Indicators of High-Level Comprehension. *International Journal of Educational Research*, 47(6), 372–391.

Tyson, L. (2015). *Critical Theory Today* (Third Edition), New York: Routledge.

Vetter, A. (2010). Positioning Students as Readers and Writers through Talk in a High School English Classroom. *English Education,* 43(1), 33–64.

Vološinov, V., (translated by Matejka, L., & Titunik, I R.) (1973). *Marxism and the Philosophy of Language* (Studies in language). New York, London: Seminar Press.

Vygotsky, L. S. (1978). *Mind in Society: The Development of Higher Psychological Processes*. Cambridge, MA: Harvard University Press.

Vygotsky, L.S. (1987). Thinking and Speech. In R. W. Rieber & A. S. Carton (Eds.), *The Collected Works of L.S. Vygotsky, Volume 1: Problems of General Psychology*. New York: Plenum.

Wee, J. (2010). *Literature Discussion as Positioning: Examining Positions in Dialogic Discussions in a Third-Grade Classroom*. (Doctor Thesis), The Ohio State University.

Wells, G. (1999). *Dialogic Inquiry toward a Sociocultural Practice and Theory of Education* Cambridge: Cambridge University Press.

Wertsch, J. (1991). *Voices of the Mind: A Sociocultural Approach to Mediated Action*. London: Harvester Wheatsheaf.

Yandell, J. (2013). The Social Construction of Meaning: Reading Animal Farm in the Classroom. *Literacy (Special Issue: Narrative and Literacy)*, 47(1), 50–55.

Yandell, J. (2014). *The Social Construction of Meaning: Reading Literature in Urban English Classrooms*. Abingdon: Routledge.

Yin, R. (2003a). *Application of Case Study Research* (2nd ed.), Applied social research methods series. London: Sage Publications.

Yin, R. (2003b). *Case Study Research: Design and Methods* (3rd ed.). Los Angeles, Calif: Sage.

Yin, R. (2011). *Qualitative Research from Start to Finish*. New York, N.Y: Guilford Press.

Yoon, B. (2008). Uninvited Guests: The Influence of Teachers' Roles and Pedagogies on the Positioning of English Language Learners in the Regular Classroom. *American Educational Research Journal, 45*(2), 495–522.

Appendices

Appendix 2.1   Critical Instant Questionnaire in the Literary Classroom
Appendix 3.1   Curriculum of English A (selected part, Danish and English versions)
Appendix 3.2   Worksheet of the Project of Literary History in Teacher S's Third-Year Class
Appendix 4.1   English B Curriculum (Selected Part, Danish and English Versions)
Appendix 4.2   Teaching Plan of Working with "Heroes, Superheroes, Heroines and Anti-heroes" in Teacher P's Class
Appendix 6.1   Chinese Version of Student Written Assignment "My Reviews" in Teacher Z's Class

Appendix 2.1   Critical Instant Questionnaire in the Literary Classroom

Literary Classroom Questionnaire

School: Class: Lesson:
Name: Gender (M/F):

(Please take about 10 minutes to respond to the questions below about these two weeks' classes. If nothing comes to mind for any of the questions, just leave the space blank. But please finish it as much as you can. Thanks for taking the time to do this. And please write your name on the form. I assure what you write will be anonymous and confidential, which will be only used in my research.)

   a. At what moment in class during these two weeks did you feel most interested in what was happening? Why?

   b. At what moment in class during these two weeks were you most distanced from what was happening? Why?

c. What action that anyone (teacher or student) took during these two weeks did you find most affirming or helpful? Why?

d. What action that you took during these two weeks did you find most confusing? Why?

e. What has been going in class during these two weeks surprised you the most? Why? (This could be about your own reactions to what went on, something that someone did, or anything else that occurred.)

f. To what extent have your expectations been achieved by attending the class during these two weeks? Large, moderate, or small? Why?

Appendix 3.1 Curriculum of English A (Selected Part, Danish and English Versions)

Engelsk A-Læreplan (Danish version)
   Eleverne skal kunne:
   — forstå forholdsvis komplekst mundtligt og skriftligt engelsk om almene og faglige emner
   — beherske et varieret ordforråd, som gør det muligt ubesværet at deltage i en samtale og diskussion på engelsk
   — give en længere, velstruktureret mundtlig og skriftlig fremstilling på flydende, korrekt engelsk af komplekse sagsforhold med forståelse for kommunikationssituationen
   — gøre rede for indhold, synspunkter og stilforskelle i forskellige typer engelsksprogede tekster og mediestof, herunder film
   — analysere og fortolke forskellige nyere og ældre teksttyper samt mediestof, herunder film, med anvendelse af faglig terminologi
   — perspektivere det givne materiale litteraturhistorisk, kulturelt, samfundsmæssigt og historisk
   — anvende en grundviden om historiske, kulturelle og samfundsmæssige forhold i Storbritannien og USA til analyse og perspektivering af aktuelle forhold
   — orientere sig i et større engelsksproget stof, herunder sortere i og vurdere

forskellige informationskilder
— analysere og beskrive engelsk sprog grammatisk og stilistisk med anvendelse af relevant faglig terminologi
— anvende faglige opslagsværker og øvrige hjælpemidler
— demonstrere indsigt i fagets identitet og metoder.

Kernestoffet er:
— det engelske sprogs grammatik, ortografi og tegnsætning
— idiomatik, ordforråd og orddannelse
— principper for tekstopbygning og tekstsammenhæng
— kommunikationsformer og kommunikationsstrategier
— standardsprog og variation, herunder elementer af det engelske sprogs udvikling og det engelske sprog som globalt kommunikationssprog
— tekstanalytiske begreber
— et bredt udvalg af nyere litterære tekster, ikke-litterære tekster og mediestof
— et bredt udvalg af litterære tekster fra forskellige perioder
— uddrag af værker af Shakespeare
— væsentlige strømninger i britisk og amerikansk litteraturhistorie
— væsentlige sproglige, historiske, kulturelle og samfundsmæssige forhold i Storbritannien og USA
— historiske og aktuelle forhold i andre dele af den engelsktalende verden.

Litterære tekster, ikke-litterære tekster og mediestof, som indgår i kernestoffet, skal være ubearbejdede og på autentisk engelsk.

(Cited from Ministeriet for Børn, Undervisning og Ligestilling, Engelsk — stx, Engelsk A-Læreplan[①])

English A Curriculum (English version)
Professional goals
Students should be able to:
— understand relatively complex orally and in writing in English about education

---

[①] The curriculum of English A (Upper Secondary School, STX, in Danish) was cited from the website of Ministry of Education, Denmark: https://www.uvm.dk/gymnasiale-uddannelser/fag-og-laereplaner/laereplaner-2013/fag-paa-stx.

and professional topics
— mastering a varied vocabulary, which enables effortless to participate in an interview and discussion in English
— give a longer, well-structured oral and written production at the liquid, correct English of complex facts with the understanding of the communication situation
— explain the content, views, and style differences in different types of English-language texts and media material, including films
— analyse and interpret various newer and older types of text and media material, including films, with the use of technical terminology
— a prospective analysis of the given material literature historically, culturally, socially, and historically
— apply basic knowledge of historical, cultural, and social conditions in the United Kingdom and the United States for analysis and perspective of current conditions
— orient themselves in a major English-language material, including sorting in and assessing the various sources of information
— analyse and describe the English language grammatically and stylistically with the use of appropriate technical terminology
— apply professional encyclopedias and other AIDS
— demonstrate insight into the subject's identity and methods.

Core fabric

Core substances are:
— the English language's grammar, orthography, and punctuation
— idiomatic, vocabulary, and word formation
— principles of text structure and text link
— forms of communication and communication strategies
— default language and variation, including elements of the English language and the English language development as a global language of communication
— text analytic concepts
— a wide selection of newer literary texts, non-literary texts, and media fabric
— a wide range of literary texts from different periods
— excerpts from the works of Shakespeare
— major currents in British and American literature
— essential linguistic, historical, cultural, and social conditions in the United

Kingdom and the United States

— historical and current conditions in other parts of the English-speaking world.

Literary texts, non-literary texts, and media material that is included in the core substance must be raw and authentic English.

(Translated from the Ministry of Children, Education, and Gender Equality, English-STX, English A-Curriculum)

Appendix 3.2   Worksheet of the Project of Literary History in Teacher S's Third-Year Class

Literary History 3e August-September 2014:
Renaissance, Enlightenment, Romanticism, Victorian, Modern, Post Modern:
Background reading material — at least: A Short History of Literature in English + copy sheet

> Background + Textual analysis (perspective).

Tasks and goals:

Each period must be covered, so each group must consist of 4–5 members.

Each group must analyse at least 8–10 pages of text — and you may choose to use a picture to support your analysis or show other aspects of your period. The groups must prepare a 45–60-minute lesson where they account for the most importants points in the literary history of their period and present a thorough analysis of their text material.

You will probably have to consult the school library and — of course — your teacher.

Suggested material: Oxford Companion to English Literature
Fields of Vision
Pictures, Prose & Poetry

	Renaissance	Enlightenment	Romanticism	Victorian Age	Modernism	Postmodern
Background reading	pp.11–24	Copied material	pp.25–40	pp. 41–56	pp.57–78	pp. 79–94

(continued)

	Renaissance	Enlightenment	Romanticism	Victorian Age	Modernism	Postmodern
Suggested literature	Shakespeare: sonnets + extracts from plays Thomas More: from Utopia (copy)	Jonathan Swift: A Modest Proposal (copy)	Wordsworth: Composed upon Westminster Bridge September 3, 1802 William Blake: The Garden of Love + The Chimney Sweeper + London Jane Austen: from Pride	(Poe: The Tell-Tale Heart + The Black Cat which we have already read) Conan Doyle:? Oscar Wilde: The Picture of Dorian Gray Poe: The	Virginia Woolf: The Mark on the Wall D. H. Lawrence: The Horse Dealer's Daughter + Snake	Julian Barnes: East Wind (read before the summer holidays) Charles Higson: The Red Line (in Now and Zen) Paul Auster:

Appendix 4.1 English B Curriculum (Selected Part, Danish and English Versions)

Engelsk B-Læreplan (Danish version)
  Eleverne skal kunne:
  — forstå mundtligt og skriftligt engelsk om almene og faglige emner
  — beherske et varieret ordforråd, som gør det muligt at deltage i en samtale og diskussion på engelsk
  — give en nuanceret, sammenhængende mundtlig og skriftlig fremstilling af alment kendte og faglige emner på et flydende og hovedsageligt korrekt engelsk
  — gøre rede for indhold og synspunkter i forskellige typer engelsksprogede tekster og mediestof, herunder film
  — analysere og fortolke litterære tekster, ikke-litterære tekster og mediestof,

herunder film, med anvendelse af faglig terminologi
— perspektivere det givne materiale kulturelt, samfundsmæssigt og historisk
— anvende en grundviden om historiske, kulturelle og samfundsmæssige forhold i Storbritannien og USA til analyse og perspektivering af aktuelle forhold
— orientere sig i et større engelsksproget stof, herunder sortere i og vurdere forskellige informationskilder
— analysere og beskrive engelsk sprog med anvendelse af relevant faglig terminologi
— anvende faglige opslagsværker og øvrige hjælpemidler
— demonstrere indsigt i fagets identitet og metoder.

Kernestoffet er:
— det engelske sprogs grammatik, lydsystem, ortografi og tegnsætning
— idiomatik, ordforråd og orddannelse
— principper for tekstopbygning
— kommunikationsformer og kommunikationsstrategier
— standardsprog og variation, herunder det engelske sprog som globalt kommunikationssprog
— et bredt udvalg af nyere litterære tekster, ikke-litterære tekster og mediestof, herunder film
— tekstanalytiske begreber
— væsentlige historiske, kulturelle og samfundsmæssige forhold i Storbritannien og USA
— historiske og aktuelle forhold i andre dele af den engelsktalende verden.

Litterære tekster, ikke-litterære tekster og mediestof, som indgår i kernestoffet, skal være ubearbejdede og på autentisk engelsk.

(Cited from Ministeriet for Børn, Undervisning og Ligestilling, Engelsk — stx, Engelsk B-Læreplan[1])

English B Curriculum (English version)
Professional goals
Students should be able to:

---

[1] The curriculum of English B (Upper Secondary School, STX, in Danish) was cited from the website of Ministry of Education, Denmark: https://www.uvm.dk/gymnasiale-uddannelser/fag-og-laereplaner/laereplaner-2013/fag-paa-stx.

- understand spoken and written English of general and professional topics
- mastering a varied vocabulary that allows students to participate in a conversation and discussion in English
- provide a balanced, coherent oral and written presentation of the universally known and professional topics in fluent and mostly correct English
- explain the content and views in different types of English-language texts and media material, including films
- analyse and interpret literary texts, non-literary texts, and media material, including movies, with the use of technical terminology
- put into perspective of the given material culturally, socially, and historically
- apply basic knowledge of historical, cultural, and social conditions in Britain and the United States for analysis and perspective on current conditions
- orient students in a major English-language material, including sort and evaluating different sources of information
- analyse and describe the English language with the use of relevant terminology
- use professional reference books and other aids
- demonstrate insight into the subject's identity and methods.

The core substance is:
- The English language grammar, sound system, orthography, and punctuation
- Idiom, vocabulary, and word formation
- Principles of text structure
- Communication and communication strategies
- Standard language and variation, including the English language as a global language of communication
- A wide selection of modern literary texts, non-literary texts, and media material, including film
- Text analytical concepts
- Significant historical, cultural, and social conditions in the UK and USA
- Historical and current conditions in other parts of the English-speaking world.

Literary texts, non-literary texts, and media substance present in the core substance must be primary and authentic English. (Cited from the Ministry of Children, Education, and Gender Equality, English-STX, English B-Curriculum)

Appendix 4.2 Teaching Plan of Working with "Heroes, Superheroes, Heroines and Anti-heroes" in Teacher P's Class

HEROES, SUPERHEROES, ANTI-HEROES, AND HEROINES

"Studieplan": This course on Heroes, Superheroes, Heroines, and Anti-heroes will introduce you to new heroes and heroines as well as deepen your understanding of the iconic figures that you already know. We will look at how we define a hero as well as the cultural influence of these figures in different periods and discuss the very idea of the hero — why do we need and invent heroes? What makes someone a hero? And what is the negative effect of elevating someone to the status of hero? Also, where does the anti-hero come in and what type of hero is he or she?

We will read texts, comic books, and graphic novels as well as watch films and look at visual material:

- Introduction: Bel Kaufmann: *Sunday in the Park* (1985).
- The superhero: group presentations.
- War heroes: S. Sassoon and the poetry of WWI. Propaganda posters.
- The anti-hero: Milton, extract from *Paradise Lost*.
- Code hero: Hemingway *The Short Happy Life of Francis Macomber* (1936).
- American soldiers in Iraq: *The Hurt Locker* (2008)

Lesson 1:
- Introduction to the course.
- Pupils discuss the concept based on my introduction and come up with keywords that they write on the whiteboard. Class discussion of a number of them.
- Reading in class: *Sunday in the Park*. Focus on the characterization of the main character and his wife, narration, and the theme. Look up the words you do not understand.
- Discussion of the short story and its connection to the "heroes" topic and comparison with keywords on the whiteboard.
- Pupils write for 15 minutes: "My hero is xxx because ..."/ "I don't have a hero because ..."
- Reading aloud in pairs and a couple in class

Lesson 2:
- Introduction to the superhero.

- Pupils invent their own superheroes (remember: superpower, weakness, look, archenemy, double identity, dark secret) in small groups and present them in class.
- Lonely heart's ad for a superhero: focus on adjectives and adverbs.
- Group work on existing superheroes that the pupils choose themselves.

Lesson 3:
- Group work continued. Students practice finding information within the time frame and cooperating in groups.

Lesson 4:
- Group work presentations. Students practice oral proficiency and presentation/communication skills. I have asked them to focus on correct language in their PowerPoint/Prezi/Keynotes and clear communication.

Lesson 5+6:
- The poetry of World War 1: Wilfred Owen and Siegfried Sassoon. Propaganda Posters. Students practice poetry analysis through various in class exercises and we discuss the poems.

Lesson 6:
- Milton: extract from *Paradise Lost*. Satan as an anti-hero. Drawing exercise to open up the topic.

Lesson 7:
- Code hero: Hemingway *The Short Happy Life of Francis Macomber* (1936). Discussion of language and characterization.

Lesson 8+9:
- Film + discussion: *The Hurt Locker* (Bigelow, 2008). Students fill out a worksheet while watching the movie. Afterwards, we discuss the film's depiction of war veterans.

Lesson 10:
- Evaluation of the topic. A test and feedback on the teaching.

Appendix 6.1 Chinese Version of Student Written Assignment "My Reviews" in Teacher Z's Class

我的点评（My reviews）

子贡问曰："乡人皆好之，何如？"子曰："未可也。"
"乡人皆恶之，何如？"
子曰："未可也，不如乡人之善者好之，其不善者恶之。"（《论语·子路第十三》第二十四章）
作业 (writing task)：阅读并思考名家评点，自选角度写出你的点评。

[**名家评点**] [Two well-known commentaries]

朱熹（Xi Zhu）：一乡之人，宜有公论矣，然其间亦各以类自为好恶也。故善者好之而恶者不恶，则必其有苟合之行。恶者恶之而善者不好，则必其无可好之实。

南怀瑾（Huaijin Nan）：孔子这个道理，说明了一件事，就是我们现在说的"群众心理是盲目的"。所以一个人对于善恶之间，很难判断。办地方选举或在司法上判案子，就要注意，有时候群众认为不对的，不一定真的不对；群众认为好的，也不一定是好的。由此可见为政之难。

Index

List of Tables

Table 1.1　Key Features of Monologically and Dialogically Organised Instruction / 23
Table 2.1　Data Collected by Type / 65
Table 2.2　Video and Audio Data Matrix / 67
Table 2.3　Defined Conventions of Transcribing / 69
Table 2.4　Types of Positioning Defined / 70
Table 2.5　Stances as Instructional Tools / 72
Table 2.6　The Integrated Framework for Data Analysis / 74
Table 3.1　Profile of Teacher S's Classes / 81
Table 3.2　Curricular Units and Activities in Teacher S's Classes / 84
Table 3.3　Third-Year Students' Responses of CIQ / 130
Table 3.4　Positioning and Envisioning in Teacher S's Classes / 134
Table 4.1　Profile of Teacher P's Class / 137
Table 4.2　Curricular Units and Activities in Teacher P's Class / 139
Table 4.3　Positioning and Envisioning in Teacher P's Class / 176
Table 5.1　Profile of Teacher X's Class / 180
Table 5.2　Curriculum Units and Activities in Teacher X's Class / 184
Table 5.3　The Difference in Student Responses / 212
Table 5.4　Positioning and Envisioning in Teacher X's Class / 220
Table 6.1　Profile of Teacher Z's Class / 223
Table 6.2　Curriculum Units and Activities in Teacher Z's Class / 225
Table 6.3　Positioning and Envisioning in Teacher Z's Class / 253
Table 7.1　The Feature of Allocation of Roles in SPS / 268

List of Figures

Figure 1.1　Bundsgaard's Cross-Model of Topic/Content-Oriented Teaching Methods and Framing / 41
Figure 2.1　The General Model of Using Discourse-Analysis Lens / 55

Figure 3.1   Seating Arrangement of Teacher S's Classes / 82
Figure 4.1   Seating Arrangement of Teacher P's Second-Year Class / 138
Figure 4.2   The Positions of the Teacher and Students in the Circle Exercise / 153
Figure 4.3   Questions for Discussing Poems of Siegfried Sassoon / 161
Figure 4.4   The Positions of the Teacher and Students in Double-Circle Exercise / 162
Figure 5.1   Seating Arrangement of Teacher X's Class / 181
Figure 5.2   Train as a Metaphor / 193
Figure 6.1   *One-to-Many Mode of* the Interaction between the Teacher and Students / 231
Figure 6.2   The *Corner of Exchanging* with the Written Task of "My Reviews" / 245
Figure 7.1   Pattern of Framing Classroom Interactions in Teacher S's Classes / 257
Figure 7.2   Pattern of Framing Classroom Interactions in Teacher P's Class / 260
Figure 7.3   Pattern of Framing Classroom Interactions in Teacher X's Class / 263
Figure 7.4   Pattern of Framing Classroom Interactions in Teacher Z's Class / 265
Figure 7.5   Modified Cross-Model of Teaching Method / 277